THE MISTRESS OF MAYFAIR

THE MISTRESS

'Will you walk into my parlour?' said the Spider to the Fly,
'Tis the prettiest little parlour that ever you did spy;
The way into my parlour is up a winding stair,
And I've a many curious things to show when you are there.'

'Oh no, no,' said the little Fly, 'to ask me is in vain,
For who goes up your winding stair
can ne'er come down again.'

Mary Howitt, *The Spider and the Fly*

First published 2016

The History Press
The Mill, Brimscombe Port
Stroud, Gloucestershire, GL5 2QG
www.thehistorypress.co.uk

© Lyndsy Spence, 2016

The right of Lyndsy Spence to be identified as the Author
of this work has been asserted in accordance with the
Copyright, Designs and Patents Act 1988.

British Library Cataloguing in Publication Data.
A catalogue record for this book is available from the British Library.

ISBN 978 0 7509 6715 0

Typesetting and origination by The History Press
Printed in Great Britain by TJ International ltd, Padstow, Cornwall

CONTENTS

Acknowledgements 8

Introduction 9

1 Doris Casts a Spell 11
2 Castlerosse is Summoned 23
3 Doris the Demi-mondaine 34
4 Castlerosse the Court Jester 47
5 Meeting at a Disadvantage 57
6 Lady Castlerosse 69
7 Doris Misbehaves 78
8 Old Habits 90
9 Beaten by Beaton 106
10 A Tangled Web 121
11 Playing to the Gallery 137
12 Doris Dreams of Stardom 147
13 A Last Resort 155
14 Out of Luck 163
15 The Jig is Up 174

Afterword 181
Notes 184
Select Bibliography 215
Index 217

ACKNOWLEDGEMENTS

I should like to thank the following individuals for their help and support during the writing of this book: my agent Robyn Drury at Diane Banks Associates; Mark Beynon at The History Press; Kathryn McKee at the Cambridge University Archives; John Brennan at the Winston Churchill Archives; Richard Ward at the Parliamentary Archives; Sarah Malcolm at the Franklin D. Roosevelt Presidential Library; Will Cross for his various archived material and for his assistance with the Castlerosse divorce files at The National Archives; Sarah Williams for her help in navigating Ancestry. com; Cameron Leslie for his assistance with archived newspaper articles; Katja Anderson for her research assistance and information on Stephen 'Laddie' Sanford; Janet Morgan for her helpful insights on Edwina Mountbatten, Doris Delevingne and Laddie Sanford; Anna Thomasson for her insights on the relationship between Edith Olivier and Doris; Alexandra Eldin-Taylor for kindly looking up references to Lord Beaverbrook and Doris; Helen Tyrell for the information on her Homan relatives; Cameron Bryant for sharing information and archived material on his Delevingne relatives; Andy Brill for sharing information on his relative, Enid Lindeman; Sofka Zinovieff for her permission to reproduce the photograph of Doris at Faringdon; Stephen Kennedy for his photograph of Doris and Paulette Goddard; Andrew Budgell, Meems Ellenberg and Kay Schuckhart for their thoughtful suggestions.

ꟼNTRODUCTION

'It's the good girls who keep diaries; the bad girls never have the time.'

Tallulah Bankhead

Little is documented about Doris Delevingne's life. A fleeting presence in the biographies of others, her name is often associated with a scandalous anecdote or a witty aside. In the 1920s and '30s she was a woman who lived at the centre of things, yet she formed almost no attachments and maintained no ties. What is known about Doris is often misquoted, misconstrued or misreported, and nobody can say for certain where a fact originated, only that it has escalated throughout the years and in the pages of various publications.

Therefore the trail that remains from a life, that was in every way a cautionary tale, is scarce. Unlike other socialites and scandalous figures of the twentieth century, Doris was discreet in print. She made no boasts of her liaisons and she committed herself to no one, not even on paper. Her letters to powerful men (Winston Churchill and Lord Beaverbrook, for example) are locked away in archives, and they tell only one side of the story.

The most important man in her life was, undoubtedly, Valentine Edward Charles Browne, styled Viscount Castlerosse and exclusively known by his courtesy title. Although from different backgrounds, both Doris and Castlerosse found a kindred spirit in one another, and they were each motivated by money: their own and other people's. To make sense of the connection they shared I have given Castlerosse his own two stand-alone chapters, as this book is very much his story too.

What we can be certain of is that Doris was unique. A nonconformist, she can neither be labelled a bluestocking, a flapper, a Bright Young Thing, or a bohemian. Her liberal attitude towards life, viewed as advanced in any era, was entirely her own. An ordinary girl who created a lifestyle of debauchery in pursuit of riches, she took life by the scruff of the neck and made no apologies for her outlook, or her behaviour.

In the last century her name was scattered like confetti, it appeared in the gossip columns at home and abroad, and it popped up in diaries and in letters – Cecil Beaton, Gerald Berners, Peter Watson and Edith Olivier, for instance, shared differing opinions of this demi-mondaine. She was photographed for *Vogue*, was painted by Winston Churchill and Sir John Lavery R.A., and she was the muse for Noel Coward's *Private Lives* and Michael Arlen's *The Green Hat*.

In today's world, where past socialites and old-world aristocrats have been brought to life as subjects in numerous biographies, Doris has lain dormant. By examining the limited sources that exist and the company that she kept, I hope I have, in some way, brought her to life.

A note on the formal titles used: to avoid confusion between Doris's friends who shared the same first names I have used formal titles to distinguish between the two: e.g. Lady Diana Cooper and Diana Guinness (later Mosley). Individuals such as Winston Churchill, Max Aitken (Lord Beaverbrook) and Cecil Beaton are referred to by their last names, including several others who were otherwise more recognisable by their last name rather than their first.

A note on the values: I have used the Bank of England inflation calculator to give the value of money in today's terms. Please see Notes for more information.

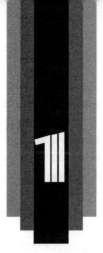

ᗞORIS ᑕᗩSTS ᗩ SPELL

'There's nothing so dangerous as a headstrong girl who knows her own mind.'

Daphne du Maurier, *Jamaica Inn*

———•◆•———

Nobody could have predicted the type of woman Doris Delevingne would become. A temptress who stirred up high society between the wars, she was as notorious for her love affairs as she was for her charm and gaiety. Her nondescript life began in October 1900 in Streatham, the south London borough of Lambeth, where she was born Jessie Doris Delevingne, the eldest child and only daughter of Edward Charles Delevingne and Jessie Marian née Homan. To avoid confusion with her mother, she would be known by her middle name, Doris. However, as she grew older, and bolder, she often listed her first name as the more elegant Jessica.

As the family's prospects advanced so did their living arrangements, and the Delevingnes left their rented home on Streatham High Street for Copers Cope House, a former farmhouse built in the seventeenth century, in the affluent area of Beckenham which had once been farmland. A thriving middle-class suburb in south-east London, it was an employment hub for craftsmen, gardeners and servants, who were engaged as staff in the nearby Victorian townhouses. With its uninterrupted greenery and a view of the river, it was a refuge from the bustling city centre. The seaside donkeys from Southend were housed in empty fields and cattle grazed on the Yokohama field, a floodplain in winter used by the locals as a lake for boating. It was a comfortable lifestyle and one that Edward and Jessie had aspired to, and through his job as co-owner of a haberdashery[1] shop which also dealt in fancy French goods, he was proud of his ability to provide for his family.

As Doris grew older, it was apparent that she was a clever child who was not only a competent conversationalist but had an ear for classical music, and such skills were encouraged by her parents. In an age when children were to be 'seen and not heard', and intelligence was considered unattractive in a woman, Edward and Jessie would have been viewed as forward-thinking by their encouragement of academic pursuits. Unlike her mother, who did not have the opportunity to complete her education, Doris attended a day school close to the family's home on Southend Road. And, by her parents' estimation, she would have gone on to higher education, but not university – for owing to the rules of the period, it was rare for a woman to sit exams and therefore they could not obtain the degree for the course they had studied. With the exception of the University of London, which, in 1880, boasted that four women were given degrees, women generally did not advance to degree status until the 1940s.

With this in mind, while Doris was given opportunities that were out of reach to many girls, it was marriage that her parents wished for her. A good marriage would have meant settling down with a middle-class young man, preferably with the means to support a wife and children, and perhaps a maid or a housekeeper. After all, through hard work and a principled life, Edward and Jessie had done well for themselves.

Social mobility and self-improvement were values which Edward held in esteem, so long as they were achieved through an honest day's work. Born Edward Charles Delevingne in France in 1875, he was a British subject said to be descended from Belgian aristocracy. Tales of nobility were a distant myth – and one which Doris was particularly keen to propagate, and in later years it would attach itself to the family name – however, the French blood was authentic. After the untimely death of his mother, Camille (née Rubay), Edward had come to London with his father, Edward Sugden Delevingne, and his two younger brothers, George and Robert, where they lived in various tenements in and around Camberwell. His father established a haberdashery shop at 4 Hamsell Street in the East End, where he and his brothers would work in the future.[2] Adapting to his new home, Edward became passionate about extolling the virtues of British life: he worked hard, he worshipped at the Church of England and, a frugal man in both his finances and recreation, his one and only hobby was chess; he was later appointed secretary of the London Chess Club.

When Edward met Jessie, she was living with her widowed mother and eldest brother, Arthur, in Lewisham. Since the death of their father, James Homan, at the age of 31, Arthur had abandoned his education to work as a woollen warehouseman to support the family. As the youngest of six children whose household was supported by James's work as a successful carver and a dealer in fancy French goods, Jessie had known hardship and, as such, she believed in the virtues of leading a frugal life. The prospect of marriage to the 25-year-old Edward, now a self-made man heading his father's business, was appealing and she accepted his proposal. His salary afforded them two servants and a lease on a Victorian townhouse on Fairmile Avenue, just off Streatham High Street, where Doris was born. Six years later, a son, Edward Dudley,[3] completed the small family and, like Doris, his middle name was used to avoid confusion with his father.

As the years passed, Doris's feelings towards her family became somewhat aloof: she was not close to her mother or father, but she had a good relationship with her brother, Dudley. The siblings shared a similar nature and aspired to a lifestyle greater than that of their parents and, as the years progressed, they would form friendships that afforded them entrée to high society. Such lack of familial ties might have been attributed to the break-up of her mother's family – Doris did not know her maternal uncles, for Jessie's three brothers, Charles, Walter and Sidney, had emigrated to Australia in their teens. Three of her grandparents were dead before she was born, and her maternal grandmother Edith Homan (née Hibberdine) had died when she was an infant, thus she did not have the opportunity to form a relationship with her. As well as having little in common with her parents, she could not relate to her extended family and their puritan outlook; her uncle, Walter Homan, in particular, was a religious man and an active member of the Anglican Church in Australia.[4] Their ordinary lives, founded on their strong working-class origins and traditional views on family life – her maternal grandparents had married aged 15 and 18 – did not appeal to her. Perhaps it was the estrangement between Doris and her relatives, due to death and distance, that instilled in her a self-sufficient nature.

As she was descended from a long line of tradesmen, Doris thought it only natural that she would follow in their footsteps. This outlook did not endear her to society's rules and, although it was not uncommon for a woman to pursue a career, it was frowned upon for a girl like Doris to possess the determination to do so. With her background and upbringing, any notions of wanting a job would have been quelled by marriage. It was the solution for many women, who had to work for a living out of necessity, and not because of fanciful ambition, as was the case with Doris.

Post-war attitudes towards working women had regressed and, after four years of running the country while men were fighting in the First World War, women were expected to surrender their jobs to returning soldiers. It was viewed as unpatriotic for a woman to take a job, even if she was qualified for it, and although unemployment benefits had been introduced through the National Insurance Act of 1911, women were not eligible for this benefit if they refused to take an available job in domestic service. There were jobs for women, in factories and in dressmaking – all considered 'women's work' – but the hours were long and the pay was low. The Sex Disqualification Act of 1919 made it somewhat easier for girls like Doris to pursue higher education, and many became qualified teachers and nurses, or sought clerical work, but they were expected to resign from those jobs when they married.

Inspired by her father's work ethic and ability to earn a living as a self-employed man, Doris chose to set up business in the rag trade.[5] Drawing on her love of clothes and her dream of earning enough money to be independent, she began working from Edward's premises on Hamsell Street. The area itself was popular with manufacturers, tradesmen and shopkeepers, but in the past it had been a controversial address given that it connected with Jewin Street, formerly known as Jews' Garden because in the medieval period it was the only place in England where Jews could be buried. The rag trade itself was predominantly Jewish and it provoked a feeling of anti-Semitism. The trade thrived in the East End, Spitalfields in particular; Jewish immigrants turned their hand to sewing garments in cramped basements, and buying and selling clothing from the deceased, or the discarded seasonal wardrobes of rich people. When fever epidemics broke out, Jews from the rag trade were blamed for spreading disease through used clothing, and unflattering rumours of stealing clothes from hospitals and workhouses were rife.

But Doris overlooked where the clothing came from and the stigma it carried. She never cared much for scorn – could this have been an early lesson for her? – and she quickly realised there was a market for chic, second-hand clothing among women who longed to look sophisticated but lacked the funds to do so. Buying second-hand evening dresses became her niche, and she turned the West End into her business domain with a clientele made up of theatrical actresses and chorus girls. She would source the dresses and travel from Hamsell Street to whichever establishment her clients asked her to meet them at, and at her father's haberdashery she could easily alter and mend the dresses to suit their tastes.

It was during this venture that Doris met Gertrude Lawrence, known as Gertie, a theatrical actress since childhood who had enjoyed minor success on the West End stage. The two women encountered one another during a period when Gertie was suffering a bout of lumbago which saw her out of work and, to make ends meet, she took any job she could find in the chorus. However, word got around that she was temperamental and difficult to manage, and the work never lasted long. Still, she was determined to look the part of a starlet, and she spent the little money she had on clothing, often getting into debt for the sake of vanity. And, given the circumstances in which they met, presumably it was Doris who provided the clothes.

Doris had never met anyone quite like Gertie before, and during her respectable upbringing in Beckenham it is doubtful that she would have come into contact with such a vibrant personality. With her dyed red hair, heavy make-up and bawdy language, Gertie had the artificial appearance of what those outside of her profession referred to as a tart.[6] To the young Doris, however, this vision of artificial femininity was intoxicating, and Gertie, on her part, embodied the sort of woman she longed to be. She gave Doris a piece of advice that would stay with her all her life. It was very bad form to ask questions, she warned her. Of course, one might know certain facts about a person but, for the sake of nurturing a pretence, it was important that one should not act on what one assumed. In other words: it was all right to judge a person privately, but one should never speak of those judgements.

Doris was attracted by this philosophy; her own childhood[7] had been a long, drawn-out age of boredom, and her parents, acutely aware of their own background, were desperate to make good and had obeyed society's rules in the hope they came across as middle-class: a step up from their original, lowly origins. The two women were, in many ways, alike in spirit, and they found common ground in their striving for independence, whether it was obtained through one's own merits or not. Despite their personalities being similar, from the beginning Gertie was much more open about her past whereas Doris appeared more enigmatic. This element of mystery may have been cultivated from Gertie's original advice. For, despite the lifestyle Doris would come to lead and the scandal it evoked, she would always maintain an air of discretion.

Although only two years older than Doris, Gertie had already experienced struggles that were, at the time, foreign to her new friend. She was born Gertrude Alice Dagmar Klasen in 1898 in Newington, close to Elephant and Castle, and her early life was marred by her Danish father's alcoholism and his inability to hold down a job as a bass singer. Her parents were to separate shortly after her birth, and she claimed she was sent to work at an early age; her first job was gnawing kippers' heads in the gutter, and in her teens she earned money by dancing barefoot to a barrel organ on street corners. By the age of 17, she was working as an understudy in a West End revue, where she met her first husband, Francis Gordon Howley, a Blackpool dance director twenty years her senior. Prior to their swift marriage, she had been engaged to Philip Bateman, a young man serving in the barrage balloon corps. Gertie herself was never certain whether her only child, Pamela, was fathered by the barrage balloon boy or her husband. However, the marriage was short-lived and she returned to her mother's home in Clapham with her baby in tow.

As their friendship developed, Doris and Gertie shared the mutual belief that their lives were in a slump. Doris, on her part, was beginning to find her career in the rag trade a bore, and she suffered the commute from Beckenham to Piccadilly every morning for a long day of selling clothes because she thought it would lead to greater things. Part of her resilience was formed from an unswerving self-belief, and throughout her life she would take charge of her life, and be mistress of her own fate. This would prove especially poignant in years to come. However, in the meantime, it was Gertie who took Doris under her wing and, as she negotiated this new lifestyle, she was content to live in her new friend's shadow. For the time being, at least.

The more impulsive of the two, Gertie acted on their plans and, leaving her baby with her mother in Clapham, she found work performing in a cabaret at Murray's, a new London nightclub on the banks of the Thames at Maidenhead. Owned by the impresario Jack May, the nightclub's reputation was bolstered by its celebrity and royal patrons, though it was also renowned for its seedier attributes. Cocaine, it was said, was the main attraction. 'It was slipped to you in packets, very quickly, when you coughed up the loot.'[8] It was at Murray's that Gertie caught the eye of the Duke of Kent and the Prince of Wales, but the royal brothers were nothing more than a passing flirtation. It was a former war hero and Household Cavalry officer named Captain Philip Astley, MC, who took the bait. Although it was Gertie whom he was interested in, Doris would inadvertently benefit from the affair, too.

The son of a wealthy clergyman, Philip Astley was born at Chequers, his family's country house in Buckinghamshire, which was later given to the serving British Prime Minister as a weekend residence. His upbringing was a world away from Gertie's and Doris's: he was christened in the robes of Oliver Cromwell, and educated at Eton and the Royal Military Academy Sandhurst. And although his family knew of his preference for young women who were not of his class, his mother hoped he would not marry one. He had romanced an actress prior to meeting Gertie, and when he approached his mother to tell her of a predicament, she simply reached under her pillow and retrieved an envelope of pound notes. 'I think you'll find that will solve it,' she told her son.

Although she did not realise it at the time, Doris's life would change forever. Having taken a lease on a flat, paid for by Philip Astley, Gertie invited Doris to live with her. Given her friend's dubious profession, her marital status and the fact she had abandoned her baby, Doris was hesitant about telling her parents the truth about Gertie. Their disapproval would not have been unfounded: it was an era when young women were expected to stay at home until they were married and, furthermore, her parents' generation believed it was bad form for a young woman to kiss a man unless she intended to marry him.[9] Naturally, she would not have told her parents that a rich man was funding Gertie's lifestyle, and that she, too, would be taking advantage of his generosity. They were reluctant for Doris to leave home, and to her everlasting frustration they continued to keep a strict eye on her. Puritan in their outlook, they believed tennis parties were an exciting enough pastime for their 19-year-old daughter.

Leaving her parents' home in sleepy Beckenham, Doris headed west of the Thames to begin her new life. The two-bedroom flat exceeded her expectations and, although small, it was located on Park Lane in the affluent area of Mayfair. The location, Gertie explained, was chosen for its close proximity to Hyde Park Barracks, where Philip Astley was stationed, and he could therefore organise their clandestine meetings at his own convenience. It was agreed that Doris would make herself scarce during his visits, but this hardly inconvenienced her, for the address was a spectator sport in itself and she spent such times observing her new neighbours. Surrounded by private mansions belonging to millionaires, dukes and princes, it was a world away from her Beckenham neighbours who prided themselves on being pillars of the community, and who 'served the town in every possible way'. Around the corner, at 18 Clifford Street, was the Buck's Club, a newly established gentleman's club with a modern American bar where the Buck's Fizz cocktail was said to have been invented. It attracted officers from the Household Cavalry and high-ranking politicians, including Winston Churchill, who, in years to come, would be a significant presence in her life.

Copers Cope House, Doris's childhood home. Courtesy of Copers Cope Residents Association

In the summer of 1919, Gertie introduced Doris to Noel Coward, her childhood friend whom she had met when they both performed in *The Goldfish*, a children's play staged at the Crystal Palace. Having been invalided out of the Artists Rifles because of headaches, vertigo and general nervous debility, Coward had reinvented himself as a playwright the year before. His new coterie included not only his show business friends from his days as an actor, but a literary set who were on the fringes of celebrity. One such friend was Michael Arlen, the Armenian author whose future novel, *The Green Hat*, was said to have been inspired by Doris. Aside from his connections which Doris thought useful, they were to become lifelong friends.

Sharing a similar background, they had both grown up in the London suburbs (Coward's childhood had been spent in Teddington), and from an early age their talent had been encouraged by their mothers. But unlike Doris, he was brought up in genteel poverty due to his father's lack of success as a piano salesman, and his mother was forced to take in lodgers to pay for his acting lessons. Their personalities were alike: capricious, witty and with an eye for imitation, they were entirely at home in the frivolous world of the upper classes as the 1920s began. On the eve of this new era, there would be room for charismatic individuals, regardless of their class, among the aristocracy. And, like Coward, Doris was determined to be the centre of attention.

In years to come, both Doris and Gertie would romanticise this period of their lives and, perhaps for her parents' benefit, Doris claimed they lived a hand-to-mouth existence and that they shared one evening dress between them. Nothing could have been further from the truth, for Philip Astley was fixated on reinventing Gertie as a society lady, and he bought her an expensive wardrobe to ensure she would look the part.[10] Doris, too, benefited from this new wardrobe and, dressed in their smart clothes, the two women would travel around London in Astley's chauffeur-driven Rolls-Royce. It would inspire Doris to want more from her current situation. To Gertie, however, it fostered an inferiority complex which reminded her of her humble background, a source of shame, and she was eager to forget her mother and daughter, whom she had left behind in Clapham.

Far from ashamed of her own background, Doris would never hide the fact she had climbed the social ladder from the bottom rung, even if she did exploit the false story that she was descended from a noble branch of Belgian Delevingnes. She would downplay her family's origins in trade and draw attention to her paternal grandmother, Camille Delevingne, who was born and raised in Paris. This, she thought, provided her with an element of chic which she felt was otherwise lacking in her ordinary family.

Having obscured the facts of her lineage, Doris then turned her attention to her physical appearance. Pale with flaxen hair, her face was set off by high cheekbones, deep-set blue eyes and a straight nose with flaring nostrils. She had thin lips which quivered when she spoke, revealing prominent white teeth with a small gap between the front ones. 'I wouldn't have them changed for anything, darling,' she said of this aesthetic flaw, which the French called *dents de la chance*. 'It shows I'm lucky and sexy ... and *how*!'[11]

Settling any qualms Doris might have had about her looks, Gertie told her that a woman's legs, and not her face, were her fortune. Believing Gertie entirely, Doris began to imitate her behaviour, and she too punctuated her conversation with expletives. Her voice, shrill in her youth, was described as 'penetrating', and it often took on a masculine pitch when she used what friends called her Thames bargee language. Although she had the appearance of an English rose, she appeared to be 'a wild rose with considerate temperament and thorns which could draw blood'.[12]

The immediate aftermath of the First World War was, to many, a dangerous age. City centres were filled with rioting ex-servicemen who felt short-changed by the country whose freedom they had fought for; crime and unrest had increased due to striking police officers; and the British government was in turmoil over Irish Home Rule and the nation's war debt. Established families harboured an uneasy feeling, prompted by the realisation that their position was not as secure as it had been before the war. It was this sense of upheaval that came to dominate society. The rise of the Labour Party was bringing the working classes and unemployed to the forefront of daily life, and the Liberal government's imposed taxation on landed families swooped in and disturbed the privilege the aristocracy had once enjoyed. Society matrons clung to a dying sense of entitlement, appearing bejewelled during the season, but they sensed their power was dwindling. But, as with any form of disease and despair, society learned to live with the affliction it could not cure, and the ruling classes, even if they refused to conform, learned to adapt.

Post-war London came to be dominated by an influx of American millionaires who were attracted by cheap property and vacant business premises, which they saw as an easy investment. Viewed as vulgar by the old world aristocracy, American millionaires and trust-fund offspring were generous with their money and, given that they were not entirely welcomed by the old guard,[13] they were open to mixing with women from lower classes. Doris, it would seem, was the sort of young woman rebellious aristocrats and playboys were attracted to. She was outspoken, opinionated and, as her confidence grew, badly behaved.

In an age when young debutantes were launched on the social scene as prey for gentlemen seeking a wife, Doris took on the role of predator. Her hunting ground became the parties which she attended with Gertie and Philip Astley, though in the early days of her social career she was still negotiating the rules of the game. As a result of these far-reaching connections, it was inevitable that her path would cross with the 25-year-old Prince of Wales, known by his intimates as P.W., for he was a good friend of Astley's. At his parties, held at his apartment at St James's Palace, she mingled with the prince's pleasure-loving friends, made up of millionaires and celebrities from the stage and screen. It was an adulterous set, but nobody was shocked by this behaviour for the prince himself was having an affair with Freda Dudley-Ward, the wife of William Dudley-Ward, a Liberal MP for Southampton.

When Doris was not attending parties at royal residences, she frequented Rules, London's oldest restaurant on Maiden Lane in Covent Garden, famous for its game dishes and opulent décor of red-plush, gilt chairs, china-globed chandeliers and marble busts of William Shakespeare and Sir Beerbohm Tree. It had changed little from the days when Edward VII gave supper parties for his mistress Lillie Langtry in the private room upstairs, and the services of certain women were recruited for exclusive parties. But, as Doris was to discover, it was a crowded market and her chances of attracting a millionaire in such settings were slim. The majority of men whom she came into contact with were either middle-aged or too young to have been in the war, and for every man there were half a dozen women vying for his attention. A valuable lesson for Doris, it became clear that she would have to stand out from her peers.

Doris's foul language and penchant for speaking her mind did not deter this set, and she found herself attracted to becoming an American man's mistress – for they were known to flaunt their wealth – but not his wife, as marriage had not crossed her mind. As Gertie could attest, certain precautions had to be taken if Doris was to act on this, and a useful source of information would have been in the form of Marie Stopes's *Married Love*, the 1918 manual on sex and contraception. There were also Hardy's Woman's Friend and Madame Drunette's Lunar Pills,[14] two of the more popular brands of 'female monthly pills' which, despite their euphemistic names, acted as an abortion aid.

Far from ashamed of this new hedonistic lifestyle, Doris aspired to more. She looked to her mother, Jessie, who had lived in a household with one domestic servant and two brothers boarding at Lucton School, and whose life had been thrown into disarray following her father's death. Although her mother had obtained financial security through the means of marriage, Doris longed for the same privileges without the long-term commitment.

At home on Park Lane the incentives for this lifestyle – the beautiful clothes and expensive jewellery – were flaunted before her on a daily basis. Standing before the mirror in her bedroom, she envisioned a similar life for herself, and touching her head, her neck and each side of her collarbone, she chanted: 'Tiara, brooch, clip, clip.' It would become known as her magic spell. And, believing entirely in the laws of attraction, Doris was prepared to repeat this idiosyncrasy every evening until she got what she desired.

But, as her naiveté gave way to cynicism, she would discover that such offerings come at a price.

CASTLEROSSE IS SUMMONED

'We are all failures – at least the best of us are.'

J.M. Barrie

———•◆•———

The square mile of Mayfair was an exclusive sphere around which the upper-class world revolved. But unlike Doris who sought glamour and excitement, the man who would become and remain an influence over her life was brought to Mayfair against his will. Castlerosse, as he was simply called, was the victim of an unscrupulous plot orchestrated by his parents, Lord and Lady Kenmare, which, at their request, also involved their friend Winston Churchill, then the Secretary of State for War, and his secretary, Eddie Marsh.

Over the course of several weeks, on the same nondescript evenings when Doris would gaze into the future and chant 'tiara, brooch, clip, clip', the fate of Castlerosse had been decided. Believing that their son was 'doing no good in Paris, gambling and keeping women',[1] the Kenmares enlisted the influence of Churchill, who ordered Lord Derby, the Ambassador in Paris, to telephone the War Office to say Castlerosse's services were no longer required. Bowing to Churchill's demands, the War Office dismissed him.

A year before his arrival in London, Castlerosse had been engaged by the Minister of Information and newspaper proprietor Sir Max Aitken, soon to be Lord Beaverbrook, in a role which entailed welcoming American firemen who were visiting Paris. Although he was a man with a frivolous nature, he thought the scheme an idiotic one. 'What nonsense is this?' Castlerosse said. 'Trying to win the war by acting as nursemaid to a lot of marked dog-collars! Bloody Tomfoolery!'[2] But he was efficient in collecting the men, delivering them to their hotels, feeding them, lecturing them, finding souvenirs, stamping their postcards and letters, and taking them to the theatres and concerts.

When peace came, in November 1918, Beaverbrook then appointed Castlerosse as liaison officer between the British Peace Delegation and the American correspondents coming to Paris to report on the post-war state of the city. He proved to be an invaluable asset to the correspondents and, with his contacts, they could rely on him to pass a message on to Lloyd George, reserve tables in smart restaurants, recommend a *cocette*, and respond to telegrams when they were in no condition to do so themselves. The *New York Herald* reported: 'Nearly all American correspondents who have now left Paris will carry away with them grateful memories of Viscount Castlerosse, whom they called "The Man Who Owns the Lakes of Killarney."'

It was in the New Year of 1919 that Castlerosse learned that his services in Paris were no longer required. He was given a farewell dinner, after which he was carried by a dozen cheering Americans to the Meurice Hotel, where he was put to bed by a beautiful American nurse. As he was oblivious to the reasons behind his dismissal, Castlerosse appealed to Beaverbrook to hire him as a correspondent for his *Sunday Express* newspaper. Beaverbrook knew of the parental influences at work, and he refused to co-operate. So, with no options and little money, Castlerosse returned to London under a cloud of gloom.

However, to understand the fate of this wayward young man and how it brought him to Doris, it is essential to start at the beginning.

He was the failure of the family, the bane of his father's existence and a thorn in his mother's side. Born Valentine Edward Charles Browne in 1891, the namesake of his father, the Anglo-Irish Earl of Kenmare★, he was a poor

---

★ At the time of his son's birth he was yet to inherit the Earldom of Kenmare and was styled Viscount Castlerosse. However to avoid confusion with Castlerosse himself, the latter title will be used.

product of his parents. Both tall, slender and extremely good-looking, they viewed their son's physical appearance with contempt. He was short and fat with small feet and stumpy legs, and had what they thought to be a 'Jewish caste' (inherited from a maternal great-grandmother), which in the Catholic Kenmare family was perceived as another flaw, or weakness, in the boy. According to his mother, he 'showed all the characteristics of a garden heap. If you turned him over and dug him up there was a certain amount of steam and smoke but not so much as a spark of fire.'[3]

He was rejected by his mother, formerly the Hon. Elizabeth Baring of the merchant banking family; she found Castlerosse 'hard to talk to and hard to understand', and claimed that engaging with her son was like 'trying to deal with a deaf mute'.[4] Had it not been for his birthright as the heir-apparent of the 5th Earl of Kenmare, perhaps she would have neglected him entirely. She had five children: two older girls, Dorothy and Cecilia, born ten months apart in 1888, and two younger sons, Dermot and Gerald, born in 1895 and 1896 respectively. After the birth of each child, Lady Kenmare sent them to Killarney, the family's estate in Ireland, to be wet-nursed while she resumed her life in London. When Castlerosse was born, she observed the confinement period after which she immediately left for Cairo with a female companion. Though, as her children aged, it was her second son Dermot whom she came to favour, and she thought him a more suitable heir than Castlerosse.

As he grew older, Castlerosse became more detached from his parents and from nursery life. Left to his own devices, his solitary days were spent on the lakes of Killarney with estate workers, who taught him to fish. To remedy what Lord and Lady Kenmare viewed as a shortcoming in his character, Castlerosse was sent to St Anthony's school at Eastbourne, where his mother hoped the 'democratic atmosphere' of an English school would correct his behaviour. Harbouring a strong sense of his own inferiority, Castlerosse's academic career proved disastrous, for his schoolmasters declared him stupid and he was mocked by his peers for his poor sportsmanship.

But he was not entirely starved of family affection; his maternal uncle, Lord Revelstoke, would arrive at St Anthony's in a motor car flanked by two beautiful women. Head of Barings and a director of the Bank of England, the flamboyant bachelor's visits were spent regaling his unhappy nephew with tales of his London adventures. One particular anecdote stood out for Castlerosse; his uncle told him of the Duke of Devonshire's mistress, Miss Catherine Walters, who was known as Skittles. The leading courtesan of her day, Skittles exercised thoroughbreds on Hyde Park's Rotten Row where she commanded attention in her skin-tight riding habits, tailored by Henry Pool

& Co., which she wore without underwear. Accumulating a legion of wealthy benefactors, she was asked by a former lover, Lord Clanricarde, what the duke was like. 'More balls than brains, my dear,' she answered frankly. Concluding the risqué visit, Lord Revelstoke placed a five-pound note in Castlerosse's hand, and departed with his two beauties in tow, leaving him to face the contempt of his schoolfellows.

As Castlerosse appeared to be an unsatisfactory student, both of his parents agreed that school was a waste of time, and Lord Kenmare thought a career in the navy would make a man of him. It was a curious choice for a boy who had never shown an interest in the sea, and barely passing the examination, he was dispatched to Osborne Naval College on the Isle of Wight. Life as a sea cadet was as uncomfortable as he imagined it to be: the hammocks in the Rodney dormitory were not suited to his bulk and the motion of the ship at sea made him sick. The tutors, hoping to instil discipline and respect, kicked him mercilessly and whipped him with the end of a rope. Fortunately for Castlerosse, his health deteriorated – congestion of the lungs was the problem – and he was sent home.

The realisation that he had once again failed his parents reinforced his belief that he was an unworthy heir to his father. Thus it became his ambition to make his mother proud, and he dreamed of sailing into Bantry Bay on an HMS cruiser, which he would command from the bridge as she looked on. As this could never be, he came to the realisation that he did not like his mother, and his diary became filled with comments such as 'my mother hates me'.[5]

Once again parental influence was not far off, and Lady Kenmare, under the guidance of Lord Revelstoke, began to think of a career in stockbroking for Castlerosse. Though she knew he did not have a head for figures, she hoped for the best and sent him to the University of Cambridge. 'His habits are beastly, and his manners are none,' observed a tutor. Failing to complete his BA, Castlerosse would say: 'I came away from Cambridge poorer financially, morally and intellectually than when I arrived.'[6] Surprisingly, given his lack of academic ability, a professor thought he would make a good barrister and had encouraged him to read for the Bar. 'The man must be a fool,' said Lady Kenmare. 'Everyone knows you have no facility as a speaker or conversationalist.'[7]

Inspired by his uncle Maurice Baring's anecdote, 'I got up in the middle of lunch once, and went to Moscow without luggage, an overcoat, money or passport – just because I could speak languages,' Castlerosse was delighted when his parents sent him to Compiègne to learn French. The following summer he went to Heuter, a small town on the Weser River north of Hanover, to learn German. Lodging with Herr Morsch, a former music teacher at Eton, Castlerosse's bedroom overlooked the local parade ground where he watched the most powerful military machine in the world being trained. For what? he wondered. He then left for a tour of Holland, where he met a young woman with whom he thought he was in love. Having taken her rowing on a canal, he attempted to sail through a narrow bridge but, owing to his large size, he became stuck. Humiliated, he abandoned his tour and returned home.

Castlerosse spent the summer of 1914 in London, where the threat of a war with Germany had become a reality. On 4 August, he noticed that the streets of London were empty except for hordes of young men singing songs as they moved along. Taking a hansom cab to his father's house in Cadogan Square, the driver told him: 'There's going to be a war. My son will go. My father was wounded in the Crimea. Those were the days.' It still had not occurred to him that war was imminent.

Letting himself into the house with his latchkey, Castlerosse spied a strip of light beneath the drawing-room door. 'Oh, old boy, there you are,' said Lord Kenmare. 'I saw George Morris today. He will take you over with the first lot.' George Morris, formerly the colonel of the Rifle Brigade, was chosen by King George V to command the Irish Guards. He then told his son: 'In an hour we shall be at war.' The hour had passed and his estimation was correct: Britain was at war with Germany.

Calling on Lord Revelstoke, Castlerosse was given forty gold sovereigns, and going to a less wealthy uncle he was given an aged revolver. He made his way to Wellington Barracks and was posted to No. 3 Company of the Irish Guards. Waiting for him at the gates was his friend, the Russian-born Countess Anastasia de Torby, in her motor car, and Castlerosse was alarmed to see that she was crying. Before they left in her car, he was told to be back at midnight as the battalion was leaving before dawn.

'Where shall I sleep?' asked Castlerosse.

'On your bloody arse,' replied the adjutant, Lord Desmond FitzGerald.

Finally, it dawned on Castlerosse that war had begun. Before the sun had risen over London, the regiment marched off via Vauxhall Bridge Road to Nine Elms Station in Battersea, and he was touched to see that his parents had come to see him off as he departed for France.

However, his prowess on the battlefield was cut short when, having been ambushed by Germans in the Villers-Cotterets Woods, a bullet struck him as he raised his right arm to swat a wasp. He collapsed from the pain and loss of blood, and when he regained consciousness he thought he had lost his elbow. And, glancing at the pool of blood next to him, he likened it to the shape of

Killarney House, Co. Kerry, Ireland. Home of the Earls of Kenmare until it was destroyed by a fire in 1913.

the lower lake of Killarney. A passing German from the Red Cross spied him and pulled him to his feet. 'If ever a German should fall into your hands be kind to him as I have been to you,' he said. He was hurled into a passing cart, whereupon two corpses were dragged out to make room for him. Spending the night at a church at Vivierres, Castlerosse was certain he would be dead by morning. He lived, but discovered that ninety wounded men had died over the course of the evening.

Two days later, a motor car arrived to ferry Castlerosse to the American hospital at Neuilly, which was managed by Mrs W.K. Vanderbilt. It was a disagreeable journey and, overcome by sickness, he vomited six times to the displeasure of a French officer who was travelling alongside him. Adding a degree of pathos to the ordeal, Castlerosse, whose uniform was destroyed, was dressed in a woman's skirt, sweater, cape and bedroom slippers. Upon his arrival he broke down in tears and was given an injection of heroin.

A few days later, Castlerosse boarded a train for La Havre with his brother, Dermot, who had been lightly wounded while serving as a lieutenant with the Coldstream Guards. Their brother Gerald, the youngest son of Lord and Lady Kenmare, would leave for the Western Front in 1916, aged 19. A deeply unhappy man, who preferred animals to people, Gerald stood still as the Germans fired. 'I can never decide,' he said, 'whether the possibility of heaven in the next world is preferable to the certainty of hell in this.'[8] On the cross-Channel ferry to England, an elderly woman eyed the two invalids with disapproval. 'I hope you have come back to get into uniform,' she hissed. Their companion, Fred Hoey, an American diplomatic courier, who was taking his fiancée's jewels to London, told her: 'Madam, you have been guilty of the gravest impertinence. Pray go away.'

It was an emotional homecoming for Lord and Lady Kenmare,[9] who were more concerned about Dermot's recovery as he was determined to return to the Front. Castlerosse, as a result of his injury, was invalided out of the Irish Guards. He was sent to convalesce at Sister Agnes's nursing home at 9 Grosvenor Gardens, named after its founder Agnes Keyser, a former courtesan and long-time mistress of King Edward VII, who invested £80,000 of her own allowance into the yearly running of the place.

When he was sufficiently recovered, he took a room at the Bachelors' Club in Hamilton Place. Dressed in his Irish Guards uniform with his arm in a sling, he was given a hero's welcome and, for the first time in his life, young women thought him an eligible bachelor. 'It was nice for once in your life to be a hero,'[10] he said. Hoping to meet the 'wounded hero', a courtesan of

Scandinavian and French descent, then one of the most beautiful women in Paris and London, asked to meet him.

Having decorated his room with flowers to impress his female caller, Castlerosse waited for hours but she never appeared. He was disappointed and embarrassed, but he did not contact her, for although he was not lacking in confidence, he had no idea of her whereabouts. Forgetting the incident, he continued to visit the hospital for bouts of anaesthetic to have fragments of bone removed from his arm, a painful procedure that was carried out to prevent amputation. Then, one day, he received a scented envelope from the mystery woman, explaining that she had been in hospital for several weeks and would he call on her at her flat in Portland Place?

The woman in question was Jacqueline Forzane, the fiancée of Fred Hoey. When they met, she expressed her regret at standing him up and told him of her illness, and that she had to have an appendectomy. Aware of her reputation as a self-proclaimed *cocette*, Castlerosse recalled: 'There was not the slightest question of love-making or even so much as a mild flirtation.' He was too shy, and she was fatigued from her bout of ill-health. Instead, they went to Mass and returned to her flat, where they conversed for hours.

'How is your fiancé, Mr Hoey?' asked Castlerosse.

'I had no idea we were engaged. His French is so bad,'[11] she said.

After several meetings, Castlerosse fell in love with Forzane and he asked her to marry him. But she thwarted his proposal by asking for the consent of his parents and, being a woman of dubious reputation, she knew it would not be given.

He went to his parents and asked for their approval to marry Forzane. Lady Kenmare thought him foolish and refused to see the woman with whom he was in love. In a rare moment of defiance against his mother, he threatened to elope with Forzane. Realising that her son might shame the family, she telephoned Lord Revelstoke and shared with him the news of Castlerosse's 'scandalous and shameful plan'.

The family conspired to pay Forzane off, but she refused the large sum of money and left for Paris. Lonely and depressed, and thinking his life was without purpose in London, Castlerosse followed her. Taking advantage of the special terms it offered to officers, he moved into the Ritz Hotel. One day a taxi pulled up outside the hotel and out stepped Forzane, now the most sought-after beauty in Paris. A few days later, Castlerosse was delighted to discover that his luggage had been transferred to her hotel. Their affair had resumed.

It was to be the happiest period of Castlerosse's life: his parents were paying his expenses, the wound was healing, and he was in love. And unlike so many occasions in his life, fate would also deal him a generous hand. Forzane, who was prone to histrionics, had developed a pimple on her nose and refused to be seen in public. Forced to take luncheon without her, he went to the Ambassador Restaurant, where among the diners was Lord Beaverbrook. Having made one another's acquaintance over luncheon, the two men formed a friendship that would benefit Castlerosse all of his days.

Several weeks later, Castlerosse was summoned to London, where he learned of the tragedy that had struck the Kenmare family. Lord Kitchener telegrammed to say Dermot had been killed at the Battle of Loos. Inconsolable over her son's death and overcome with grief, Lady Kenmare thought 'the light of her life had gone out'.[12] It was apparent that she could have easily sacrificed Castlerosse to the war, but not her beloved Dermot.[13]

Returning to Paris, Castlerosse resumed contact with Beaverbrook, now the Minister of Information. With his fighting days long behind him, Beaverbrook gave him a job in the Ministry, and Castlerosse reverted to his pleasure-loving lifestyle. Forzane had flitted out of his life; now a popular model and actress, she was feted by men richer than Castlerosse. Although fond of him, and possibly in love with him, she was honest when she said she could not wreck his life. She also sensed parental disapproval, and the plot to retrieve Castlerosse from Paris was proof enough that she would never be accepted as his wife. The affair fizzled out as the conflict on the battlefields of France drew to an end.

During this period, Castlerosse met Enid Cameron (née Lindeman), an Australian wine heiress. Enid, who in her late teens had been the mistress of Bernard Baruch, a middle-aged American financier and presidential adviser, was a young widow living in the French capital with her baby son. Her rich American husband, Roderick Cameron, had died a year after they were married, and with her inherited millions she left New York to drive an ambulance for the war effort in Paris. With her beauty, charm and charisma, she became popular with officers, and it was reported that five men, having found her so intoxicating, committed suicide. One blew himself up with sticks of dynamite; another threw himself under Le Train Bleu while she was on board; and during a cruise an admirer had jumped overboard into shark-infested waters when she showed a marked preference for another man. Or, as Enid put it, 'They were not able to take the strain.'[14]

Castlerosse was enchanted by Enid and her money, and they began an affair. A millionairess in her own right, she was incapable of managing her finances and maintained an expensive drug habit; she smoked opium and injected herself with heroin.[15] The romance came to a halt when her old boyfriend, Lord Derby, expressed concerned for the havoc she was causing among the officers and, hoping to remedy this, he suggested she remarry. Enid agreed and, to relieve her of her fiscal responsibility, Lord Derby produced her next husband, Brigadier General Frederick Cavendish, known as 'Caviar'. They were married in 1917, and Castlerosse was once again broken-hearted and alone.

The London Castlerosse returned to in 1919 was not the happy place he recalled from wartime. The city's patriotic spirit had diminished, and around the restaurants and dance-floors the young men stared like lost souls. Some became bitter, even cynical towards society and their place in it. Others were determined to forget the horrors of war and have a good time. Castlerosse belonged to the latter.

First he had to learn to live with his injury and adapt to doing everyday tasks with his arm bent at a permanent angle. Eating and drinking (his two great pleasures) were clumsy endeavours, and he was embarrassed by the spills down his front. When people offered their sympathies for his disability, he would say: 'If you ask me, I was very lucky.' And, demonstrating how well his arm held a glass of whisky to his mouth, he added: 'When everyone else around me was dying, wouldn't you have settled for this?'[16]

Losing himself in the nightclubs of Mayfair, Castlerosse ran up an enormous tab and surrounded himself with beautiful women. 'What's the good of being a viscount if you can't live on credit?'[17] he often said. This rootless existence was inspired by something greater than the war. Following Dermot's death and Lady Kenmare's intense grief, Castlerosse was faced with his own inferiority complex. Thinking himself an ugly duckling and a source of shame to his parents, he realised that he could never replace Dermot in his mother's heart. To compensate for this inadequacy he became more extravagant than before, and his evenings were spent eating, drinking and gambling. He lost money he did not have, and was forced to approach his father for handouts. Having convinced himself he was a failure, he became prone to self-sabotage, and in his desperate state he looked for love or some semblance of affection. In turn, he became a scapegoat for ambitious young women who exploited his generosity and offered him little by way of kindness.

In those early days, Castlerosse and Doris were destined not to meet. While he frequented the St James nightclub in Mayfair, she slipped through the doors of the Four Hundred and Ambassador nightclubs with Gertie and their louche set. The end of his affair with Jacqueline Forzane and his rejection by Enid had instilled in him a lack of confidence, both in himself and with the opposite sex. With this in mind, an aggressive seductress like Doris was not the type of woman he sought. However, in those early days, Castlerosse was not the type of man Doris wanted, or needed.

DORIS
THE DEMI-MONDAINE

'Every Harlot was a Virgin once.'

William Blake, *For the Sexes: The Gates of Paradise*

———◆———

As the 1920s began, Doris's presence on the social scene remained cloaked in Gertie's shadow. More than a friend and a mentor, she became an example of what Doris aspired to be. Sources indicate that she took a similar path to Gertie in her quest to find a rich man, and it appears that she found work of sorts as a chorus girl at the Grafton Galleries in Mayfair. Not only was it a way for Doris to support herself but it gave her the opportunity to meet affluent men, for when the chorus girls were not performing, they were expected to socialise with the clientele and, in doing so, they earned a hostess's fee. If the dance floor was a hive of opportunity, then the dressing room was a cesspit for gossip and scandal. Many of the young women had fallen victim to enterprising men – 'backstreet doctors' – who hosted sex parties and would then offer to abort those who had got into trouble.

A basement in an art gallery, the Grafton Galleries became a nightclub after dark, with nude paintings covered with tissue paper to preserve the clientele's modesty; or was it the opposite? Since the Licensing Act of 1921 was passed, permitting alcohol to be served until 12.30 a.m. as long as it was accompanied by food, nightclubs were growing in popularity. Its owner, Captain Gordon Halsey, was said to have 'enjoyed a stroll down the Primrose Path'[1] with Doris, though she was not the only young woman for whom he had a special affection. Sylvia Hawkes, a Cochran Revue chorus girl, actress and lingerie model, was another of his conquests. Under such circumstances it would have been fair to call Sylvia a rival of Doris's, but a camaraderie existed between the two women and they became friends. Sylvia, it should be noted, would go on to blaze ahead of Doris, collecting five celebrated husbands: two British noblemen, a Russian prince, and two Hollywood stars: Douglas Fairbanks and Clark Gable. Far from jealous, as the years advanced, Doris looked to Sylvia as a great connector of people, and someone who could open doors for her.

Doris's early affairs are shrouded in secrecy and little is known about her beginnings as a courtesan except that comments regarding this lifestyle of choice range from admiration to contempt. 'A little bit more than a tramp,'[2] said a gentleman who wished to remain anonymous. How did an ordinary girl from Beckenham, who had a seemingly nice – if dull – family and upbringing, come to settle for a life that, in the beginning, was just above the lowest rung of the oldest profession? Was it her greed for money and beautiful things which had inspired the young Doris to sleep with men in exchange for the aforementioned? Or did a deeper malice drive this ambition? Some thought her a nymphomaniac, others a ruthless temptress. Chances are that she had not been exposed to anything improper in the family home, so what provoked her to take such a path? Did Gertie merely plant a seed in an impressionable young woman's mind, showing her how one could attract a rich man and live in luxury? Caught up in the brave new world of post-war London, it is possible that Doris was swept away on a wave of excitement which made her realise that she enjoyed this lifestyle. Capturing men had become a game and, until her looks and spirit withered through time, she thrived on the chase.

Although there is a fragment of truth in both statements regarding Doris's engagement as a chorus girl, she was, perhaps, hired as a hostess, as pretty girls were sought to entertain affluent men in popular nightclubs. The first indication of this stepping-stone is a photograph that was among Gordon Halsey's personal collection, of Doris posing in an evening gown with a fan of feathers behind her head, affectionately signed, 'To Gordie, with my love, Doris'.[3] The second clue is that he was a close friend of Gertie's and his flat abutted hers, thus it was inevitable that he would have crossed paths with Doris.

As she became a familiar face amongst London's nightlife, she was known as 'the girl with the gloves' because she always wore black or white opera gloves. It was a trait she had learned at the Grafton Galleries, for the women were required to wear gloves on the dance floor. Although short-lived, Doris's spell at the Grafton Galleries is a reminder of Gertie's influence over her as she negotiated her way through high society. She was introduced, by Gertie, to Café Society – the set in which Halsey moved. It was a rarified social group composed of international socialites and aristocrats who were known to one another personally, or by reputation.

In spite of her connections, Doris did not attach herself to any particular set or movement; she associated with its members, but she did not commit herself to a category. Perhaps she was not entirely welcomed as a verified member. Take, for instance, the Bright Young Things: a set that had sprung up in the aftermath of the First World War. They had seen their brothers and fathers slain on the battlefields and, hiding their heartbreak, they were determined to have a good time. Their good times were tame in comparison to their wild reputation; they sought pleasure in throwing themed parties, running amok in London and stately homes, conducting treasure hunts by motor car, and creating elaborately staged photographs. They were also the offspring of the aristocracy with a few exceptions in the form of talented individuals, such as Cecil Beaton.

With her open-mindedness towards sex and holding a vocation for little else, Doris lacked the capacity to be a Bright Young Thing. Fascinated by her, they became her friend, but their version of bad behaviour was mischievous ('sick-making'[4]) and not sordid. Her sexual freedom might have endeared her to the Bloomsbury set, a generation before. But her fundamental morals, although similar, veered to the opposite end of the spectrum. Sex for a Bloomsbury was for spiritual fulfilment, and even though they swapped partners ('what does it matter who puts what where?'[5]) they did not do it for materialistic or monetary gain. Given Doris's honesty about her motives, there were few places she would have fitted in, outside of a nightclub.

The flirtation with Gordon Halsey was brief, if the timeline of his dealings with the Grafton Galleries is anything to go by. The nightclub was raided by the police and closed down in 1923 for violating the Licensing Act, through its alcohol-fuelled parties lasting until 4 a.m. Halsey then bought a 33 per cent interest in the Quadrant, a nightclub in Air Street, between Regent Street and Piccadilly, co-owned by Desmond Young and Captain Dawes. There was a strict rule that only members could order alcohol at the club; however, it was ignored by Sylvia Hawkes and a friend, who were not members. The women had the drinks on their table when the police came to raid the Quadrant. But Doris, although she would retain a fondness for Halsey, was looking to the future.

It was an era when respectable girls wore lipstick, cut their hair and smoked cigarettes, though well-bred women did not smoke in the street.[6] Doris was eager to fit in and she mimicked what was in fashion:[7] she cut her long hair into a chin-length bob, dyed it golden blonde,[8] and took up smoking. Clothes became more daring; the corset was abandoned, hemlines were raised to below the knee, and flesh-coloured stockings were introduced to give the illusion of bare legs. And realising that her legs were her best asset, Doris began to wear shorts, altered shorter than what was deemed proper, as part of her everyday clothing, before it was acceptable to do so. 'Young Doris may go far on those legs of hers but, mark my words, she doesn't know how to make a man comfortable,'[9] remarked Rosa Lewis, proprietor of the Cavendish Hotel.

The Cavendish had become Doris's newest haunt. A crumbling *grande dame* from a bygone era standing on Jermyn Street in Mayfair, it was once a respectable dwelling place for the gentry. It had begun to experience something of a renaissance amongst the children of its past residents and regulars, reviving its business if not its reputation. Opening in 1902, the hotel was purchased by Rosa with the money given to her by King Edward VII, an admirer of her cooking and, if the rumours are to be believed, her lover. The king had kept a suite at the hotel until his death in 1910. Decorated to resemble a country house, the hotel contained fine pieces of furniture, including Chinese Chippendale mirrors bought by a long-time resident, the Liberal politician Lord Ribblesdale. A mixture of a private house and a club, with over a hundred bedrooms, it was rumoured that Rosa ran Britain's most famous high-class brothel[10] and that prostitutes were provided for Members of Parliament, high-ranking military officers, and the aristocracy. After dark, the place was said to have a menacing atmosphere, owing to the salacious goings on behind closed doors. As the 1920s began, American millionaires were slowly being accepted at the hotel; their money could at least buy them entry, even if some long-term patrons viewed them with contempt. Rosa herself had since decided that her guests should belong to the three As: Aristocratic, Affluent, or American.

It was at the Cavendish that Doris began to flutter her wings as a social butterfly. Along with Gertie and Barbara Cartland, she was invited to raucous parties given by the American millionaires, Jock Whitney and Stephen 'Laddie' Sanford, who had taken suites at the hotel. Her first serious affair was with Laddie Sanford, a famous ten-goal polo player, who was the heir to the Bigelow-Sanford Carpet Company and a $40 million[11] fortune. Discretion was paramount at the Cavendish, and Rosa would deliberately muddle up her patrons' names to protect their privacy. The correct name, however, was always placed on the bill. It was a quality which Doris herself would practice; from her earliest days of coming to London and selling clothes to chorus girls, she knew that it paid, literally, to be discreet. Ramsay MacDonald would later sum up society's views on the topic, when he said: 'The people do not mind fornication but they loathe adultery.'

However, unlike the men who played a part in her later affairs, Laddie was not married. Like Doris, he lived for pleasure and his moral compass was askew. At the time, and with a degree of hindsight, they were both described as 'sexual adventurers'. It is true that their morals – especially Doris's, who was expected to remain a virgin until marriage – were frowned upon. This was an age when women, particularly if they were married, looked upon sex as a tiresome duty, and wives were known to boast if they had a husband who 'doesn't bother me very much'.[12] She was viewed as wanton, and he a corrupter of respectable women. Her views were modern and advanced for their time; she did not hesitate to attack the standards of the age, which forced women to bow to the social, sexual and economic dominance of men. Doris felt that men ought to pay some tribute for being allowed to maintain the position of their superiority, and she delicately exploited the male sex without, it must be noted, any complaint from them.[13]

The clandestine nature of their relationship, conducted at the Cavendish Hotel, began in 1923. That same year, Laddie had come to England for the Grand National and his 13-year-old gelding, Sergeant Murphy,[14] won the race. Feted in the press, Laddie was featured on the cover of *Time* magazine, accompanied by the controversial headline: 'An American wins where kings and peers have failed.'

The magazine cover has been the topic of much speculation regarding Laddie, the author F. Scott Fitzgerald and his 1925 novel, *The Great Gatsby*, whose plot was inspired by the flamboyant parties thrown by the rich on Long Island. Fitzgerald's fictional character, Tom Buchanan, a wealthy polo player was said to have been modelled on Tommy Hitchcock, another mallet-swinging American from that era. However, with the publicity surrounding Laddie and his soaring popularity as a celebrity playboy and sportsman, it is possible that Fitzgerald saw the famous *Time* cover and, as he planned the novel in 1923, this might have influenced his own polo-playing character.[15]

It was Tommy Hitchcock's biographer, Nelson Aldrich, who inflamed the speculation that he had inspired *The Great Gatsby*. Although Hitchcock would become a friend of Fitzgerald's, it was Laddie who dominated the Long Island scene. Was it possible that both Laddie and Hitchcock served to inspire the author? At the time the similarity between the two men was striking. Both had gone to Ivy League universities (Laddie to Yale and Hitchcock to Harvard), they came from old money – by American standards – and could afford to pursue their love of sport full-time. Like Laddie, Hitchcock's father was a keen steeplechaser and a renowned racehorse breeder and, unlike Laddie, Hitchcock himself pursued employment – in 1937 he became a partner in the Lehman Brothers investment firm. The excessive wealth and social mobility – in Laddie's case his association with the aristocracy – were more relevant to Laddie than to Hitchcock. And, certainly his lifestyle could have influenced a number of Fitzgerald's books.

Was it this freedom of new money that appealed to Doris? In comparison to English attitudes and respect for tradition, the American dream and the privileges it bore were as vast as the ocean that separated the two countries. Money equalled power, and with power came respect, unlike English values where an immense fortune, if founded in trade, was frowned upon. The *nouveau-riche* and their decadent displays of wealth were an intoxicating combination for a young woman like Doris, who thrived on materialism. She sought privilege but, at the time, she was unaware that with such riches came disapproval from the very class she was trying to infiltrate.

Apart from his interest in steeplechasing, Laddie's frequent trips to England were in the interests of his polo team, the Hurricanes, named after his father's cattle farm in Amsterdam, New York. During this period he began to hunt at Melton Mowbray with the Quorn, Belvoir and Coltsmore packs, after which he advanced to shooting stag in the Scottish Highlands before going to India and South Africa for big game hunting. For the sum of 750 guineas, an individual could participate in 'tiger shooting, deer stalking, leopard shooting, pig sticking, an elephant drive, and other fascinating diversions', as promised by a brochure for Shoot Your Own Tiger from Orient Tourist Holidays of Regent Street. Attracted by the prospect of hunting with an Indian prince, Laddie set off for India with the Grand Duchess Marie Bonaparte, who brought with her a brace of Purdey guns. The skins of exotic animals were shipped home to not only adorn the trophy rooms of grand houses but to be given as gifts to godchildren for their nursery walls.

Although Philip Astley's appeal to Gertie was not only his money but his connections, Laddie was somewhat naïve in comparison. Not as connected as Astley, Laddie was still making a name for himself in London's high society circles, where English gentlemen found him and his wealth repellent. They called him a bounder, and in turn he played up to his roguish reputation when he charmed the wives of his naysayers, who thought him 'sweet: a nice, charming American … a bit dim but a very good polo-player'. He was said to have known every demi-mondaine in London, a remark that was meant as an insult but Laddie took it as a compliment.[16]

It was Doris whom he chose to be his demi-mondaine and, impressed by the luxurious lifestyle Gertie had created for herself, she was content with this arrangement. Bidding farewell to Gertie who, having revived her career, was off to Broadway in Noel Coward's *London Calling*, Doris packed up her small bedroom on Park Lane and headed around the corner to 6 Deanery Street,[17] where Laddie installed her in a townhouse close to the Dorchester Hotel. He bought her a Rolls-Royce and hired a chauffeur, and paid for a small staff, which included a lady's maid named Swayne, and a young man by the name of Martin who arrived every day to style Doris's hair. Not even Gertie had those privileges.

The pressure of having to earn her own living, in the traditional sense, became a distant memory. Laddie loved to spoil Doris and, unlike Philip Astley who taught Gertie to be a society woman, she was presented as one of his trophies. She was a plaything, something to be shown off, and a physical example of his wealth. He bought her diamond jewellery from Cartier and clothing from the leading couturiers; Schiaparelli was to become a favourite. She developed a preference for handmade Italian leather shoes imported from Rome, ordering more than 200 pairs at a time. 'Idiotic to wear shoes more than three or four times,' she would say. The same philosophy was applied to her habit of buying silk stockings from Paris, which she wore once and then discarded. The incessant need for beautiful things did not endear her to other women who were titled from birth and secure in their place at the top of the social ladder. They thought her vulgar, as 'nothing was considered so common as to be dressed in the height of fashion. Harlots and actresses could flaunt the current clothes, it was quite all right for them, and indeed a mark of their profession.'[18]

Greed gave way to generosity and Doris never forgot her old friends, the chorus girls she had met in the rag trade and her colleagues from the Grafton

Galleries. She gave away her old clothes to those girls, and the barely worn stockings[19] and shoes, too. When she had money, she treated those whom she thought were in need. Randolph Churchill remembered her taking out a gang of young officers from the Brigade of Guards, whom she entertained, and then footed the bill.[20] On a winter's night, she encountered the future Duke of Bedford at a dinner party and, giving him a lift home in her Rolls-Royce, she observed that he was without a coat. The coat, the young man said, was left behind at the party. But Doris knew better. 'You haven't got an overcoat, have you?' she asked him. He admitted that his eccentric father kept him short of money, and he could not afford to buy one. Writing an address on a piece of paper, she told him: 'You go tomorrow to this address, buy an overcoat and put it on my account.'[21]

Doris was determined to make people like and accept her. She was kind to old people[22] and tempered her bad language in their presence, but she never sensed when she had made a bad impression. Rosa Lewis, in particular, took a dim view of Doris and her lifestyle, and eyeing her strips of diamond bracelets, she sniped: 'You should write a book and call it round the world in eighty beds!' Rosa herself was a forward-thinking woman; a former servant from the East End, she had risen to prominence as a celebrated cook in Edwardian England, and forged a successful career as a freelance chef before opening the Cavendish Hotel. Her disapproval of Doris was well-known, and she made no secret of disliking her as a person. So this stance should be taken as a vendetta against her character, and not her lifestyle.

The manners and morals of the young women of Doris's generation were freer than their mothers, but even scandalous behaviour tends to be exaggerated. Such behaviour was not, according to popular belief, a social epidemic. It was confined to an exclusive set in London, the well-heeled areas of Mayfair and Belgravia, where drug-taking,[23] hard-drinking and promiscuity were the preferred forms of recreation. Not everybody approved, or partook, and there was a resistance from Britons who wished for social mores to be restored to their pre-war sensibilities.

As a response to this outcry, fraud had risen and was especially rife among religious profiteers masquerading as faith-healers who promised to rid society of its evils. One in particular was Aimee Semple McPherson, a celebrity evangelist popular with Hollywood stars, who had cured 'a red-haired Jezebel who could not make her hips behave'. McPherson came to London and rented the Royal Albert Hall for her Four Square Gospel Alliance but, despite McPherson's rousing speeches and gimmick of wearing angel wings on stage, ticket sales were mediocre. During this period, the Mormon Church sent over a legion of missionaries as they sought British converts but this, too, had floundered. Less glamorous but more convincing was the Oxford Movement (later known as MRA – Moral Re-Amendment), a Christian sect which Frank Buchman brought from America to Mayfair.

The maelstrom of Mayfair and society as a whole were moving closer together, though not entirely merged as one. It was a new era for those exclusive areas of London as new money and Americans swept in, bringing with them a brash, more daring form of self-entitlement. For an ambitious girl like Doris, it must have felt as though she was in the right place at the right time.

In the second week of August 1925, Doris accompanied Noel Coward and his American boyfriend, Jack Wilson, to Le Touquet, an elegant holiday resort in northern France, to stay with Syrie Maugham, the society decorator and wife of the writer, W. Somerset Maugham. Famous for her white rooms with mirrored screens, the interior of Syrie's villa was decorated in her signature style, and it was a hub for aristocrats and artists. She was also credited with introducing 'diet luncheon parties', where weight-reducing pills were served instead of food.

On Doris's visit, the guests included the former musical comedy star Gertie Millar; Lord and Lady Plunkett, who were killed in a car accident not long after; Ivar Kreuger, the Swedish match millionaire; Beverley Nichols, a handsome young man then at the start of a literary career; and Frankie Levesson, a Danish decorator whom Syrie would hire to manage her London shop. Laddie remained in London and, in his absence, Doris brought her 19-year-old brother, Dudley, who had begun to socialise with the same crowd as his sister. Later, when he was working as an 'impoverished' insurance broker,[24] he would befriend the Prince of Wales and move with his raffish set.

Two weeks into Doris's stay, Maugham and his lover, Gerald Haxton, returned from their holiday in Capri. Their arrival coincided with a party Syrie was throwing, and their presence evoked an undercurrent of tension between husband and wife. The guests felt embarrassed for Syrie, particularly when she flung open her arms and cried, 'Darlings!' at the two men, and blew a kiss at Haxton, which he disregarded. Haxton then attempted to shock the guests when he told them how he had seduced a 12-year-old girl in Siam for a tin of condensed milk. Leaving the party, Doris, Noel Coward and Jack Wilson walked to Paris-Plage to swim, while the others remained on the terrace, playing backgammon and gossiping.

Doris had been present during a pivotal moment in the disintegration of the Maughams' marriage. He disliked her friends – 'kept women' – and their vapidness, he felt, rubbed off on Syrie. 'All you do is sit about in beautiful clothes and look "picturesque". It isn't very much, is it?'[25] It was a cheap shot, for Syrie was an intelligent woman who was admired by the aesthetes[26] of the period. Her first protégé was Rex Whistler, and she was among the first London hostesses to recognise the genius of Noel Coward and had endorsed his play, *The Vortex*. Over luncheon, Maugham branded her a loose woman, a cheat and a liar.

Their bickering continued, and on Sunday, the last day of Doris's visit, the couple had a petty argument provoked by Syrie giving Maugham and Gerald Haxton a bill for bath towels. After the argument, she went outside to the garden to find Doris playing tennis with Jack Wilson. Noel Coward and Beverley Nichols were spectating from a court-side bench, and bypassing her guests, she chose to sit alone, her pale face still wet from the tears. Later that evening, Syrie departed for England with Beverley Nichols, leaving her guests at the villa and walking out on her marriage.

Although their circumstances were vastly different, Doris would return to London to discover that she, too, had been dealt a similar fate.

Laddie was a vague presence in Doris's life and he lived for most of the year in his native America. On his visits to England, for the Grand National and for polo tournaments, he resumed his affair with her. It was unconventional, and his admiration was expressed from afar. But this did not deter Doris, and she fell deeply in love with him and would continue to think of him as the love of her life, long after he had broken her heart. Fixated with Laddie, she thought his generosity was an indication of his love for her, and she hoped such feelings would lead to marriage.

However, since returning from America in the summer of 1925, he had grown aloof towards her. Perhaps to show him how loyal she was, she continued to go to Hurlingham and Ranelagh to watch him play polo; she knew his teammates, and his friend, Kenyon Goode, became a willing escort on occasions when Laddie was otherwise engaged. Besotted by him, she was content with this arrangement, and she did not think he would fall in love or be unfaithful with another woman.

But it would be another woman who would take Laddie away from Doris. Her name was Edwina Mountbatten and she was the 23-year-old wife of Lord 'Dickie' Mountbatten, the former Prince Louis of Battenberg. After almost three years of marriage, the Mountbattens' relationship had grown stale;

their personalities were ill-suited, and Dickie's naval career took him away for long periods at a time. Looking for excitement, Edwina had experienced her first extramarital dalliance with Lord Molyneux. On the rebound from Molyneux, she met Laddie, to whom she had been introduced at a house party on Long Island in 1924, months after giving birth to her first child, Patricia. Pathologically jealous of her daughter, who was the centre of her husband's attention, she dismissed the baby as 'a divine little daughter. Too thrilling, too sweet'[27] and, in the care of her nanny, she sent her to the south coast. Now she was free to live as she pleased.

Leaving Doris in London, Laddie travelled down to Uxbridge where he had leased a house for the summer. And, unbeknown to Doris, he invited Edwina for luncheon and to swim in his open-air heated swimming pool. She took her husband's friend, Fruity Metcalfe, to the luncheon but, smitten by Laddie's charm, she quickly discarded him. As the visit concluded, it was clear that Laddie and Edwina had started an affair.

Unlike Doris, who depended on Laddie financially as well as emotionally, Edwina was an heiress in her own right. The favourite granddaughter of a wealthy Jewish financier, Sir Edward Cassel, friend and financier to King Edward VII, she had inherited a £2 million fortune when he died in 1921. Beautiful, stylish, and financially independent, Edwina made Doris look 'shop-worn and insignificant', and she was ruthlessly dropped by Laddie.[28]

Humiliated at being replaced with Edwina, Doris went around telling everyone she was heartbroken. Although described by her admirers as arrogant and self-assured[29] – an attribute they found attractive – her confidence was shaken by Laddie's rejection. She could not convince him to stay with her, and she could not compete with Edwina, whose social sphere was a world away from her own.

Laddie remained a constant presence in Edwina's life, whether Dickie was there or not. He attended the Mountbattens' third wedding anniversary, which occurred during the same month they had begun their affair. When Dickie took Edwina to Deauville, Laddie followed them and was photographed by her side, wearing his dapper clothes. They attended Cochran's Revue, *1926*, and were seen together at the Embassy Club, which was Doris's nightly haunt. He sent her jewellery and expensive gifts, as he had done with Doris. And it was reported in the press that an admirer had asked a Bond Street jeweller to send several thousand pounds' worth of cigarette cases to Adsdean (the Mountbattens' home) so that Edwina might select one.

Wherever Doris looked, she was taunted by their affair. She must have felt as though she was being usurped by more accomplished women, who not only rivalled her looks, but had better backgrounds and breeding than she. However, there was one consolation from the break-up and that was the house on Deanery Street, which Laddie had given her. She paid for its upkeep by pawning her Cartier jewels, the total value of which had been compared to 'a Maharanee's dowry'.[30]

Looking for a rich man to fund her lifestyle, Doris began to frequent the Café de Paris, then the smartest nightclub in London. Her face became a familiar sight among the regular patrons, and the hostesses referred to her as a 'balcony girl'. The term was used to describe the young women who attended the bar and restaurant on the balcony, a replica of the Palm Court on the ill-fated *Lusitania*, the passenger-liner torpedoed during the First World War. On the balcony, distinguished people could dine in less formal clothing, but they were not permitted on the dance floor where a strict dress code was enforced. The latter was a hunting ground, with eligible bachelors and married millionaires circling the room with a pretty girl on their arm. Stalking the horseshoe-shaped balcony, Doris watched over the dance floor like a bird of prey.

Opening in 1924, the Café de Paris was built over three storeys below street level on Leicester Square, on top of which sat The Rialto cinema. Its manager, the impresario Harry Foster, persuaded the Prince of Wales to patronise the establishment. When the news spread that he went there in the afternoons, the balcony was overrun with beautiful young women hoping to catch his eye. It was also famous for its employee, Louise Brooks, then an unknown American, who brought the Charleston to London. The head-waiter from the Embassy Club, Martin Poulsen, was recruited as maître d' and, familiar with the clientele, he would 'dress the room'. This meant that a divorced couple would be placed at neighbouring tables, giving the diners a floor show to watch until the cabaret started.

It was here that Doris met the 50-year-old Sir Edward MacKay Edgar, known as Mike, a Canadian who had come to London in 1907 to join the merchant bankers of Sperling & Co. Like Doris, he possessed enough arrogance to believe that he could buy his way into the British aristocracy, and in the 1920 New Year Honours list, largely due to his services to British-Canadian trade, he gained entry to the peerage with his new status of baronet. Known as 'the man with the load of millions', he served as chairman of British Controlled Oilfields until 1925.

Bereft after the death of his only son, John, who was killed in a car accident in July 1925, Mike turned to Doris for a good time. That same year his finances ran into trouble and he declared himself bankrupt. They used one another to mask their mutual heartbreak; she provided him with sex and companionship, and he paid for the upkeep of her house and her living expenses. But ill-health and excessive spending caught up with him; in 1926 he declared himself bankrupt for a second time and was forced to give up his home on Park Lane, and his country house, Merton Hall, in Thetford. Speaking of his past fortune, he said: 'If you win you're marvellous; and you will have friends standing in a queue a mile long. If you lose, it means facing the punishments – or death.'[31] It was a prophetic statement, and one Doris was inclined to agree with.

There was no question of continuing the affair with Mike now that he was penniless. He lived in poverty until his death a few years later in 1934, and he was said to have died 'broken in health and utterly disillusioned'.[32] Having failed to revive his fortune and repeat his past success, the city of London did not forgive his mishandling of the public's finances nor did they overlook his gambles, many of which plunged companies into debt and provoked the suicide of a close associate.[33] When he was rich, he showered his friends with money and gifts, and he dabbled in breeding racehorses, which proved moderately successful. Doris was on the receiving end of his generosity, though not for long. But it could be said that she got the last of his dwindling fortune before the well ran dry. Money became her priority and to make it easier for the men willing to part with it, she changed her name to Delavigne (often printed as de la Vigne in various publications). 'Easier to spell on a cheque,' she said.

The experience with Laddie had hardened Doris's heart, and having proclaimed him the love of her life, his betrayal would leave a mark on her personality.[34] She had become bitter, even cynical, towards romantic relationships and she was determined to use men, the way Laddie had used her, to get what she wanted. 'She was arrogant and extremely intelligent,' recalled an admirer. 'She had a quality which attracted men to her – a contemptuous and challenging air of superiority to them. She gave the impression, in her speech and attitude and from the expression in her knowing blue eyes, that she had much to give but that no man or woman would ever get it all.'[35] In time it proved a valuable lesson, for there was one thing a courtesan could not do, and that was to fall in love.

CASTLEROSSE THE COURT JESTER

'There they laugh: they do not understand me; I am not the mouth for these ears.'

Friedrich Nietzsche

———•◆•———

The name Castlerosse was on the tip of polite society's tongue and, owing to his reputation, he had become a celebrity on the Mayfair nightclub scene. Many thought him a flamboyant figure: his protruding stomach encased in a brightly coloured waistcoat, a cigar dangling from his mouth, and he conformed to the general belief that he was trying to drink everyone under the table. Gambling at the St James nightclub had become his favourite pastime, and he spent more than he earned and lost more than he could afford. Women, too, swarmed around him, but he formed no attachments and pursued no affairs.

In the interim between leaving Paris and coming to London, he had taken a job at Rowe and Pitman, the stockbrokers for his uncle Lord Revelstoke's bank, Baring Brothers, and tried to adapt to a schedule that demanded he

Castlerosse and his companions.

was at the office by nine o'clock each morning. It took him only a few weeks, dressed in a frock coat and striped trousers, to realise the clothing and corporate mindset were not to his liking. He hated the job and his colleagues, and with little regard for the rules and regulations, he arrived late to the office. One day, his colleague, Jock Bowes-Lyon, remarked: 'It's a disgrace how late you come in.'

'But think how early I go,'[1] Castlerosse replied.

To relieve his boredom, Castlerosse spent his afternoons gambling what little money he had on the stock market, and his mounting debt grew to £20,000.[2] As he was apt to do in times of trouble, he approached Beaverbrook for help.

'Not a penny you will get from me,' Beaverbrook rebuffed him. 'Never, never again will I help you out of your scrapes.'

As crestfallen as he was, Castlerosse sensed it was an empty threat. 'The little beggar was pretty hot in what he said, but never mind, he will pay up,'[3] he said. Going against his word, Beaverbrook sent him a cheque for £20,000 the following day.

His career in finance was not to last, and the pivotal moment came when Castlerosse went to the Savoy for lunch. Having finished his meal, he made his way to the cloakroom with a cigar in his mouth and his left hand struggling to reach for the matches. In his pocket he felt for some papers and upon pulling them out they fell to the floor. An official from Baring Brothers bent down to help him gather them up, and smiling with 'the triumphant smile of a man who had peered at the secrets of Lady Godiva', he handed them over. Castlerosse realised he had absently stuffed £200,000[4] of National War Bonds into his jacket pocket and had taken them to lunch with him. Watching his colleague slither out of sight, and certain he would report his gaffe, Castlerosse helplessly downed another brandy and smoked a cigar.

Returning to the office, Castlerosse walked into Lord Revelstoke's office and boldly threw the war bonds on his desk. His career as a stockbroker was over. He thought about returning to Killarney, where he could farm, but word reached him that Lady Kenmare was building an elaborate chapel in Dermot's memory[5] and they both agreed it was for the best if he stayed away.

Deeply unhappy, Castlerosse yearned for someone to love him or, at least, for someone he could love as he had Jacqueline Forzane. In spite of this, he remained suspicious of women and, with the exception of Forzane, they did not feature in his life at all. However, he was not averse to inventing stories of debauchery and he told a story of how he had spent the weekend gambling for chorus girls' garters, in which he fibbed: 'The girl was thrown in if you won.'

This reluctance towards women began at an early age, when he had decided that women were perfidious and would always betray him. At the age of 19, he had fallen in love with a 14-year-old girl who had come to learn sewing and domestic science at an industrial school founded by Lady Kenmare. Every Sunday, during the holidays, he would wait for the nuns to bring the girls to St Mary's Cathedral in Killarney, hoping that his beloved would catch a glimpse of him and see that he loved her. During the annual summer outing to the shores of the Lower Lake at Killarney, he accompanied his mother who would make a speech and mingle with the girls. During such pleasantries, he edged towards the girl and, taking her hand, he bowed. Trembling, he said: 'Perhaps you do not know who I am. My name—'[6] He could not finish, for he had emitted a painful screech because a girl had stabbed him with a pin. Turning back to the object of his affection, he was disheartened to discover that she was laughing at him.

With this in mind, Castlerosse decided to pursue wealthy married women, for as emotionally unattached as they were to their husbands, they still had access to their money. One such woman was Millicent Hearst, a former vaudeville star and wife of the American newspaper magnate, William Randolph Hearst. A handsome woman in her mid-40s, her marriage to Hearst existed in name only, due to his public affair with the Hollywood actress Marion Davies. She travelled around Europe and set up residence in London, where she surrounded herself with the British aristocracy and the royal families of Europe.

Indulging Castlerosse with attention, she enjoyed his absurdity and laughed at his jokes. He in turn appreciated her good humour, and her wealth. She referred to him as a 'great big bouncing elephant', and she felt 'almost ashamed' when they stepped out in public for the first time. Dressed in his usual elaborate style, 'he wore a suit with striped pants, spats and a white waistcoat, and he positively flaunted his stomach. He spent hours over his food. And what language he used.'[7] Yet his vibrant personality succeeded in charming her.

Castlerosse always fell deeply in love with the women who flattered him and, as his passion for Millicent deepened, he invited her to visit Killarney. Arriving with her American friend, the gossip columnist, author and famous society hostess Elsa Maxwell, the two women were thrown into the forbidding world of his birthright. It was a striking contrast to his own lust for life. Advising the women to 'keep their voices down' and to 'eschew lipstick and powder', Castlerosse warned them that the staff and tenants would not approve of such flamboyance. They were told to refrain from acting with too much familiarity towards him, especially Millicent, as he had not revealed the true nature of their relationship. 'We had to behave ourselves more carefully in front of his servants and tenants than we did in front of the Prince of Wales,' Millicent later recalled. Castlerosse delighted in showing them around the estate, taking in the views of the lakes and the surrounding hills. But when Millicent stumbled over a rabbit hole and uttered, 'Oh damn,' he looked at her with a mixture of fury and disgust, and for a moment she 'thought he was going to send me back to rinse my mouth out'.

The hedonistic lifestyle Castlerosse enjoyed in London did not merge with his life in Ireland. At Killarney he adhered to the religious customs he had been brought up with – his prayer-book was, in fact, a pornographic book, which he read in chapel – and he expected his guests to rise at half past seven every morning for prayers. Millicent obliged him, but the protestant Elsa was not as courteous, and hammering on her door one morning, Castlerosse bellowed: 'You wicked hag, if you don't come down, I swear I'll come in and drag you down in your nightgown.'[8] Although he meant what he said, it would have been an impossible task given that Elsa was as heavy as he.

Although the affair was brief, Millicent remained fond of Castlerosse and she convinced Hearst's principal editor, Arthur Brisbane, to print his opinions of America on the front page of the *New York American*. And, telling Hearst himself of this 'journalistic find', she persuaded her husband to give Castlerosse a job. Asking Brisbane of his opinion of Castlerosse's talent as a writer, Hearst agreed that he would be paid £40[9] per article, to be published in the Sunday edition of the *New York American*.

However, the contract with Hearst was turned down in favour of Beaverbrook's offer to hire him as a travelling companion – a source of entertainment – who would accompany him around the world, all expenses paid. '[Beaverbrook] has become my never-ending lord of appeal,' Castlerosse said of his friend. 'He is always there, and always indulgent, when I have made a fool of myself.'[10]

Many viewed Castlerosse as nothing more than a court jester[11] for his new employer. Although Beaverbrook's upbringing as one of ten children born to a Scottish minister in Ontario, Canada, was a world away from Castlerosse's aristocratic background, the two men understood one another. Both of them had something the other wanted: Castlerosse coveted Beaverbrook's money and power, and Beaverbrook envied Castlerosse's inherited title and breeding. A self-made millionaire by the age of 30, Beaverbrook was a shrewd man who rarely pursued something without the premise that he would gain something in return. In Castlerosse, he recognised the malicious wit and jovial sense of fun that had gifted him with a natural talent for gossip. Prior to this arrangement, he had envisioned hiring someone who could chronicle the doings and sayings of important people, not just a gossip writer but an observer of social upheaval. He had engaged Leslie Hore-Belisha to write a column titled the Londoner's Log, but his writing was not to Beaverbrook's liking. Still, he continued to entertain the idea of featuring the column in his newspaper, the *Sunday Express*.

An opportunity arose while they were staying at the Hotel de Paris in Monte Carlo, and Castlerosse off-handedly remarked that he wanted to write an article on the principality for one of Beaverbrook's newspapers. 'Why don't you have a go?' Beaverbrook said. 'Look. You sit in one room and write the article on this subject. I'll sit in another room and write on the same theme.' When they were finished, he dismissed his own attempt and told Castlerosse, 'Your article is better.'

Beaverbrook stood by his statement and Castlerosse's article was printed in the *Sunday Express*, the newest of his fleet of newspapers. And, reviving his original idea of including the Londoner's Log in the newspaper, he offered Castlerosse £3,000[12] per annum plus expenses to write the column. At three thousand words, it occupied half of page two and, breaking from tradition, Castlerosse wrote under his real name. It had been the custom in Fleet Street to use a nom de plume for newspaper diaries, a discreet system that allowed the writer to report on their peers without being discovered. His decision was unconventional, and he became a gossip columnist 'when it was still thought extraordinary and in bad taste to do either'.[13]

However, Castlerosse cared little for social etiquette, and he openly gossiped about others in his column. Mischievous as opposed to muckraking, it was a clever ploy for his readers to live vicariously through him. In return, they became emotionally invested in his life. His column was largely a self-portrait: an aristocrat, a *bon viveur*, a confidant of millionaires and the companion of princes. Most of all, it presented a man who seemed to be living at the centre of things and it was the sort of lifestyle his readers aspired to, and envied. But owing to his damaged arm, he found writing to be a painful chore and, after several false starts, he discovered that he could write comfortably if he lay horizontally with a pillow propped under his right shoulder. Thus, all of his reporting for the Londoner's Log was done from his bed.

This new career did not suppress Castlerosse's pursuit of pleasure, and he continued his role of Beaverbrook's travelling companion, though he could now disguise his debauchery as 'work'. There was an expedition to Germany with Beaverbrook, Venetia Montagu, Lady Diana Cooper and Arnold Bennett.

It was a raucous bunch and the women, as highborn as they were, were well-versed in the art of vulgarity. Lady Diana, brought up as the daughter of the Duke of Rutland, was the product of an affair between her mother and the Unionist politician, Henry Cust. Renowned for her beauty and popularity as a socialite in both London and Paris, she had moved in the pre-war circle known as The Coterie, a group of intellectuals whose young men had been killed in the First World War. In 1919, she married Alfred 'Duff' Gordon Cooper, one of the few survivors of the group – an unpopular choice, for her parents had expected her to marry the Prince of Wales. Venetia, too, was accustomed to scorn from the members of her class. Strikingly beautiful, as a young debutante she had been a close friend of the former prime minister H.H. Asquith's daughter, Violet. In 1910 she had begun a lengthy correspondence with Asquith himself, which some assumed to be an affair.

Arnold Bennett recoiled at Castlerosse's explicit language, especially in front of the women, and was further mortified when Nancy Cunard approached him on the golf-course and asked what his handicap was. 'Drink and debauchery,'[14] Castlerosse answered. And, upon noticing Bennett's shocked expression, he added: 'I mean physical love.' Far from offended, the equally irreverent Nancy was amused by the response. It was beyond the pale for Bennett, and he refused to join them on a tour of Berlin's transvestite nightclubs. But he could not escape his travelling companions entirely, as they were in Berlin to discuss a film he was to write, Beaverbrook to finance, and Lady Diana to star in. The idea was 'no more than an idle fantasy', and nothing came of it.

After their Berlin trip they ventured to Brazil, and Venetia was replaced by Beaverbrook's long-term mistress, Jean Norton, the wife of the film producer Richard Norton, the future Lord Grantley. Lacking the gaiety of Berlin, the Brazilian trip was destined to be a failure from the moment they left Paris. Beaverbrook was in a cantankerous mood, dwelling on his wife Gladys's endless letters pleading with him to give up Jean. Married for almost twenty-four years, by her own admission she lived an 'Anna Karenina existence' alone with their three children. She had tolerated his past dalliances, but resented Jean's influence over her husband. This insecurity was partly due to her ill-health, as she had been diagnosed as suffering from a brain tumour. Although concerned for his wife's health, this did not prevent Beaverbrook from pursuing his travels, and he engaged the King's doctor, Thomas Horder, to look after her in his absence.

However, with his mind on Gladys and plagued by her letters to him about Jean Norton, Beaverbrook expressed his frustration by controlling every minute detail of the trip. Before they had left Paris, he had bullied Lady Diana into drinking champagne even though she had declined, claiming she did not like it. 'Of course you like it,' he told her and, summoning the waiter, he demanded, 'Some champagne for Lady Diana.' Beaverbrook then attacked an unsuspecting Castlerosse, who had boasted of the novel he was writing. Ordering him to read aloud the eight thousand words he had written, Lady Diana questioned whether he could read well. 'Like hell he can, the worst in the world,' said Beaverbrook. Humiliated, Castlerosse struggled through the manuscript, and Beaverbrook planted the final dart when he remarked: 'Not worth a damn, is it?'

Arriving in Rio, they were given the news that yellow fever, typhoid, cholera and leprosy had broken out in the city. Castlerosse took precautions and wore gloves to handle the money, and Lady Diana wallowed in a melancholic mood. Afraid of flying, she fretted about an aeroplane ride across the Andes, and she refused to join the party. It spoiled the sight-seeing trip for Beaverbrook and, further adding to his misery, Jean fell seriously ill and all of their excursions were cancelled. Following her recovery, they boarded the next ship home, and were met by Duff Cooper on their arrival. 'Personally I would rather spend six weeks in Wormwood Scrubs,'[15] he quipped when Lady Diana told him of the trip.

It was the era of the aristocratic columnist; Lady Eleanor Smith had her column in the *Weekly Dispatch*, Patrick Balfour was Mr Gossip of the *Daily Sketch*, and Tom Driberg was The Dragoman ('an interpreter or guide in eastern countries') for the *Daily Express*. Castlerosse had become a celebrity writer and the popularity of the Londoner's Log contributed to an increase in circulation for the *Sunday Express*.

A part of popular culture, his fame reached other echelons, and he appeared to epitomise the character of Adam Fenwick-Symes in Evelyn Waugh's future novel, *Vile Bodies* (published in 1930). The comparison was striking: Adam must find a job if he is to marry, and he lands a journalist post writing a gossip column under the guise of Mr Chatterbox for Lord Monomark's newspaper, the *Daily Excess* – shades of Beaverbrook and his *Express* newspapers. However, unlike Waugh's fictional character, Castlerosse lacked the moral compass which drove Adam to do the honourable thing for the woman he loved. Not one to let something as petty as money stand in the way of a romantic relationship, when the time was right, Castlerosse would look for a potential bride with her own money to support them both.

The Londoner's Log endeared Castlerosse to the type of woman he sought, and the column was well received by the very people he was writing about.

Mrs Belloc Lowndes reported that in one country house eight copies of the newspaper were delivered, one for each lady staying there. It became a platform for ambitious young women to promote themselves, and they aspired to have their names and photographs featured in the column. Enterprising socialites were approaching John Gordon, editor of the *Sunday Express*, with bribes of a weekend's entertainment with the 'most alluring amenities' if he would ensure they appeared in the Log.

Capitalising on the success of the Londoner's Log, Beaverbrook promoted Castlerosse to the role of editor of the column, which gave him more freedom to write about whatever he pleased. It was a simple decision for Beaverbrook, who often ordered his journalists to 'get more names into the paper, the more aristocratic the better. Everyone likes reading about people in better circumstances than his or her own.' The abandon with which Castlerosse wrote about his contemporaries appealed to Beaverbrook, and Castlerosse himself remarked: 'I don't care a tinker's curse about the troubles of a society journalist, and less than half of that for the feelings of those who are hurt by what is said about them in the newspapers. I don't care if all the dukes of England go dotty and all the barons become transformed into bloates.'

Despite Castlerosse's statement, it would be a misrepresentation to dismiss his writing for the Londoner's Log as flippant. He was sensitive to the fact that he had been a 'drop-out', and his parents never ceased to remind him that he was a failure in comparison to Dermot, who, unlike Castlerosse, had returned to the trenches after being wounded. The disability which prevented him from seeing out the war, dead or alive, plagued him with guilt. Relating to the men who had come back from the war, Castlerosse believed he could give them a voice and, as the years advanced, he realised that journalism gave him the power to broaden a man's sympathies. He worked hard, continuously revising, and he would write thirty thousand words in order to have enough material to edit it down to the three thousand that were required.

Once he had established his literary voice, Castlerosse became more self-assured in his editing and the speed at which he altered a feature, imposing his personality on to the narrative and giving it an entirely original approach. The topics which fascinated him appeared early on in the Log: his interest in money and the men who owned it, and the unstated feeling that he could have a happier time squandering their fortune than any of them ever could. To think of himself as an immensely rich man excited his imagination. Had Castlerosse been in possession of the riches he longed for, he would have frittered them away. As a gambler, his sympathies always lay with the victim, and in the Londoner's Log he told of a French aristocrat, the Marquis de

Gouy d'Arcy, who lost a considerable amount at the gaming tables that he was forced to retire to Florence, where living was cheap. And offering advice to his readers, Castlerosse issued such warnings as: 'If I were you, I should not bet with George Morton of 58 Pall Mall for he does not pay.'

The Londoner's Log had become a topical diary of his life, and he was viewed as an eligible bachelor of sorts – an endearing, overweight romantic who was looking for love. Photographs of his pudgy, smiling face adorned women's bedroom walls, and they began to write him letters, sexually explicit in their tone. Some sent detailed arrangements for their assignations, others were pathetic in their pleading to meet him. 'Darling, I am yours. Florence,' telegrammed one such lonely woman from Preston. The next day she sent another: 'I am so much in love I cannot even breathe. Florence.' Castlerosse's reply was simple: 'Try choking.'[16] There were harebrained, humorous letters too. 'My dear husband,' wrote a woman from Ealing. 'It's time that we set up house together. Please communicate with me at once.'

Proceeding to the address in Ealing, Castlerosse was ushered into a room where an old woman was reading the Bible. 'Madame,' he said, 'I have come in reference to a letter you sent me in which you state that I am your husband.'

The woman looked at Castlerosse, and replied, 'Your insolence is astounding. I have divorced you and have married the Emperor of China.'

Taken aback by this statement, Castlerosse said, 'I trust, madam, that you are quite happy.'

'All empresses are happy,' the woman retorted. 'Please leave the room.'[17]

Following the strange encounter, Castlerosse was inspired to write about a subject he knew nothing about: marriage. He confided to his readers:

> I am beginning to think that I ought to get married. I live in one room and eat out. This leads to incidents … but not to a standardised life. On the other hand, I carry my worries under my hat and nobody seems particularly interested in arranging a marriage for me. I should like to marry a good-natured, jolly woman.[18]

For his women readers the Londoner's Log had become an exciting serial. They approved of Castlerosse's appraisal of his ideal wife, and they longed for him to find romance with the type of woman who would appreciate his talent, overlook his physical shortcomings, and love him unconditionally. And having created such a parable in print, not even Castlerosse himself knew how the story would end.

⑨EETIN(5 AT A ⑩ISADVANTA(5E

'The way into my parlour is up a winding stair,
And I've a many curious things to show when you are there.'

Mary Howitt, *The Spider and the Fly*

———•◆•———

Doris's emergence as a socialite can be measured against the ebb and flow of
social issues and the part she played in them. Not yet at the forefront of the
set she would later associate with, she found herself overshadowed as topical
events unfolded. This might have served as an incentive for her to take on a
significant role but, as her actions during the Second World War would later
show, she was not chauvinistically minded. That is to say, she only took an
interest in current affairs when they posed a threat to her lifestyle.

But in 1926, as the Roaring Twenties ground to a halt with the General
Strike, Doris was not of adequate social prominence to be in a position
to help. The gulf between the rich and the poor was wider than before,
and unemployment, a crisis following the war, had turned into a national
epidemic. The parallel world of Belgravia and Mayfair, once immune from
such unpleasantness, could not escape the topic of the strike when 1.7 million

workers went out, predominantly in transport and heavy industry. It was prompted by the council of the Trade Union Congress (TUC), who had attempted to force the government to prevent wage reduction and worsening conditions for some 800,000 coal miners.

Political chat and threats of shutting down British industry by brute force excited young society women, and politics became a fashionable topic of conversation. Edwina Mountbatten led the crusade of socialites who helped to keep Britain afloat when renegade workers dared to hold the country to ransom. She worked on a switchboard alongside her best friend Jean Norton, and across the city of London those who had never worked a day in their lives were stepping into the roles normally filled by the working classes. A game to them, it was great fun to drive Tube trains and buses, and to serve tea and sandwiches to strike-breaking lorry drivers, and to answer telephones on a switchboard. It encapsulated the attitude of the Bright Young Things: that anything could become a joke. However, the fun came to an end after nine days when the TUC was defeated by the British government.

With order restored, the season continued in full swing, and the white stucco houses of Belgravia and Mayfair opened their doors to eligible bachelors, peers, heirs and spares of the aristocracy, who were looking for a wife. Doris was not a debutante and, edging out of her mid-20s, she was slipping towards what her mother's generation would have called an old maid. She began an affair with David Carnegie, the 11th Earl of Northesk, a skeleton competitor who would go on to win a bronze medal at the 1928 Winter Olympics. With his money, Doris nurtured the ostentatious idea of commissioning Rex Whistler to paint on her bedroom wall a mural design of *trompe l'oeil Corinthian*, consisting of columns and pilasters on a high base with interspersed niches and scenes depicting the Judgement of Paris. For reasons unknown, the design was not executed.

The affair was a distraction of sorts for them both: Northesk's four-year marriage to his American wife, Jessica (née Brown), a former Ziegfeld girl, was on the rocks, and Doris continued to pine for Laddie. She had heard through the grapevine that relations between Laddie and Edwina were fraught. For a month, in January 1927, Laddie had pressed Edwina to leave Dickie Mountbatten and, after a series of rows fuelled by her indecisiveness, she distanced herself from him and joined her husband in Malta. Upon learning that Laddie was back in London, free and unattached, Doris hoped for a reconciliation. But it was not to be: he had taken a two-month lease on a house in Osterley, and busied himself competing in polo matches with the Hurricanes, and brooding over Edwina.

To Doris's disappointment, Laddie and Edwina reconciled but they continued to argue about their future, and at the end of June he left for America. Learning of his whereabouts and that he was in New York without Edwina, Doris took a bold step and made plans to go there. Once again, Edwina was not completely out of the picture, and she joined him at his home on Long Island. It was a disastrous reunion: Edwina discovered she was pregnant, the baby having been conceived during her brief separation from Laddie, and now there was no hope of her leaving Dickie. Doris, on her part, remained in London, and continued to carry a torch for Laddie, though she knew he would never take her back.

Castlerosse was at a loss too, and although he was surrounded by beautiful women, attentive to him and revelling in his celebrity, he was yet to find love. He was desperate to love someone, and to be loved in return. To compensate for his loneliness, he turned to his old vices: food and alcohol were consumed more heartily than before, and his weight increased. With his enormous stomach, balding head and double chin, he looked older than his 37 years. He flaunted his gluttony and took pride in guzzling wine, drinking whiskey from a glass as big as a vase, and spilling the contents of his meals down his front due to his bad arm. His corpulence became a joke, thus setting the tone for the teasing he endured from the newspapers. The cruel jibes and the jokes made at his expense crossed over to his private life, and his appearance became the punchline of many a dinner-party anecdote. An acquaintance, Sir William Orpen, had attended a party where Castlerosse was a guest, and he asked: 'Is this green thing a waistcoat?'

'Yes,' said Castlerosse. 'What did you think it was?'

'A tennis court,' Sir William replied.[1]

In October, Castlerosse went to Newmarket to attend the races. 'How amusing racing would be,' he wrote in the Londoner's Log, 'if it were not for the horses. They take people's minds off conversation.' The conversation in question was with a gentleman who told him to back a horse named Nipisiquit. He failed to do so, and backed another horse. As was his luck, Nipisiquit won.

The wasted opportunity was not to be in vain.

Social events such as the races and agricultural shows brought the gentry out in droves, but it was the festivities afterwards which appealed to Doris. After the main event, men often went to nightclubs without their wives, and women like Doris would be at the establishment where, away from the glare of the public and being photographed for *The Sketch* and *The Bystander*, the recreation was unrestrained.

On one particular evening, after the Newmarket Races, Doris went to the St James nightclub. Castlerosse was there, with an elderly companion, drowning his sorrows after failing to bet on Nipisiquit. 'You want cheering up,' said his companion, as he sulked. 'Look at that woman who has just come in.'

It was Doris – blonde, beautiful and exquisitely dressed – and Castlerosse's heart was momentarily lifted. Gambling and women were a perfect recipe, he concurred. His point of view was simple: if one was a woman, gamble heavily; if one was a man, subscribe to the party funds. 'The woman will be endowed with a past, and the man with a title,' he wrote.[2] It was an insightful remark, for Doris was a woman with a past and she sought a man with a title.

'Apart from anything else,' his companion remarked, 'it must be fun to afford a dress like that.' If only his observant companion had known how Doris acquired such a dress, they might have been hesitant in encouraging Castlerosse to make her acquaintance.

When they met, he told Doris how 'exhilarated' he felt by her appearance.[3] Knowing of his fame and his affluent readership, she responded to the flattery. It became a question of who was flattering, or exploiting, whom.[4] Their meeting was brief and perhaps one which Doris did not wish to repeat. But Castlerosse would make a gesture that would turn her head, and following their encounter he included her photograph alongside several society beauties in the Londoner's Log.

At first, Doris was charmed by Castlerosse's 'great big rascally towards life', for it was a similar outlook to her own. 'He was a little boy with a warm heart, and I find that comforting,' she told a friend. He was, as she discovered, easy to manipulate because he was 'wonderfully susceptible to flattery'.[5] The men she had known, and those who had given her money and gifts, possessed a ruthless streak that was attached to their fortune, and how they earned and maintained it. Although Doris benefited from their (often fleeting) arrangements, she knew it was they who had the upper hand. However, in Castlerosse she found a man whom she could play to her advantage. Aware of his shortcomings, he wrote in the Londoner's Log:

> I suppose that among all living things, there are no such conceited animals as men. As a poor fool of a pheasant will gobble down raisins till it dies of indigestion, so will men consume flattery from women until they find themselves married. All the successful women in the world have been mistresses of flattery.

From the moment they met, Castlerosse's passion burned brighter than Doris's, though she was fond of him and admired his jovial sense of humour. He acknowledged his growing obsession with her, and each day he longed to hear her voice, or to catch a glimpse of her. It had become a sickness in him, and one which only Doris could cure. From his flat on Brook Street, just off Hanover Square in Mayfair, he monitored her comings and goings, and he began to follow her to wherever she went.

Far from flattered by the attention which Castlerosse was paying to her, it embarrassed Doris. She continued to see other men casually, as was her wont, in exchange for money and gifts, and she feared his meddling would sabotage such arrangements. As he was one of the most famous figures in London and on the continent, it was difficult to disguise her association with him. Revered by royalty – his family, the Kenmares, had a long association with the British royal family – he held the key to those doors that remained closed to her. Knowing that it was this which Doris desired, many men in his position would have exploited this power. But not Castlerosse, for in those early days he was too besotted to care about such a dynamic, and he played into her hands.

In an attempt to compete with Doris's admirers – his rivals, as he viewed them – Castlerosse began to send her jewels, furs and paintings, which plunged him further into debt. Aware that he was out of his depth, she bluntly told him that he was making a fool of himself. 'I know I am,' he said. 'But I can't help it. I am not just in love. I am obsessed.'[6]

It was not the romance he had imagined and, when he was in Doris's company, they quarrelled. Castlerosse refused to acknowledge it as a sign of how unsuited they were; perhaps he had not met a woman quite like Doris before. Although she shared a similar lifestyle to Jacqueline Forzane, their temperaments were entirely opposite. Far from submissive, Doris matched his infamous temper, and during their arguments she attacked him physically. Setting the tone of their future relationship, he retaliated.

It was more than Doris could bear and, one afternoon in 1927, she paid Beaverbrook a visit. She was angry and distressed by Castlerosse's treatment, and pulling up her sleeve she showed him a mass of bruises on her arm. 'I want you to warn him, as a friend,' she told Beaverbrook, 'that if he behaves like this again I shall inform the police.' Certain she would have no further dealings with Castlerosse, she asked Beaverbrook to force him to return the key to her house, which he had stolen.

Summoned by Beaverbrook, Castlerosse appeared and was reproached for beating Doris. 'How dare she,' he said, spilling his drink as his anger mounted.

Rolling up his trouser leg, he revealed a bandaged calf. 'Look what she did to *me*, with her *teeth*, too!'

Although taken aback by the impassioned wound, Beaverbrook said: 'Even this is no reason for you to hammer Doris like that.'

'We are utterly unsuited,' he agreed with Beaverbrook. 'I won't see her again.'

There was more than an ounce of deceit in Castlerosse's promise to Beaverbrook, for he could not stay away from her. And she too, despite her better judgement, was drawn to him. Doris became the subject of a piece in the Londoner's Log,[7] when Castlerosse expressed his thoughts on romantic relationships, the topic of which was inspired by his views on marriage.

Appealing to his female readers, he wrote of a woman named Doreen who, like Doris, had a changeable nature. 'Eighty-percent of what Doreen says is true. The remaining twenty is illuminating embroidery.' Drawing on Doris's heartbreak prompted by her love affair with Laddie Sanford, he confided to his readers that Doreen's experience of love had been a bitter one. 'The embrace of a man had been too closely allied to the kiss of Judas.' He invented a nameless daughter for Doreen, whom she advised: 'Marry the greatest man in the world, even if nobody but you thinks so. Faith may not move mountains but it has a wonderfully steadying effect on husbands. Never bore him and always greet him joyfully.'

Offering his own advice for a harmonious marriage, Castlerosse said: 'When you come down to breakfast, remain silent but be perfectly dressed. Put your husband's comfort before your own.' Quick to emphasise his own flaws, perhaps a ploy to tug on the heartstrings of his female admirers, he warned against marrying a high-spirited man, for 'a disillusionment may await her … beware when you marry a clown that the black vulture of despair is not fluttering in his wake'.[8]

Doris could ignore him no longer, and she began to entertain his proposal of marriage. Years before, when she lived with Gertie, the two women spoke of their aspirations. Gertie told her, 'I am going to be the most celebrated actress in London,' to which Doris reputedly said, 'And I am going to marry a lord.' Castlerosse was the first lord she had known to propose marriage and, given that she was prone to meeting married peers, perhaps he was the only one who was unattached. Furthermore, he had led her to believe that he could afford her expensive tastes. With his devotion, her ability to manipulate him, and (what she thought to be) his wealth, there was little to convince her that marriage to Castlerosse was a bad idea.

Approaching her friends for their advice, she was warned that marriage to such a profligate and selfish man would be impossible. Castlerosse, too, sought counsel from his friends. Their response was less than inspiring, and they told him to avoid marrying a self-centred, arrogant and attractive woman, for it would end in disaster. Hoping to dissuade him from committing a mistake, the Countess of Tolby listened to his plea that he and Doris were suited, to which she answered: 'Discontented wives were usually the victims of love matches.'[9]

Neither Doris nor Castlerosse listened, for each individual had their own motives for marriage. From the beginning, he was hypnotised and thought her 'breathlessly lovely to look at, with the delicate features of a nervous and sensitive deer and the mobility, strength and grace of a panther'. And he was equally attracted by her 'outspoken, outrageous and shameless' behaviour. It was an age when decadence was admired, and Doris embraced this furore. Rather than dressing outrageously (women were painting their fingernails green and copying the dark and menacing looks of Pola Negri and Alla Nazimova), she made scenes in public. Restaurants were her platform to misbehave and she took pleasure in demanding to see managers and chefs, in order to berate them for the position of the table, the temperature of the wine, and the quality of the food. 'No one seemed to resent this,' recalled an admirer. 'The men she was with seemed to think it gave them a sort of cachet.'[10]

Castlerosse himself had become embroiled in outrageous behaviour, though on this occasion he was the victim rather than the instigator. It was revealed that an anonymous man was using his name to write passionate letters to a young woman, whose aunt wrote to him at the *Sunday Express*, asking how soon the wedding could be expected. A private detective was put on the case, and the man turned out to be a Mr Murray, who belonged to a Highland regiment. Confronted by Castlerosse as to why he had done such a thing, Murray smiled ruefully and replied: 'Romance, my lord, romance.'

Their exchange had inadvertently piqued Castlerosse's conscience, and Doris was the recipient of his response. Marriage, he told his readers (before he told Doris), was on the cards. 'After all,' he looked to the future, 'they might change the divorce laws.' Though, careful not to be viewed as controversial, he added: 'Marriage is a great institution but we don't all wish to spend our lives in institutions.'[11]

Doris had played her hand too foolishly and, in her haste to find someone to protect her, she impulsively agreed to marry Castlerosse. Had she waited, she might have become the next Countess of Northesk, for the earl's divorce had been granted on the grounds of his misconduct and, a year later, he married Elizabeth Vlasto. Laddie, too, was also single after Edwina had finally severed ties with him to remain with her husband, though she would continue to have numerous affairs.

Although there were more eligible men available to Doris when she accepted Castlerosse's proposal, she admitted that she felt an unexplainable attraction to him. He felt the same way about her, and in an effort to explain their compatibility, he said: 'I am a downy old bird and Doris is a downy young chicken.'[12] But this was an attraction which ran deeper than Castlerosse's colloquialism. Regardless of their age difference and backgrounds, in all manner of relationships they took what they could and gave little away. Throughout the years, after bitter feelings and hatred tore them apart, they gravitated towards one another. It was a force that neither Doris nor Castlerosse could explain, or resist.

The name Doris Delevingne and all that it symbolised had reached the Kenmare fold by way of gossip. She had not met her future mother-in-law, nor had she been introduced to the members of Castlerosse's family. He had refrained from telling his parents about his fiancée and, owing to their response to the Jacqueline Forzane affair, was there a possibility that he thought Doris would accept payment to disappear from his life?

Lady Kenmare travelled from Killarney to London to confront her son, and knowing Beaverbrook was an influential figure in his life, she hoped to gain his support. As she had done when Castlerosse proposed marriage to Forzane, she involved her brother, Lord Revelstoke. Their conspiracy to close rank only reinforced Doris's importance in Castlerosse's life, and he viewed them both as victims of parental authority and provocateurs against social convention. Further wounding him was the betrayal of his oldest ally, Beaverbrook, who agreed with Lady Kenmare's sentiments that he should be dissuaded from marrying Doris.

Privy to their arguments, which had escalated into public brawls – they argued in restaurants, their voices growing louder until all eyes were on them – Beaverbrook appealed to Doris to leave Castlerosse. But neither Doris nor Castlerosse would admit they were ill-matched. His resentment towards his mother for her rejection of his future wife, and Doris's own ambition to join the aristocracy, inspired the couple to play Lord and Lady Kenmare, Lord Revelstoke and Beaverbrook at their own game. As for Doris's parents' reaction, there is no evidence to suggest that they either approved or disapproved of her marrying a peer. Given the feeling of semi-estrangement between their daughter and themselves, perhaps they felt her world was one in which they were not welcome. Her brother, Dudley, however, was enthusiastic about the marriage and he would form a close friendship with Castlerosse, who treated the young man with a paternal air and often dispensed advice on his love affairs and finances, whether it was solicited or not.

Having committed themselves to deceiving the Kenmares and Beaverbrook, Doris and Castlerosse failed to consider the press and their habit of periodically checking the marriage notices with the intention of reporting on prominent individuals. As a result, Beaverbrook's *Express* journalists discovered their notice of marriage, which had been posted at Hammersmith Register Office. John Gordon, the editor-in-chief of the *Sunday Express*, queried it with Beaverbrook, who then approached Castlerosse for verification. Having promised Lady Kenmare that he would do all he could to discourage the couple, Beaverbrook made one last appeal to Castlerosse. The reason for sabotaging the marriage was founded on their belief that Doris would corrupt Castlerosse and bring shame to the Kenmare family.

However, Castlerosse himself had experienced his own share of sexual deviance. Though, unlike Doris, his being a man meant such behaviour was not ridiculed, even if it was frowned upon due to his faith and the fact that his father had not strayed from Lady Kenmare. He had once been in love with Mabel de Forest, the daughter of the Baron de Forest and his first wife, Mathilde Menier, the rich widow of Albert Menier, scion of the chocolate family. At almost ten years his junior, Mabel would have nothing to do with him and, in an attempt to impress her, Castlerosse engaged her stepmother's influence. This resulted in a brief affair between Castlerosse and the stepmother, Ethel, who was ten years his senior and renowned for her infidelities with younger men. The affair ended the year Castlerosse met Doris, and friends wondered why he had left Ethel, a rich woman, for Doris, an opportunist. 'I didn't,' said Castlerosse, 'she did.' When they asked why, they were told: 'Oh, I taught her French practices, and once, while she was engaged in them, she looked up and found me reading the *Evening Standard*.'[13]

Appealing to Castlerosse's self-indulgent nature, Beaverbrook invited him to the French Riviera. Then, he booked two tickets on the Golden Arrow, aware that the train departed London before the register office opened. To his surprise, Castlerosse seemed to forget his plan to marry Doris, and citing that he had experienced 'a worrying time', he looked forward to 'some rest and sunshine'.

Before leaving, Castlerosse and Doris had conspired for her to discreetly join him in Cannes. Arriving the same day as the men, Doris used

Beaverbrook's account and booked into a room on the other side of the hotel. They met each afternoon for secret assignations, after which they ordered champagne, and revelled in fooling Beaverbrook. When the bill was presented to Beaverbrook, he made investigations and was disappointed to learn that his friend had deceived him. But, as he had assured Lady Kenmare, they were *not* married.

While Doris was enjoying the flurry of scandal that she had created within the Kenmare household, she did not stop to think of the repercussions. Castlerosse himself had failed to warn her of the ruthlessness of his parents, his mother in particular. A devout Catholic (she had converted before marriage), Lady Kenmare took sadistic pleasure in helping the priests round up the sinners who were lackadaisical in their devotion to Christ. And during the annual religious processions, she saw to it that some of the more notorious sinners knelt on stone until their kneecaps bled in penance. To her, Doris was a sinner, a wanton woman who would lead her impressionable son to rack and ruin. She knew how to punish Castlerosse, and she twisted the knife where it would hurt most. His allowance, although meagre from his father's estate, was supplemented from the Baring trust fund, and should he marry 'this notorious woman', it would stop.

Doris, it can be assumed, was unaware of Lady Kenmare's threats to cut Castlerosse off financially. He felt like a small boy again, unloved, and a thorn in his mother's side. As he was apt to do when he was most unhappy, he overindulged in food, wine and Doris. Returning to gambling with more fervour than before, he lost hoards of money and his debts escalated. As the creditors chased him all over London, he sought comfort in the arms of Doris, who momentarily restored his confidence.

In spite of this turmoil, his writing for the Londoner's Log had become more energetic than before. His piece on love and marriage was not lost on his friends, but it slipped past the watchful eye of Lady Kenmare (did she read his column?). Publishing a fictional conversation with a woman named Margaret, he wrote:

> I threw down my pen, took up a telephone, and asked a woman to luncheon. This woman is beautiful, experienced, richly successful, extravagant in her clothes but I fancy not over-lavish in her morals. 'Supposing, Margaret,' I said to her, 'you fell in love with a man who had a reputation of being a waster. What would you do?'
>
> 'Well,' she said, 'providing I was sufficiently in love with him I should marry him, because my experience is that a woman who falls in love with

a waster as a rule goes on being attracted by the same type. It is the same with men. Some men like bad women. And this they will continue to do so all their lives. It is an unhappy fate, but it is better to have a few months' happiness with a waster than forty years' misery and boredom with what others would call a bad man … I would marry the man I love and the man who loves me. Like Diana Cooper,[14] I would go out into the world hand in hand with my husband, confident that poverty can be overcome by wit and hard work.'[15]

Although Doris provided the inspiration for Margaret's beauty, experience and extravagant clothes, she could never be content in a marriage to a poor man. Nor would she have endorsed the belief that poverty could be 'overcome by wit and hard work'. The latter part of Castlerosse's sentiment, it appears, was wishful thinking on his behalf.

The subject of Doris and Castlerosse's engagement, tinged by parental disapproval, became a topical piece of conversation. Those readers who were his friends read the Londoner's Log as the saga unfolded, believing they knew what the outcome would be. Thinking he would never defy his mother, the thought of him marrying Doris became the source of much hilarity. The Prince of Wales spied the couple in the Embassy Club and whistled with admiration. 'Congratulations, my Lord!' he scribbled on a note to Castlerosse. Castlerosse was delighted, Doris even more so. All eyes were on her. Newspapers, too, speculated about the woman who had captured his heart, and the Londoner's Diary of the *Evening Standard* wrote:

> I see that Lord Castlerosse has been writing about marriage. He is a modest man who, however, does occasionally allow us glimpses of his adventures, which include being left for dead by the retreating Germans after the Marne, fighting on the Somme and at Passchendaele, finance in London and New York, and finally journalism. From the last adventure of matrimony, however, though he is now 37, he continues to shrink. But, confirmed bachelor though he professes to be, he cannot avoid the topic, and there are moments when his disquisitions on it irresistibly remind me of the bird and the snake.[16]

It was an insightful appraisal, particularly the closing sentiment for, as Castlerosse was to learn, Doris was 'a regal beauty with a viper's tongue'.[17] With her penchant for bad behaviour, further inflamed by the attention of the press and Castlerosse's friends, she was determined to maintain the momentum. However, she knew Castlerosse was an impressionable man, and that Beaverbrook's persuasion of money could threaten her position. As newspaper diarists mocked him for his bravado in print, Doris appealed to his ego and prompted him to prove his naysayers wrong.

Prove them wrong he did, and on 15 May 1928, a notice of marriage was pinned to the board of Hammersmith Register Office. The following morning, Doris and Castlerosse were married.[18]

₵ADY CASTLEROSSE

'The terrible thing is done.'

Lady Kenmare

———•◆•———

The bravado of the newlyweds began to falter and, twenty-four hours after their secret marriage at Hammersmith Register Office, discontentment set in. After the wedding they moved into 8 Balfour Place, on Park Lane, due to Castlerosse's dislike of the two steps leading down to the lavatory at Doris's house on Deanery Street. It was a small upheaval for Doris who was pleased with her new title, if not her husband, and she busied herself by ordering viscountess coronets to be stitched on to her crêpe de Chine sheets and pillowcases, which she sent to Paris to be laundered.[1] Coronets, too, adorned her notepaper and were embossed on her luggage.

Castlerosse, however, was less flamboyant and the fear of breaking the news to his parents sobered any marital bliss he had previously felt. 'How can Goethe say that he knew only ten days of happiness in his life?' he had written in the Londoner's Log before committing himself to Doris. Now, with those ten days of happiness a distant memory, he sensed the storm clouds were closing in.

Aside from parental disapproval, Castlerosse was exasperated by Doris's spending. A frivolous man himself, his own taste in clothing had become more extravagant as he aged. His shirts cost £5[2] each and had to be monogrammed; there were evening suits in dark inky-blue Viana, jewel-coloured velvet smoking jackets, gold embroidered and coronetted slippers, acres of white pique waistcoats; heavy satin cravats were stuck with a large pearl-shaped tiepin, one of his overcoats was lined with sable and another had a collar of astrakhan. With his own bills, many of which went unpaid, he could not afford Doris's 'casual expenses'[3] of £100 a week.

It was not long before they had their first domestic quarrel, which was about money, the foundation on which their marriage and lives were built. But regardless of his title, he believed by marrying a woman from an ordinary background, he would 'by the stroke of a wand or the signature of a marriage register go back to the simple pleasures of their youth'.[4] Despite Castlerosse's wishful thinking, neither he nor Doris were willing to compromise. Far from sympathetic towards her husband's financial woes, she told him: 'All right, don't give me any money, then. I'll pay for everything myself in future.'[5] Aware of how Doris intended to get this money, he relented and increased her allowance.

The argument marked a pivotal moment in their relationship, and they soon found one another's recklessness hard to forgive: Castlerosse and his dependence on others for money, and Doris's dependence on others for attention. It did not help when Doris made a joke about his beloved Killarney, and was astonished by his furious reaction. He berated her for the exact things which had attracted him in the beginning: her behaviour, her language, and 'the way she snapped her fingers at the morals of the day'.[6] Their dynamic was established early on and, to those observing their rapport, she appeared to be 'a virulent blonde shrew-mouse goading an elephant'.[7]

Eventually, as he was inclined to do, Castlerosse turned to Beaverbrook for help. Lacking the courage to face his friends, he asked Beaverbrook to break the news of his marriage. 'Tell me now,' asked their mutual friend, Tim Healy, the Viceroy of Ireland, 'what sort of a woman would this Doris be?'

After some thought, Beaverbrook replied, 'She is a woman of the world.'[8]

Although Beaverbrook disapproved of the marriage – since his wife's death he had grown possessive of his cronies and was reluctant to share them – he was interested in sexuality, his own and other people's. A woman like Doris who was uninhibited and unfaithful would have intrigued him, and so there was an element of fascination where she was concerned. Owing to this deviance, he had once convinced a group of friends to hide with him in the garden to peer through a bedroom window 'to watch Castlerosse perform'.[9]

Weeks before he had asked Beaverbrook to break the news of his marriage, Castlerosse himself had been afraid to confess to his friend what he had done. Hiding behind his column, he had written about the subject of weddings in the Londoner's Log, where he brooded over the question as to why crowds turned out to see two people marry. Hinting at his own problem, which was yet to be aired, he came to the macabre conclusion: 'We can all rejoice that executions are now held in private.' He must have sensed his own metaphorical execution was in the near future but, unlike his journalistic musings, his would be a public affair.

After a series of rows, instigated by Doris who threatened to reveal the secret, Castlerosse relented and decided the appropriate timing to tell Beaverbrook would be at his birthday luncheon held at his country house, Cherkley Court. Leaving Doris behind in London, he motored down to Surrey to find Beaverbrook dining alone with Lady Diana Cooper. Over the course of the luncheon, she teased him about his infatuation with Doris, and ridiculed his plans to marry her. Irritated by her comments, he could not eat or drink, and halfway through the meal he rose from the table and abruptly left.

A comedy of errors would follow. Returning to London, he called on his friend, Lady Bridget Paget, to tell her of his dilemma. Younger than Castlerosse (he was a friend of her mother's), Lady Bridget moved with the Bright Young Things and thought him a great buffoon of a man. Amused that he had married Doris, and of his terror about confessing to his parents what he had done, she offered to break the news to Beaverbrook as though it were a piece of society gossip. Agreeing with her plan, Castlerosse sent her down to Cherkley where, as Beaverbrook's birthday party continued, she broke the news that Castlerosse had married Doris in secret. Explaining that Castlerosse did not have the courage to tell him in person, Lady Bridget asked if Beaverbrook would 'kindly pass on a message' to Lady Kenmare.

Beaverbrook himself had promised to keep Lady Kenmare informed of all developments, and in turn Castlerosse had given his word that he would not act without telling him first. Knowing of his friend's impressionable nature, he presumed Doris had forced Castlerosse into the marriage, and it did not inspire feelings of endearment towards her. Betrayed and hurt, and infuriated at the position he had been forced into, Beaverbrook telephoned Castlerosse to express his disappointment. Sensing that he already knew the folly he had committed, Beaverbrook's defences weakened. 'Please tell my mother,' Castlerosse pleaded. 'And please break it gently.'[10]

The following morning, Beaverbrook made an appointment to visit Lady Kenmare and, knowing how distraught she would be, he ordered her doctor to stand by. After listening to how her son had married 'that woman' at Hammersmith Register Office, the colour returned to her complexion. 'Thank God,' she said. 'That means they're not really married.' Beaverbrook did not agree with her religious outlook that marriage outside of a church was not binding, and he pitied her optimism, for he knew that Doris and Castlerosse were, indeed, legally married. Before he left, he suggested she meet with Castlerosse to hear his reasons for marrying Doris.

It was Doris who urged Castlerosse to visit his mother who, upon learning that he was avoiding her, felt angry and disappointed all over again. But this was not done out of love for her husband or respect for her mother-in-law. She was amused at how afraid he was of Lady Kenmare, and the situation had become a joke to her. However, Castlerosse's fears were genuine. His sisters, Lady Margaret and Lady Cecilia, had formed good marriages; the former to Lord Edward Grosvenor (she also participated in the coronation of King George V), and the latter to Colonel Hon. Thomas Eustace Vesey. Furthermore, his mother's health, which had declined since the death of Dermot, troubled him and he worried how his actions would affect her weak heart.

Prompting Castlerosse to see sense, Doris warned him that the marriage of a famous peer would not remain a secret for long. Formalities aside, and caring little for Castlerosse's dilemma, she wanted everyone to know that she had married into the peerage. With her marriage came certain responsibilities, and she must have known she would be expected to provide her husband with an heir. And Castlerosse was correct when he predicted that Lady Kenmare did not think highly of the woman he had chosen to secure the Kenmare bloodline.

It further pained Lady Kenmare when she discovered that Doris was not a Catholic, nor would she consider converting, as she had done when she married her own husband. But Doris was not the first viscountess to attract attention for the wrong reasons. Castlerosse's friend, Jean Skeffington, the Scots-born wife of the 11th Viscount Massereene, a famous beauty renowned for her dark, exotic looks and flamboyant dress sense, was once mistaken for a streetwalker.[11] However, unlike Lady Massereene and her penchant for low-cut dresses, backless gowns and bejewelled head-wear, it was not Doris's clothing that Lady Kenmare was worried about. She had heard the rumours about her new daughter-in-law and, like all of Mayfair, she knew that Doris was 'an exclusive *poule de luxe*'.[12]

The meeting between Castlerosse and his mother was as painful as he imagined it to be, and it evoked his boyhood memories of feeling unloved and rejected. 'I must tell you,' began Lady Kenmare, 'that I am against the alliance you have made and will never approve of it. Nor will your father. As for me, I shall never meet this woman, and you must not bring her to Killarney in my lifetime.' She hoped, by exerting her authority, that Castlerosse would agree to divorce Doris, and they could continue with their lives as though nothing had happened. Although her religious beliefs did not condone divorce, she felt, in her son's predicament, it was the only answer. After all, in her own mind, she was saving him from a sinner.

Castlerosse respected his mother's wish that he refrain from bringing Doris to Killarney. It caused him a considerable amount of anguish, for he loved the estate and he had hoped that his wife would too. Not only had their different outlooks on money caused a degree of conflict in their marriage, now his inability to introduce Doris to Killarney, a place that was not only his birthright but had given him so much happiness, would intensify those feelings. Amid the tension, he found the courage to tell his mother: 'I love my wife, Doris, and there will never be any other woman.'[13]

Breaking her foreboding silence, Lady Kenmare abandoned her original plan of instigating a divorce and suggested that an announcement of marriage must be made to the press, prompting their quarrel to escalate from a family matter into an Irish farce. They disagreed over the wording. Lady Kenmare wanted the notice to say that a marriage between Viscount Castlerosse and Doris Delavigne★ had been 'celebrated' at Hammersmith Register Office. Privately, she announced the marriage to her friends and close family as 'the terrible thing is done'. But Castlerosse insisted the correct term should be 'solemnised', as it was listed on the marriage certificate. His mother thought it sacrilegious, as she felt it could only apply to church weddings. With their tempers fraying, they dispatched a footman to locate a dictionary, where they proceeded to disagree over the correct terminology. In a rare victory over his mother, it was Castlerosse who had the final say.

Finally, they parted amicably with Lady Kenmare kissing her son as he left. The maternal warmth was a fleeting gesture, for she told Beaverbrook: 'I will never meet the woman he has married. And she will never enter my

---

★ The press used Doris's modified spelling of 'Delevingne' to report on her.

home while I am there.'[14] More than a threat, it was a promise she intended to keep.

The following morning, Doris got her wish. All of London woke up to the news that she had married a lord. Among the newspaper notices, the *Daily Mail*'s was the most positive, paying tribute to her physical charm:

> The announcement of a secret marriage between Lord Castlerosse and Miss Doris Delavigne has come as a great surprise to the West End, for Lord Castlerosse has publicly outlined on several occasions the advantage of remaining a bachelor. Miss Delavigne is tall, fair and very pretty with a wistfully cynical smile and a very quick brain. Mr Michael Arlen thought that she would become a leading hostess in London if she ever married.

The humour that Doris had once found in deceiving her parents-in-law had become unfunny, and she realised the consequences of their marriage. As for Castlerosse, he 'tiptoed through the first weeks of matrimony like a dog with a raw pad walking through a field of nettles'.[15] Perhaps as an indication to how he felt about his choice of wife, he included Edna St Vincent Millay's couplet in the Londoner's Log: 'Safe upon the solid rock the ugly houses stand; Come and see my shining palace, built upon the sand!'

Their union, although burdened by setbacks from the beginning, had weakened after the news broke. Still disapproving of Doris, Lord Revelstoke followed through with his threat and he stopped Castlerosse's allowance from the Baring trust fund. Beaverbrook, too, thought his friend deserved to be punished, and he refused to see him. The estrangement from his richest relative and his benevolent friend became a topic of gossip, which circulated through Mayfair. Once faithful friends betrayed any loyalty they had felt towards Castlerosse, and they tattled to Beaverbrook all the scandal they had not dared to reveal before.

Doris was furious; she resented Beaverbrook's financial ascendancy over her husband and how he did not hesitate to exert his power. Having lost his two most generous benefactors, Castlerosse had only his salary as a journalist to keep himself and Doris. She berated him for his lack of money, and for bowing to Lady Kenmare and Lord Revelstoke's authority. As far as Doris was concerned, he had given in too easily, and she thought him a coward. 'Marriage is an involuntary association of an impermanent nature between two people of weak minds!' Castlerosse said. Far from weak-minded, Doris was looking to the future, and to a solution to relieve her of her limited income. In a bid to appease Doris, and to settle the friction between the two,

Castlerosse bought her a Rolls-Royce Phantom, a car he could not afford,[16] and hired a chauffeur from William 'Billy' (later Sir William) Rootes's motor-car agency to drive it.

Castlerosse's secretary, Gwyn Lewis, was privy to his financial irresponsibility, and like Doris, although under different circumstances, she also suffered from his lack of income. Reporting to Castlerosse every Thursday, she would find him in bed, relaxing or reading, surrounded by a fortress of books. After a morning brandy and cigar, he would offhandedly attempt to quote something ('As Caesar once said …') and point to a pile of books and say, 'It's in that lot.' He was supposed to contribute £5[17] a week to Gwyn's salary, and she often had to prompt him to do so. Sometimes he would write an introduction for the Londoner's Log, and ask her to finish it. She would have to find out which socialites were popular, and submit a list of their names to Castlerosse. He had something acid to say about each of them, especially if they had snubbed Doris.

Marriage for Doris had symbolised nothing more than a change of name. Her outlook and morals remained as before, and she did not think it necessary to change her friends, or reform her behaviour. She dabbled in charity work, as many peeresses did, but her efforts were overshadowed by the gaiety of the fundraising. One event in particular was Barbara Cartland's (then Mrs Alexander McCorquodale) idea of enhancing an otherwise formal dinner dance at the Kit-Kat Club in aid of Queen Charlotte's Hospital by transforming it into a Queen Charlotte's Birthday Dinner, complete with fancy dress. Keeping within the culinary theme, Lady Dunn was the white wine; Lady Scarsdale was the goose; Barbara was the champagne; and Doris was the fish course – her costume was fashioned from a tight dress of shimmering sequins and chiffon fins. Barbara then threw a Hallowe'en ball and invited Doris to come as one of the thirteen superstitions,[18] and there was an opportunity for her to re-enact a lido scene at a later event.

Overlooking his wife's charity work, albeit an excuse to go to parties, Castlerosse criticised her behaviour and accused her of infidelity. Many of her affairs were so casual that Doris herself did not view them as adultery, and she innocently told him that she was 'a magnet to men'.[19] Humiliated by her promiscuity, Castlerosse demanded that she show some obedience and discretion. 'She is quite blatant,' he remarked to a friend. 'She will soon have all of London laughing at me behind my back.' But Doris's reaction was to laugh in his face. In truth, she could not fathom why he was so angry.

Within weeks the arguments they were having in private turned into public spectacles, and they became the talk of Mayfair. When Doris and Castlerosse entered a restaurant, all eyes followed them. With his enormous stomach, he had trouble squeezing past the tables, while she looked ethereal in comparison, 'giving a shining impression of white and gold'.[20] The table at which they sat became the focal point for their fellow diners. Doris's voice would be raised, its shrillness piercing through the restaurant and, despite the disturbance, onlookers thought 'she looked at her most beautiful when her cheeks were flushed in temper'.[21]

In retaliation, Castlerosse would inflate his elephantine body until he was puce in the face and curse his wife and throw things at her to try and force her out on to the street. Doris was unflinching, and she outdid his swearing and outsmarted his tactics. She would throw things back at him, and they scrapped and rolled around on the floor, hitting and biting one another until they drew blood. She knew his weaknesses – his weight, his gambling debts, his failure as a son, and his disappointing Beaverbrook – and where to plant the dart. When she had triumphed over him, she would let out a shrill laugh as she left the room.

After their arguments, Castlerosse was left breathless and wounded from Doris's verbal barbs. He collapsed on to his bed, his body covered in sweat and his face soaked with tears, and after a time, he would take a bath, into which he poured an entire bottle of eau de cologne. With his body rested and his mind restored, he reappeared with a cigar in his mouth, dressed in his usual flamboyant style, ready to face an evening's entertainment at one of his favourite haunts. Publicly he was 'Gay Lord Castlerosse',[22] but privately he was a wreck.

Not one to admit defeat, Doris would be waiting for him at those restaurants and, sensing that his persona was an act, she resorted to a new tactic to break his temper. She would show up, wearing a new piece of jewellery that was not a gift from her husband, and flaunt it before his eyes. He would ask where she had got it, thinking it a token of admiration (or thanks) from a wealthy admirer, and often he was right. She would refuse to tell him where it had come from, knowing that he would erupt with fury. He beat his fists on the table and his voice bellowed through the restaurant, to which she remained defiantly mute. When she did respond it would not be with the answer he had wanted to hear, but to make fun of his appearance, to laugh at his jealousy, and to diminish his ability as a lover in comparison to the many men she had slept with. It did not help Castlerosse's pride when the smart set of Mayfair began to refer to Doris as 'Mrs Goldsmith and Silversmith'.[23]

During their arguments across the restaurant table, Doris directed Castlerosse's accusations back to him. She suspected he was having love affairs with his women friends, many of whom followed the Londoner's Log and felt a certain fondness towards him. There were outrageous scenes, and he would slap her across the face to silence her, and she reacted by biting him wherever she could sink her teeth into his bovine flesh. Afterwards, Doris would leave the table and summon her Rolls-Royce to collect her, whereupon she fled to an understanding friend. Daphne Weymouth, in particular, knew how Doris truly felt and she recalled her arrival at the Palm Court of the Ritz Hotel for luncheon, where she revealed the bruises and scars that Castlerosse had given her. 'She even managed to carry off a black eye with a certain *brio*,'[24] said Daphne.

Castlerosse thought of himself as a victim, and he did not consider Doris's feelings, or how the conflict might have troubled her. His old flame, Millicent Hearst, was also privy to their public fights, and she said: 'I wouldn't say Doris was as bad as all that. She was just a flighty, nervous, pretty girl who was not the right company for [Castlerosse].'[25] The fights were instigated by Doris who, according to Millicent, 'never knew when to keep her mouth shut'. Castlerosse's friends did not like her, and they were not shy in expressing those feelings to him, whether she was in their presence or not.

To avoid a scene, Millicent tried to warn her, 'Now you know what will happen if you have a row, dear. His friends will be pleased as punch.' Doris was not the retiring type, and no man, not even her husband, would tell her what to do. This won her scorn and admiration in equal measures from her female contemporaries. After falling for Castlerosse's tactics to provoke her, Doris would go to Millicent[26] and say: 'Well, Millicent, it happened again. I tried my best, but the things he said, I couldn't help it. We had a flaming bloody row over the dinner table.' However, as she related with a certain amount of pride, 'I gave him as good as he gave me.'

Although no match for Doris in person, Castlerosse began to use the pen as his weapon and he fought back in print. More than a gossip column, the Londoner's Log had become an insight into their marriage. When Doris was behaving herself, Castlerosse waxed lyrical about the beauty and purity of womanhood, and when he attacked the fairer sex, it was a clue that his wife had resorted to her old ways. It was the latter that would become the norm. For there was one thing Doris could not do, and that was to devote herself to only one man.

ĐORIS ĞAISBEHAVES

'Money is like a sixth sense without which you cannot make complete use of the other five.'

W. Somerset Maugham

———•◆•———

After six weeks of marriage, Doris moved out of 8 Balfour Place and returned to her house on Deanery Street, which she had leased out. The separation was prompted by an argument which had, once again, ended in a physical fight. Weary from Doris's insults and the violence she provoked in him, Castlerosse removed himself to the International Sportmen's Club at the Grosvenor House Hotel, where he hoped his wife would not find him. He blamed himself entirely and, although miserable, he said: 'I went into this marriage with my eyes open. Doris was always honest.'

News of the couple's marital discord reached the Kenmares, and Lady Kenmare continued to hope that the marriage could be annulled on religious grounds. Although she had once wished for Castlerosse to divorce Doris in secret, now the marriage had become common knowledge, she could not tolerate the shame of her son being the topic of gossip. Or, more importantly, disobeying the Catholic Church. Disapproving as she was of Doris, she ordered Castlerosse to fix his marriage and to control his wife.

Disillusioned with marriage, Doris herself longed for a divorce, the consequences of which meant little to her, for she would keep her courtesy title of Viscountess Castlerosse unless she were to remarry. But she would not give her husband or her in-laws the satisfaction of seeing herself named as the guilty party.* Sensing that forces beyond her control, perhaps the influential figure of Beaverbrook, might in some way portray her as the instigator of a divorce (such as her adultery), she began to visit her lawyer to have her bruises photographed for evidence. This step initiated both Doris and Castlerosse's attempts to build a case against one other, a long-winded battle that would continue for a decade.

Reverting to her old ways, Doris drove around London in her Rolls-Royce, following the natural order of Mayfair society from dress shop to restaurant, to cocktail party to dinner party, to nightclub. Throwing open the doors of 6 Deanery Street, she reinvented herself as an aristocratic hostess, but this new guise of Viscountess Castlerosse did not equate respectability. 'All sorts and conditions present at Doris Castlerosse's party,'[1] wrote Sir Robert Bruce Lockhart in his diary. She gave dinner parties for the Hollywood star Douglas Fairbanks, Lord Carlyle, Lady Oxford, Sir Philip Sassoon, Lady Cunard, Lord and Lady Weymouth, Lord Alington, Lord Stanley of Alderley, Sir John and Lady Lavery, and Lord and Lady Ashley; the last was her old friend Sylvia Hawkes, whom she had met at the Grafton Galleries.

Interestingly, among her guests during this period were Evan Morgan, who would succeed as the 2nd Viscount Tredegar in 1934, and his wife, Lois. Hailing from what the Duke of Bedford described as 'the oddest family I have ever met', the Tredegars were tainted by scandal after Morgan's sister, Gwyneth, a drug addict, went missing and her body was discovered washed up in the Thames. It was rumoured that the family had exercised mind control which, along with Gwyneth's opium addiction, led to her untimely death in 1924. Aside from Lois's indiscretions (she became a close friend to Doris,

---

* A Private Member's Bill introduced in 1923 – which was passed as the Matrimonial Causes Act – made adultery by either husband or wife the sole ground for divorce. A wife no longer had to prove additional faults against the husband, but evidence of adultery was required.

and the two women were said to have 'slept their way through high society'), Morgan was a homosexual whose sexual orientation was listed in a discarded divorce petition, and he was an accomplished occultist. He would go to great lengths to bribe Castlerosse with money to prevent him from reporting on his private life.

Doris's ever-changing coterie included millionaires and sprigs of the aristocracy, rebellious princes from the House of Windsor, and deposed European royalty. Despite her association with royalty, society matrons who were aware that she was of questionable morality began to view 6 Deanery Street as something as notorious as a brothel.[2] This was not a confined opinion, for Prince George boasted that 'he had got into trouble with his father for going to Lady Castlerosse's party'.[3] And regardless of her lack of money, she entertained on a lavish scale, and the magnums of champagne and food were 'put on the bill', which was in Castlerosse's name.

In the meantime, Castlerosse's attention was devoted to amassing debts greater than before, to which he charged his suits, shirts, cigars, wine and spirits, food, gambling, and the expense of his trips to and from Killarney. He convinced himself that he was economising by paying for nothing in ready cash but charging it all to his account. 'Any bloody economist will tell you it's cheaper to order in bulk, old boy,' he would tell concerned friends who knew the truth about his finances.

Doris's escalating bills, combined with his own, was a crippling combination and with no handouts coming from Beaverbrook or the Baring trust fund, Castlerosse found it difficult to avoid the creditors. When they caught up with him, he told Doris of the situation, and she urged him to approach Beaverbrook: the only remedy, she felt, to the problem. Surprisingly, to Castlerosse, she accepted her share of the responsibility and, perhaps seeing no other solution, she pawned her jewellery to fund her own personal expenses.[4]

It was not a new experience for her, but it was one which Castlerosse viewed as selfless, and a testimony of her love for him. He was reading too much into the gesture and, owing to his vulnerability, he suggested they reconcile. However, it was not love or sentimentality that inspired Doris to reunite with her husband. Beaverbrook was back in Castlerosse's life, the former having taken the initiative to restore their friendship. Having never warmed to her, or so he told Castlerosse and his contemporaries, Beaverbrook rescued him from the 'poison of Doris's tongue', and suggested they go away 'for a breath of fresh air'.[5]

In the near future, Doris and Beaverbrook would reach an understanding of sorts but she would never be close to his family or privy to his home life the way Castlerosse was. She had met Beaverbrook's daughter, Janet Aitken, the 17-year-old bride of Ian Campbell, the future 11th Duke of Argyll, and had advised her to have a passionate love affair in order to lose weight.[6]

In the present day, Beaverbrook concerned himself with Castlerosse and his failing health. He was suffering from liver trouble and was seeing black spots before his eyes; and he was hag-ridden by debt and by Doris. In his fatherly way – he always treated Castlerosse as a mischievous son – Beaverbrook ordered his yacht to be made ready and they sailed to France, away from the gossipmongers of Mayfair. The holiday was a ploy to 'jolly him, bully him and diet him back to his normal health and good humour'. Also on board the yacht were Lord and Lady Weymouth, who had recently lost a child.

They sailed along the Seine, docking in Paris and visiting the famous restaurant, Josef's, where Castlerosse presided over the party in a foul mood. Doris was on his mind, and he spent his time wondering what she was doing and who she was with. He had been trying to reach her by telephone, with each attempt proving unsuccessful. Doris herself was not at home, and if she was at home she was not taking his calls, knowing how it would inflame his jealousy and induce him into a rage. Frustrated by the situation and knowing that Doris was goading him from afar, he hurled the telephone across the restaurant, knocking his plate of chicken off the table as he did so. With no Doris and no food, his simmering bad temper turned into a blind rage. When the party left Josef's, he remained behind and introduced himself to the head waiter as Lord Beaverbrook. 'About the telephone and the crockery,' Castlerosse said, ashamed of his behaviour. 'If there is a bill for damage, send it to that well-behaved small man going out. His name is Lord Castlerosse.'[7]

When Doris met Castlerosse on his return to London they were confronted with the reality that he was facing bankruptcy. She convinced him to approach his favourite uncle, Maurice Baring, whom she hoped would speak to Lord Revelstoke on their behalf and ask for him to loan Castlerosse money from the Baring trust fund. Maurice was forthright when he told them it was unlikely that his brother would help, and he was right.[8] With no one else to whom they could turn, they both agreed to involve Beaverbrook in their latest crisis and, since he had been generous in the past, Castlerosse assumed he would offer him a loan. The loans, however, were never repaid in spite of Castlerosse promising to do so, and Beaverbrook came to accept such terms.

For weeks, Beaverbrook corresponded with the Kenmares who hoped that, amid Castlerosse's financial ruin, they could salvage something, even if it was only their good name. Through their various letters and meetings,

Beaverbrook came up with the idea that he could mortgage Castlerosse's Irish inheritance in return for his own ready money. A Canadian property company was to be founded to take over the Kenmare trust and Killarney estate, which allowed Castlerosse to have shares in the company; and the money would also fund Lord and Lady Kenmare's present income. When the deal was finalised, it was agreed that £20,000 would be released to pay Castlerosse and Doris's debts, and, in return, Beaverbrook sought complete control of the company. Although the Kenmares expressed their gratitude for his help, they were reluctant to sign over the estate and their descendants' birthright. A shrewd businessman, Beaverbrook respected their decision, but he was frustrated by the situation. He closed his cheque book and was determined to make Castlerosse take responsibility for his actions. The fact that Doris was his wife, and that Castlerosse had deceived him in marrying her, contributed to this new, heavy-handed approach.

Although it was not what Doris and Castlerosse had expected from Beaverbrook, they welcomed his offer to look at their liabilities. They devised a list of their debts and expenditures for his review but, upon reading it, he discovered that their claims were contradictory. Castlerosse's debts were easy to trace, as he kept an account at various establishments in London. Doris, however, downplayed her spending to make her husband look reckless and irresponsible. Bypassing her own personal debts, Doris's list was entirely self-centred and she chronicled the loss of her precious jewels, which had gone to the pawnbroker earlier in the year. Rather than accepting it had been a necessity to pawn them to ensure a healthy cash-flow, she asked Beaverbrook to pay £750[9] to the pawnbroker and buy them back for her. He must have been surprised by her request, and by her candour, for he wrote to ask what she planned to do with the retrieved jewellery.

Doris replied that she planned to sell the jewellery to supplement her annual income, which she estimated to be about £1,000 a year.[10] And, hoping to prove that she was economising, Doris added that her income was previously £3,600[11] a year. Far from deceived by her figures, he was not convinced she could live off that figure,[12] and he warned it would more than likely cause her to run into debt again. In her response to Beaverbrook, Doris admitted that the jewellery she had pawned came to the value of £4,000.[13] Again, Beaverbrook told her that Castlerosse should bear the responsibility of having it released from the pawnbroker. He asked if any other jewellery should be treated the same way, and if it ought to be retrieved from the pawnbroker.[14] She did not agree that she could rely on her husband to buy it back, and she hinted that Beaverbrook should do the honours.

Beaverbrook admired boldness, but Doris's blatant opportunism left him cold. Once again, he suggested that Castlerosse buy the jewellery and recover the original figure of £750 from its eventual sale. Then, he told her that the debt owed to the pawnbroker should not be included in the list of liabilities, and he advised her to sell the house on Deanery Street, including its contents. To his surprise, she agreed. Her decision was partly influenced by the realisation that the creditors would seize the house to settle Castlerosse's debts. To distance himself from the situation, and disliking Doris's personable approach, Beaverbrook told her that he understood his arrangement with her was to the effect that she transfer the house and furniture for purpose of liquidation not exceeding £4,000 of all existing debts.[15]

However, in addition to the couple's personal debts, Castlerosse produced a statement of liability to the income tax collector. 'It is a very large sum,' Beaverbrook warned Doris. 'I think it quite likely this additional disclosure may wreck everything.' His presumption was correct, and Castlerosse was threatened with bankruptcy court. Beaverbrook then told her that everything depended on whether or not he could 'carry through a scheme of debts settlement with all persons concerned'.[16]

The settlement came from an unlikely source when, to keep their son out of bankruptcy court and to save the family from 'disgrace', Lord and Lady Kenmare paid £100,000[17] towards Castlerosse and Doris's debts. The amount 'crippled' them financially and it 'broke up their home'.[18] Lady Kenmare was adamant that Castlerosse would not inherit any money she might leave after her death, and she changed her will so that his brother and two sisters were her sole heirs.[19]

Although the Kenmares had graciously refused Beaverbrook's original proposal, Lady Kenmare had thought of a new solution to Castlerosse's financial problems. She agreed to help him on the condition that he got rid of Doris, whose share of the debts she resented. Beaverbrook, too, agreed with her logic. But with his loyalty toward Castlerosse, he hoped it would not be obvious to either party, and it put him in a delicate position.

When Castlerosse realised that his mother and oldest friend were conspiring to banish his wife, he became 'abusive and impossible'. Doris might have been a thorn in his side, but he resented their meddling. However, it was Beaverbrook, and not Lady Kenmare, who managed to convince him that a separation from Doris was a 'necessity' – financially speaking.

Doris was no fool; she sensed the underhand tactics at play and, in an attempt to have the last word, she went to Castlerosse with the news that Beaverbrook found him 'a nuisance and a bore'. Hurt by his friend's apparent betrayal, Castlerosse wrote a sombre letter to Beaverbrook. 'You used to find me amusing,' he bemoaned – and was sent the cold response: 'You have always known that it would not be right of you to take your news of my opinion of you from Lady Castlerosse.'[20]

To settle the remaining debts, Doris followed through with her agreement to sell the Deanery Street house, and she listed it with the estate agents Lane and Savill. She told Beaverbrook that two people were interested in buying it, but if they declined, she would lease it to the Guinnesses for six months. Was this a subtle hint that Beaverbrook should offer her some money? He must have thought so, for he told her to forget about leasing it to the Guinnesses and to sell it promptly.[21]

Beaverbrook disliked her calculating approach, and how she had assumed he would be as foolish with his money as her admirers had been with theirs. He was not one of her admirers, and in order to get his money she would have to provide a service that benefited him and his business interests. But he underestimated Doris, and the lengths she was willing to resort to.

In the early days of her marriage, when Castlerosse and Beaverbrook had ended their period of estrangement, Doris kept a respectful distance from him and addressed his letters to 'Dear Lord Beaverbrook'. Their first existing letter,[22] although formal in tone, suggests they had come to an agreement that would benefit them both. He liked to know people's weaknesses, and Doris's was money.

In mid-November, before she had confided her debts to him, it was agreed that Doris was to spy on well-known socialites, many of whom were her acquaintances. Then she was to inform on their antics to Beaverbrook, who would print the gossip in his newspapers. Without it appearing blatantly obvious, she was instructed to throw dinner parties at Deanery Street (prior to her selling the house), with her socialite friends and Beaverbrook in attendance. She called herself a shepherd's dog and complained that her flock was so scattered that she could not assemble them on the 15th; however, she assured Beaverbrook they would be available on the 21st.[23]

By December, the 'flock' was assembled at Deanery Street and Beaverbrook was present. It is assumed the effort was not in vain, for Doris was paid £5[24] for her trouble. Having 'worked assiduously' and successfully, she thought it put her on an equal footing with Beaverbrook, and she began to address him by his first name, Max, hoping she did not come across as too bold in addressing him thus.[25]

Doris enjoyed her new role of society spy, which she felt was on par with Castlerosse's Londoner's Log, though without fame or recognition in print. Castlerosse himself did not know of the arrangement she kept with Beaverbrook, presumably because he would have been jealous, or suspicious. He liked to keep Beaverbrook to himself and was 'piqued if [Beaverbrook] pitched into anyone else'.[26] Keeping her eyes peeled for displays of debauchery and her ear to the ground for gossip, she targeted old friends and became a shoulder of comfort during their difficult times.

Having gathered the information, she would write to Beaverbrook, or telephone him. But he did not like to be reached by telephone nor did he approve of her overly familiar letters, and he often had his secretary respond. Still, Doris remained enthusiastic. 'Arthur's daughter Mrs Plunket-Greene was married in Berlin to Anthony de Bosdari,' was an example of the information she gleaned for him. 'He has just heard the news … he is terribly upset. I don't think anyone knows yet.'[27] And, 'I telephoned your secretary, telling her about Jock Whitney's engagement, hoping it might be of some interest to your newspapers.'[28]

Things did not always work in Doris's favour, and in the summer of 1929 she risked her arrangement with Beaverbrook when Lady Diana Cooper was insulted at one of her dinner parties. Lady Diana was six months pregnant with her first child, conceived after almost a decade of marriage, and it had become the topic of society gossip. Her contemporaries whispered that Duff Cooper was not the biological father (he was), and they joked that the baby would be 'dark skinned' like all descendants of those 'who went even for a trip to the West Indies' – a reference to her holiday in Nassau before she had announced her pregnancy.

Doris told Beaverbrook, 'I hope you do not think that I allowed Diana to be insulted in my house by that song.' The song of which, she assured him, she had not heard until that evening. Pleading her innocence, she told him she had heard it at many parties – this contradicts her original claim – including one which Eleanor Smith was at, because she had written about it in the *Dispatch*. It was apparent by Doris's reaction that it was a song about Lady Diana and her circle, for she claimed 'the whole song is a joke' and she said no real names were mentioned in it.[29] The song in question appears to have been *Burlington Bertie from Bow*, and the offending lyrics were: 'I've just had a banana with Lady Diana.' Although written in 1915 as a parody of the music-hall song *Burlington Bertie*, it seems the lyric was recycled to suit the context of the gossip, and was used as a reference to the untrue rumour that her baby was fathered by a West Indian.

There was further disenchantment between Doris and Beaverbrook when she travelled to Paris, knowing that he and Castlerosse were staying at the

Ritz Hotel. She took a suite two floors above the men, whereupon she began to besiege her estranged husband with abusive telephone messages, which succeeded in breaking Castlerosse's temper and prompted him to retaliate with equally vitriolic remarks. 'The telephone is going by night and by day and the turmoil never dies,' Beaverbrook wrote to Lady Diana Cooper. Having departed the Ritz, he added, 'It is beyond my power to get to the bottom of the well or cesspool.'[30]

Later in the year, Doris travelled to Germany to stay at Dr F. Dengler's sanatorium in Baden Baden, a palatial building overlooking evergreen hills. Dr Dengler 'had the most aristocratic clientele in Europe and had made a fortune compelling the very rich to go for a walk before breakfast and be in bed by 10 p.m.'.[31] With the sanatorium crammed with 'princes, lords and ladies, millionaires, Jews, Germans, Americans', she used her six weeks of rest to mingle with the various interesting guests, hoping to discover a scandalous anecdote or topics of interest that might appeal to Beaverbrook. She 'took the cure', which was a menu of 'huge chunks of meat, dishes of cream, lots of butter',[32] devised to help the inmates lose weight and overcome fatigue.

Writing from the sanatorium, Doris told Beaverbrook that the current gossip from Paris was that the Aga Khan's engagement announcement was not true.[33] It was one of the rare occasions when she related false news to him, for the engagement was true and the Aga Khan would marry Andrée Joséphine Caron that December in Aix-les-Bains. The visit proved unremarkable and, except for Lady Zia Wernher, there was 'really nobody interesting'.[34]

The excitement, however, was created by Castlerosse who had accompanied Doris to Baden Baden, where he checked into a hotel. Doris left the sanatorium in the evenings to dine with Castlerosse, and they met Douglas Fairbanks and his wife, Mary Pickford, who were staying at a local hotel. The party went to a golf club, where they met 'the Cooch'* who, Doris told Beaverbrook, had just received her marching orders and would have to leave for India in a week or two.[35] The group had their photograph taken on a terrace, standing next to wicker furniture, with a smiling Doris and Castlerosse appearing as a happily married couple, and it was printed in the *Sunday Express*.

---

* Indira Devi, the consort of Jitendra Narayan, Maharaja of Cooch Behar, and a princess of Baroda State in her own right.

While staying in Baden Baden, Castlerosse met two women at his hotel and had fallen for one of them, and with Doris at the sanatorium during the day, he was free to explore Bavaria with his love interest. The affair would have gone unnoticed had it not been for him crashing his car with the two women in it. In a letter to Beaverbrook, Doris underlined the 'two women', and wrote that 'one is still laid aside'.[36]

Beaverbrook, too, was unwittingly caught in the middle of Castlerosse's fling. The day after spending the night with this mystery woman, Castlerosse asked the hotel manager to find him some orchids. Upon being told that Baden Baden had no orchids, he flew into a rage. 'There must be some orchids somewhere – send for some, I don't care where, or at what expense,'[37] he roared at the hotel manager. The orchids were found, and they were brought by air from Berlin, Munich, Paris, Amsterdam and Brussels. The following day, Castlerosse was given a bill for £200.[38] He sent it to Beaverbrook, along with a bill for bottles of Vichy water, which he had used to fill his bathtub.

When Doris left Dengler's sanatorium, she and Castlerosse went to Paris, and she wrote to Beaverbrook, imploring him to join them.[39] It was a happy time for Castlerosse, who promised Doris that he would control his temper, and in turn she promised to control herself. Her behaviour was not satisfactory, as far as he was concerned, but in the aftermath of his car crash in Baden Baden, he did not feel in a position to demand more. 'I was continually at war with myself,' he later said. 'I hated Doris lividly and I loved her too. The wise men say that the passion of love and hate burn themselves out and eventually die, but with me they are a deuce of a time a-dying.'[40]

The truce did not last long, and on their return to London they were, once again, at war with one another. The money had run out, and Castlerosse's spirits were low. In the evenings, Doris took to playing poker with Beaverbrook and, being a talented card player, she often won. 'Lord Beaverbrook requests me to send you the enclosed cheque for £3.9.0[41] in settlement for his debt incurred last night,'[42] wrote his secretary. But it was not enough to keep the proverbial wolf from the door.

Castlerosse owed his tailors £555,[43] and was subsequently sued by one firm. He pleaded misfit, saying that the suits, custom-made for him, 'were fit only for the Mappin terrace at the zoo'.[44] Failing to reduce his expenses after his parents had paid to keep him out of bankruptcy court, Castlerosse continued to spend frivolously, with his annual bill for flowers amounting to £250[45] and his bill for wine coming to £700.[46] He was issued with a writ from a creditor, for which his debt was listed as £453,[47] including £11[48] interest. His bank manager asked him to make a list of liabilities, as Beaverbrook had previously requested, and he gave his debts as £3,747, 5s 3d,[49] including the £500[50] he had borrowed from the *Daily Express*. It was considerably larger than his calculations and, although he could not afford the things he had purchased on credit, he also owed his staff several months' worth of wages. Due to this, he would often suffer from a guilty conscience, and remark to his valet and chauffeur: 'I must owe you some money. Why don't you ever let me have your account books?' The account books were kept under Castlerosse's bed, and were seldom looked at. He would retrieve £100 from his pocket, which he often carried in a screwed-up ball, and divide it into three piles: one for himself, and two smaller amounts for his staff. 'I'll give you some more when Lord Beaverbrook pays me what he owes me,' he would say.[51]

As he had done before, Castlerosse asked Beaverbrook for help. This time he did not refuse, and he gave Castlerosse the money to pay off his debt. 'I will not run up accounts again nor will I go to moneylenders, and will live within my income,' he told a cynical Beaverbrook. His handling of money can be attributed to how he measured wealth, his own and everybody else's, against Beaverbrook's fortune. And since he would never be in possession of such a fortune, the money, he felt, had no value. Castlerosse once scoffed at a description of a New York socialite as 'a rich man', and he was reminded that the gentleman in question had a fortune of $20 million. 'Beaverbrook,' he said, 'wouldn't consider that as wealthy unless it's yearly income.'

If Beaverbrook was frustrated by his wayward friend, he did not show it, and he felt sympathetic towards Castlerosse and the misery he felt in his marriage. His own wife had been a passive woman, and his mistresses never attempted to have the upper hand, or caused him misery. Castlerosse, however, seemed to be at the mercy of Doris, and she thrived on this dynamic.

Having sold her house on Deanery Street to pay off Castlerosse's creditors, Doris felt bitter and betrayed by his rising debts. He could not suppress his spending, and she could not ignore her need for attention, regardless of where it came from. There were those who believed Beaverbrook took her as his mistress[52] around 1929, when Castlerosse was in a vulnerable position with his health and happiness. And, judging by her letters to Beaverbrook, Doris appeared to enjoy this status, mistress or not.

But it was a dangerous game that Doris was playing. It was unusual for Beaverbrook to be generous without expecting something in return and, like many self-made men, he resented the privilege his money afforded other people – something his children could attest to. Even his favourites were not exempt from this treatment, best displayed through his handling of Daphne and Henry Weymouth who, although fond of them as he was, had unwittingly become his victims. They had filmed themselves 'cavorting naked'[54] in their boat off the Lido at Venice, and the film had been retained by Kodak. When the Weymouths appealed to Beaverbrook, who recaptured the film, they learned that he had screened it for his cronies as a piece of after-dinner entertainment. However, Doris was willing to take risks, and she appeared to understand the rules of the game. She, too, was a shrewd character who expected a pay-off, regardless of if it was under different circumstances.

Over a period of time, Doris wrote to Beaverbrook to ask him to stop Castlerosse from publishing articles on her friends; one in particular was Loelia Ponsonby, who was engaged to the twice-divorced 2nd Duke of Westminster. 'Implore you not to let Valentine's Log go into print as it stands. Important,'[55] read one such telegram. Indeed, Castlerosse was making enemies of his friends within Beaverbrook's circle,[56] and he had begun to use the Londoner's Log as a poison-pen letter against his contemporaries. Furthermore, the 2nd Duke of Westminster was a nephew-by-marriage of his eldest sister Lady Dorothy, who was the widow of Lord Edward Grosvenor, the youngest son of the 1st Duke of Westminster. Since Beaverbrook had obliged Doris and prevented the articles from going to print, their exact content remains unknown. Envious towards those who were in love and happy, Castlerosse had reacted in an uncharacteristic fashion. Although, throughout the years, his column had often contained jibes at his enemies and snippets of acid wit, he had never attacked an influential figure in print.

It was Doris who was on the receiving end of Castlerosse's inferiority complex. Blaming her for all that had gone wrong in his life, as she had done to him, he attacked her insecurities. He told her that she was losing her looks, and he accused her of giving a false date of birth on their marriage certificate. After a particularly volatile argument, Beaverbrook intervened. He tried to reason with Doris, but she had a mind as quick as his own, and he privately admired that quality in her. 'Max,' she told him, 'I would have you know that an Englishwoman's bed is her castle.'[57] Beaverbrook did not argue with her philosophy, but he approached Castlerosse to offer his advice: 'Live amicably with your wife or leave her.'[58]

But Doris was not a woman who would let a man decide her fate. To spite Castlerosse, whom she knew was at the mercy of Beaverbrook, she took the initiative and made up his mind for him. She would be leaving him but, as she told her unsuspecting husband, she would remain in their leased house. So, having listened to Beaverbrook and accepted his counsel, Castlerosse found himself without a wife and without a home.

OLD ḈABITS

'Sex … is not a sovereign cure for everything, you know.
I only wish it were.'

Nancy Mitford, *Love in a Cold Climate*

———— • ◆ • ————

The New Year of 1930 began as a solemn one for Doris. In February, her father, Edward Charles Delevingne, died unexpectedly at the City of London Chess Club. Since resigning in 1925 from his post as managing director of the haberdashery and the fancy French goods business he ran with his brothers, he had been residing at the Queens Hotel in Upper Norwood. Presumably, Edward had been suffering from ill health, for the hotel, located in 'the fresh air suburb', was a desirable location for those with respiratory ailments. He left an estate of £12,573 11s 9d[1] to his wife, Jessie.

Doris was not close to either of her parents; she rarely mentioned them in her correspondence, and little information exists to gauge what sort of relationship they shared. Shortly after her father's death, Doris mentioned her mother in a letter to Beaverbrook. She wrote that her mother, whom she had not 'seen for ages', had visited her home, and by the time she had got rid of her, and got up and dressed, it would have been too late.[2] She was referring to an invitation from Beaverbrook, which she had missed because of her mother's visit. This lone reference to her mother, and remark about spoiling her plans, is telling.

It is evident from Jessie's background and her principles – a religious woman who believed hard work, in the traditional sense, was the key to advancing in life – that there was no room for her in Doris's life. Perhaps Doris felt her mother was a reminder of the woman she was behind the smokescreen of couture clothing and title, a sham though the image was. Either way, an unspoken element of discomfort lingered between the two. Jessie eventually left London and spent her widowhood in a small house in Kent, where she managed her inheritance with the frugality she had known all her life.

Rumours of Doris and Castlerosse's estrangement reached Lady Kenmare, and she summoned her son to hear his version of events. Assured that Doris would have no access to his money now they were separated, aside from the allowance he paid to her, Lady Kenmare reinstated certain funds from her Baring inheritance that she had previously withdrawn. But Doris was no fool, and having learned that Castlerosse was back in the family fold, financially speaking, she suggested they reconcile.

A romantic at heart, his one longing in life was to be loved unconditionally and, thinking Doris had reformed her outlook and that she felt an ounce of love for him, Castlerosse agreed. She returned to his flat on Culross Street, but in spite of his optimism, neither were prepared to change their ways. As was their wont, Castlerosse chided Doris about her behaviour, and in turn she went to great efforts to send him into a jealous rage. The end result was a domestic arrangement that neither of them relished.

Beaverbrook intervened, by request of Castlerosse, and attempted to reason with Doris. As she had done before, she expressed little tolerance for his counsel – an outburst she came to regret. She sent a letter of apology to Beaverbrook, claiming that Castlerosse had accused her of being rude to him over the telephone. And, furthermore, she admitted she had raised her voice to him. It was the last thing she had wanted to do, and she explained that Castlerosse had been 'winding' her up, which she said was a clever trick he often used. She asked for Beaverbrook's forgiveness, as she had never intended to cause offence.[3]

Although Doris had a reputation for being bad-tempered – 'She is the most arrogant, temperamental, foul-mouthed, and ecstatically beautiful woman in London'[4] – she realised Beaverbrook was a powerful ally. Through Beaverbrook, she had come to know Winston Churchill, and their friendship began in the spring of 1930.[5] His first impression of Doris was favourable, evident when his son Randolph said 'bloody' in her presence and, disapproving of Randolph's language, he was reported to have said: 'Wash out your mouth, my boy.'[6]

Out of Parliament following the Conservatives' defeat in the 1929 elections, Churchill himself had become preoccupied with a headier social life than before, for which he received criticism. He holidayed in America and in Europe as the guest of Beaverbrook and William Randolph Hearst, and he drank and gambled, chiefly with Brendan Bracken, a young man rumoured to be his biological son. Having lost much of his American investments[7] in the Wall Street Crash of 1929, Churchill supported himself by writing articles and books, and low on funds but not on friendship, he called this period 'the wilderness years'.

The circumstances in which Doris's and Churchill's paths crossed, it can be assumed, happened when she encountered him at Beaverbrook's villa in Le Touquet. Churchill's own attitude towards adultery was conflicting;[8] during his lifetime he was dogged by rumours that he had fathered his sister-in-law's son, Esmond Romilly. To his wife Clementine's frustration, he did not dispel the stories and appeared to revel in them. It was said that he took 'a particular dislike to overt sexual predators',[9] which conflicts with the rumour that he and Doris enjoyed a brief fling, for affair is too strong a word.

According to much-repeated gossip, Churchill was reported to have slept with Doris at the Ritz Hotel in Paris where, after their encounter, he said: 'Doris you could make a corpse come.'[10] Again, Churchill did not dismiss the rumour, and perhaps he enjoyed the boost it gave to his ego. Likewise, his fellow statesman Harold Macmillan later remarked after reading the nineteenth-century courtesan Harriet Wilson's memoirs, that Doris 'was one of the last demi-mondaines'.[11]

It was during this period, in which the rumours of Doris and Churchill's affair were circulating, that she turned her sights on to younger men. She met Tom Mitford, the only son of David Mitford, the 2nd Baron Redesdale and brother of the six Mitford girls, who nicknamed him 'Tuddemy' to somewhat rhyme with Tom and adultery. Although he had experienced homosexual affairs in his youth, he dismissed it as a phase and turned his attention towards the opposite sex. At the age of twenty-one, he had already gained a reputation for having affairs with older, married women.

Aged 21, Tom was nine years Doris's junior, and what he lacked in years, he made up for with experience. Regarded as one of the most handsome men in society, blonde-haired, blue-eyed Tom was said to resemble a Saxon king. He had attended Eton, graduated from Oxford, and before reading for the Bar he had toured Vienna and studied in Munich, where the rise of Nazism was spreading through Germany. Although not rich – money was a constant worry for his parents – he received an allowance from his father, and he dined at the best restaurants and was the guest of the brightest and most important people. His beautiful sister, Diana Mitford, was the young wife of the brewery heir Bryan Guinness, and it was through Tom that Doris became friends with the Guinnesses. She was particularly fond of Diana, then a dazzling society hostess whose coterie revolved around the Bright Young Things. The novelist Evelyn Waugh, who was on the cusp of literary fame, found a muse in Diana and dedicated *Vile Bodies* to her, and her older friends included Emerald Cunard, Lytton Strachey and Dora Carrington. Doris also became acquainted with Tom and Diana's eldest sister, Nancy Mitford, who nicknamed her 'Dolly'.[12] Churchill's son, Randolph, moved within this set; his mother, Clementine, was David Mitford's cousin, and the adolescent Randolph had been in love with Diana, and continued to carry a torch for her.

While in London, Tom lived with Randolph Churchill at Edward James's townhouse. And, unbeknown to James, both young men were simultaneously sleeping with Tilly Losch, a Viennese dancer who found fame on the West End in Noel Coward's *This Year of Grace*, and with whom James had become obsessed. A rich man, who was a poet and patron of the arts, James had stalked Tilly for two years until she agreed to marry him, but marriage did not alter her promiscuous ways. Through her association with Tom and Randolph, Doris became friendly with Tilly and the two women would maintain a polite friendship over the years. Perhaps, in one another, they recognised a kindred spirit.

With their marriage once again on the rocks, and neither Doris or Castlerosse willing to sacrifice their old habits, they agreed to part. He spoke openly about divorcing her, though their mutual friends did not take his threat seriously. 'I doubt, however if he will ever carry it through. He is so much under her influence, and she will not hesitate to hold him if she can,' wrote Sir Robert Bruce Lockhart in his diary.[13] Doris, Sir Robert said, had 'guts', and in the same diary entry he wrote that she had 'informed [name omitted] that she will slap her publicly the next time she sees her'.

Once again, Castlerosse moved into the International Sporting Club, where he stayed for several months until he was driven out 'by the depressing sound of young men's muscles flexing and old men's arteries collapsing'.[14] He then moved with his valet, Welch, into an apartment on the top floor of Claridge's; the hotel bill was partly paid for by his Londoner's Log salary and supplemented by Beaverbrook's generosity. Although consumed with jealousy, he distracted himself from Doris's infidelities by eating enormous dishes sent up from the kitchen, and mingling with his fellow guests.

One guest in particular caught his eye; it was the Hollywood film star Constance Bennett, who was between marriages and at a low ebb in her acting career. She had heard of Castlerosse's column and of his genius for courting publicity. And Castlerosse himself graciously welcomed Bennett's friendship, with his persona radiating the chivalry and charm of his background and breeding, all the while keeping his hand open for the rewards of the financial scheme he was plotting. Bennett confided her plans of making a comeback in films, and conferences were held at Castlerosse's suite, where agreements were made and the result of which was that she could hardly drink her morning coffee without the incident becoming headline news. Castlerosse, on his part, 'just opened wide his palms and let the Hollywood money pour in'.[15] As it turned out, Bennett met the French nobleman Henri de la Falaise, returned to Hollywood, and Castlerosse found himself momentarily richer.

After this spell of good fortune and 'with his new richly lined wallet',[16] Doris invited Castlerosse to return to the marital home. She had promised Beaverbrook that she 'would try hard', but she confessed that her husband did not make it easy for her. She accused Castlerosse of being the 'most annoying of all men', and claimed he did not handle women but manhandled them. Nevertheless, she could not stay mad at him for long and, as she explained, she did care for him.[17]

The affair with Tom Mitford had been nothing more than a fleeting fancy; his pockets did not run deep enough for Doris, and on his part he was busy travelling around Europe and conducting affairs of his own. In August she left for the continent with Castlerosse, where they joined Sir Oswald Mosley – before his foray into fascism – and his wife Lady Cynthia at their villa in Antibes. They all went to Maxine Elliott's villa (before she had built the famous Château de l'Horizon in 1932) along with Cecil Beaton, Beatrice Guinness and her daughters, Baby and Zita Jungman, Sylvia Ashley and Michael Arlen. The women wore beach pyjamas and pearls, and the men were in linen trousers and Aertex shirts, except for Castlerosse, who maintained his flamboyant appearance of velvet and brocade, in spite of the Riviera's climate.

On one particular evening, at a party given by Maxine Elliott, a woman climbed up an 80ft ladder and dived into a narrow tank 4½ft deep with petrol burning on the water. At another party, given by the courtier Captain Edward Molyneaux, a jazz band from the Monte Carlo Casino played on a dance floor especially constructed for the occasion. 'Everyone in the world [was] there', and Noel Coward played the piano, and at the end of the festivities there were fireworks. Lady Mendl (formerly the actress Elsie de Wolfe) stood on her head, and the stage and costume designer Oliver Messel was 'caught in an incriminating position'[18] with several men.

When Doris and Castlerosse returned to London they found themselves the subject of Noel Coward's latest play, *Private Lives*. The plot revolved around Elyot and his new wife Sybil, who are on honeymoon at a hotel in Deauville. In the adjoining suite, Amanda and her new husband Victor are starting their new life together, although Victor is consumed by thoughts of the cruelty Amanda's ex-husband had displayed towards her. Ex-spouses Amanda and Elyot have been divorced for five years, but upon realising they still love each other, they run off to her flat in Paris. After several days together, Amanda and Elyot begin to fight, and during a particularly volatile argument, Amanda breaks a record over Elyot's head and he retaliates by slapping her across the face – shades of Doris and Castlerosse. They appear to be trapped in a cycle of love and hate – Elyot says, 'I don't hate her. I think I despise her' – where neither can live with or without one another.

Traits of Doris's personality were blatantly obvious in that of Amanda. The character was described as 'uncontrolled, and wicked, and unfaithful',[19] or as Coward himself said of Doris: 'Her wit when she's in a good mood can be devastating, but she doesn't give a damn about people's feelings.'[20] Amanda's physical appearance also resembled Doris's: Coward wrote she was 'pretty and sleek, and her hands were long and slim, and her legs were long and slim'. Like Doris, Amanda flaunted her promiscuity: 'It wasn't an innocent girlish heart. It was jagged with sophistication.' Furthermore, she challenged Elyot's comment, 'It doesn't suit women to be promiscuous,' and remarked, 'It doesn't suit men for women to be promiscuous.'[21]

It was a daring exchange, even for the London stage. Lord Chamberlain thought so, and he objected to a love scene in the second act, deeming it too risqué due to the fact the characters were divorced and married to others. Coward went along to St James's Palace to plead his case by acting out the play himself and assuring the censor that, with an artful direction, the scene would be presented in a dignified and unobjectionable manner.

In the spirit of Doris and Castlerosse's behaviour, far from the dignified display that Chamberlain sought, Coward had Amanda and Elyot reminisce about certain arguments. They speak of a fight in Venice which 'went on intermittently for days', and the worst one ('a rouser') was in Cannes, 'where your curling tongs burnt a hole in my new dressing-gown'. Amanda remembered, 'That was the first time you hit me.' To which Elyot responded,

Doris and Noel Coward on their way to Venice.

'I didn't hit you very hard.'[22] 'I've been brought up to believe that it's beyond the pale for a man to strike a woman,' mused Amanda. 'Certain women should be struck regularly, like gongs,'[23] Elyot replied. The visual quality of their argument evoked Doris and Castlerosse's physical fights, when Amanda and Elyot laugh about the hotel manager finding them 'rolling on the floor, biting and scratching like panthers'. Like Castlerosse, Elyot had taken offence at Amanda accepting jewellery ('a trivial little brooch') from other men, and said: 'You went out of your way to torture me.'

Produced by C.B. Cochran, the play began its provincial tour on 18 August 1930, with Coward directing the play and acting in the part of Elyot; Adrienne Allen was Sybil; Laurence Olivier was Victor; and, in an ironic parallel of life imitating art, Gertrude Lawrence played Amanda. When *Private Lives* opened on 24 September 1930, at the Phoenix Theatre in London, Lady Kenmare was introduced to the playwright. 'Quite amusing,' she told Coward. 'But those quarrels and rollings around on the floor – quite unreal. No couple could possibly quarrel like that in real life.'

'Couldn't they?' replied Coward. 'You obviously don't know the Castlerosses.'[24]

It was not the first time Doris had inspired a literary character. Michael Arlen, a neighbour of Doris's during her relationship with Laddie Sanford when they had both lived at Deanery Street, was said to have used her as the model for Iris Storm, the *femme fatale* of his bestselling novel, *The Green Hat*. Published in 1924 when the 'twenties were beginning to roar, Arlen's portrait of a woman with loose morals and living independently dazzled those who aspired to or lived a similar lifestyle, and shocked those who held on to a bygone perception of English womanhood. Iris zips around town in her yellow Hispano-Suiza without a care in the world, but behind her bonhomie lies a tragic heroine. She was a social outlaw who 'kicked through every restraint and of caste and chastity, there's the whole world open to her to play mischief in, there's every invention in the world to help her indulge her intolerable little lusts'. Much like Doris in those early days on Deanery Street, Iris mirrored her outlook on life: 'There is one taste in us that is unsatisfied. I don't know what that taste is, but I know it is there. Life's best gift, has not someone said, is the ability to dream of a better life.'[25]

Castlerosse, too, had inspired a number of literary works. His traits and profession were apparent in Evelyn Waugh's fictional character Mr Chatterbox from his 1930 novel, *Vile Bodies*. Waugh, who had little contact with the aristocracy in the late 1920s, insisted that his characters were not based on real people. This was not entirely true; he had met Diana and Bryan Guinness through Nancy Mitford in 1929 and, at the time, he was the husband of the Hon. Evelyn née Gardner (known as She-Evelyn to his He-Evelyn). During this period, Waugh existed on the fringes of the set he would later satirise, and Castlerosse was no exception. It was, after all, the era of the aristocratic gossip columnist, and Castlerosse was, at that time, the most prominent.

Two years after its publication, *Vile Bodies* was staged as a play. By then, Evelyn Waugh had befriended most of the aristocracy, many of whom he thought terrific bores and ferociously self-centred. When the tickets of the play were made available for sale, Lady Cunard did not like her seats and she complained of having to take Prince George to the eighteenth row. 'Old trout,' Waugh said about Lady Cunard, 'who was only an American anyway'.[26] Doris was bolder in her treatment of him and the play: she simply refused to pay for her ticket. Perhaps she felt he owed something to her (by then estranged) husband, and a dash of artistic homage to herself. 'Oh dear,' Waugh remarked, 'these great ladies.'[27]

As with Noel Coward's fictional characters in *Private Lives*, Doris and Castlerosse were on the brink of divorce themselves. And Castlerosse, serious about his desire to be rid of her, moved back into Claridge's. He was convinced Doris was seeing a young baronet and, leaving her alone at their home on Culross Street, he hoped to catch her in the act.

Within days his suspicions were confirmed. Far from discovering the truth himself, the information came from an unlikely source. One evening, a pretty young streetwalker approached him for business and, declining her services, he asked how a nice young girl had got into such a sordid trade. The girl explained that she was employed as a downstairs maid at the home of Lord Castlerosse – he had since departed and knew nothing of this arrangement – whom she had never met because 'the silly old bugger is always out chasing the ladies'. Mortified, he asked why his wife allowed one of their maids to ply the streets, to which the girl retorted: 'The old cow's always upstairs in bed with her bookmaker boyfriend.'[28] Although she had mistaken the baronet for a bookmaker, Castlerosse discovered that the part-time prostitute was, at least, an honest reporter.

As night fell, Castlerosse hid in the bushes outside their flat on Culross Street and waited in ambush on the dark street until the gentleman in question re-emerged. Looming in the shadows, he attacked him with his blackthorn stick and gave the suitor 'a merciless hiding'. Hearing the noise, Doris ran on to the street, shouting, 'Murder!' Castlerosse was said to have enjoyed himself thoroughly; perhaps all three of them did.

The young baronet was Sir Alfred Beit – nicknamed 'the belching baronet'[29] – who was three years Doris's junior. In 1930, the year they began an affair, he had inherited a fortune of £3,651,247 following the death of his uncle, his namesake, Alfred Beit, the South African mining millionaire and art collector. Aside from the millions and the diamond mine, Sir Alfred inherited works by Goya, Vermeer, Rubens and Gainsborough. He had since left his white stucco townhouse at 49 Belgrave Square to live in a mansion at Kensington Palace Gardens, the most exclusive area of London, where he displayed his paintings. A year later, and still in the throes of an affair with Doris, he would be elected as a Conservative Member of Parliament for St Pancras South East.

The assault Sir Alfred received from Castlerosse did little to quell his infatuation with Doris, and they continued to see one another. However, unbeknown to Sir Alfred, Castlerosse had set the detectives on Doris and he began to keep a log of her comings and goings, and the places where she had met with him, in anticipation of a divorce. But it was a short-sighted reaction, for he ought to have known better than to think she was having an extramarital affair with only one man.

In the spring of 1932, Doris's Churchill connection had come full circle. Just six months after his twenty-first birthday, she began an affair with Randolph Churchill, a rival of sorts to Castlerosse, who thought him an usurper. Randolph had begun writing for the *Sunday Dispatch*, and with his salary he rented the best suite at the Mayfair Hotel and hired an enormous chauffeur-driven limousine. Like Castlerosse, he was a spendthrift, and the two men shared the burden of knowing they were the wastrel sons of great men. But, unlike Castlerosse – renowned for his topical wit and jovial sense of humour – a dose of venom lurked in Randolph's words.

Alarmed by the affair, Winston Churchill intervened and, perhaps thinking it bad form to go where he had once trodden, he attempted to instil common sense in his son. 'What are you doing?' Churchill asked Randolph. 'When I was your age I was reading five hours a day. You spend most of your time in nightclubs, staving off a vast army of debtors by eking out a precarious living as a hack journalist.'[30]

It had become a topic of gossip in London, and Doris did little to hide the affair from Castlerosse. Though, in the beginning, she had reportedly refused to sleep with Randolph because he smelled of castor oil. Before Castlerosse suspected anything, Doris and Randolph's affair was discovered by Anthony O'Connor, the maitre d' of the Calvary Club, when he opened the door to the ante-room and was 'confronted by a pair of long, gorgeous legs waving happily in the air'. Doris, whose face he could not see, let out a gasp, and when the 'man between the legs looked up', O'Connor saw it was Randolph Churchill. 'Get out!' Randolph yelled. A few weeks later, he was supervising a party given by Beaverbrook for Castlerosse, when Doris approached him and congratulated him on the excellence of the food. 'She was an absolute stunner,' O'Connor recalled. 'Tall, a beautiful face and a lovely figure,'[31] and observing her famous legs, he then realised they were the same pair he had seen in the ante-room.

Soon the secret affair had become common knowledge among London society, and Doris enjoyed wounding Castlerosse from afar (they continued to live apart), even if she was not present to witness it. Randolph shared her sadistic approach, and he placed a collect call to Castlerosse. 'Guess where I am?' He proceeded to torment Castlerosse by telling him that he was in bed with Doris. Another story, existing from that period, was told by Castlerosse in a bid to protect his pride and to portray him as taking charge of the situation. He supposedly telephoned Randolph and said, 'I hear you're living with my wife.'

'Yes, I am,' replied Randolph, 'and it's more than you have the courtesy to do.'

The exchange bred in Castlerosse a lasting grudge against Randolph, and he attacked his character whenever the opportunity presented itself. Once, when Randolph spoke badly about a former statesman, Castlerosse told him: 'Young man, it will be time enough to start abusing others when you have stopped abusing yourself.' On another occasion, at the Kit-Kat Club, Randolph diminished the occupation of gossip writers and declared he was going to form a society to exclude them from parties. Castlerosse eventually lost his temper when Randolph declared Beaverbrook's latest book, *Politicians and the War Vol. I*, as the work of a 'sneak guest'. He sought revenge by telling Randolph that his father had murdered a quarter of a million men at the Dardanelles.[32] When Randolph retaliated with an angry remark, Castlerosse said, 'For two pins, I'd hit you.'

'Don't do that,' replied Randolph. 'I'm not your wife.'[33]

Eventually Castlerosse did react to Randolph's insults and, at the opening of the San Carlo restaurant, he lifted a vase and hurled it in his direction. According to Evelyn Waugh, Randolph moved in time and narrowly avoided the assault, but the vase hit Lady Birkenhead and knocked her out. Those present thought this an 'act of cowardice', and their already ominous opinion of Randolph dimmed after that.

Following their heated encounters, Castlerosse launched an attack on Randolph in an article published in the *Daily Express*. Under the headline 'Pity These Great Men's Sons', he wrote: 'There is Randolph Churchill. He is a charming youth, but he is late in keeping appointments, and his powers are even more latent, though quite possibly they may also be there.'

In his own send-up of Castlerosse, Randolph wrote that his foe was 'supposed to be amusing. I have always found him more amusing to look at than to listen to.' Referring to Doris, he added that Castlerosse had 'a wife who is so much more amusing than him'. Why did Castlerosse write this article? Randolph implored his readers, before concluding it was 'because he is jealous'.

Doris herself had been the subject of an article printed in the *Daily Express*, but unlike the treatment of Castlerosse and Randolph in print, this paragraph was full of admiration:

> I once crossed the Channel with Lady Castlerosse. She has simplicity, a rare quality in a society woman. It sometimes leads her into absurd mis-statements. And, too, you can never be quite sure. When you think you are making fun of her, you are being made fun of. She is constantly striving after useful knowledge and culture. She would like to be well read. This she will never be, for she will not go through the labour. Like Lord Rosebery, she wants 'the palm without the dust'. Lady Castlerosse is cynical but, unlike cynical women, thoroughly good-natured and reliable. She is one of those strong characters who arouse bitter hostility or inspire friendship and affection. She is well turned-out but with no exaggeration. She has no habits. She does not pick the varnish off her fingernails. She does not twist her ring around her finger. She does not smoke cigarettes. She does not drink champagne. She does not disdain bad language. She makes full use of the common idiom in her speech.[34]

This character description of Doris must have struck Castlerosse as ironic, and somewhat grovelling. Before he could confront Doris, or indeed the author (it was written anonymously), she left for Venice with Randolph, where her voice echoed through the bridges and canals as she called out 'Fuzzy-wuzzy' – her pet name for him.

They went to Lady Diana Cooper's birthday party, organised by Chips Channon on the Venetian island of Murano, where a brawl broke out between the American tobacco heiress Doris Duke and Sir Richard Sykes, after he lit a Lucky Strike cigarette and purposely burnt her hand. Randolph intruded on the scene and Sir Richard hit him, whereupon Randolph retaliated by wrestling him to the ground. The birthday party became one of the smartest brawls with broken bottles, broken jaws, and considerable outrage from the general public, who had read about it in the British newspapers.

For Doris, however, her association with Chips Channon would be a memorable one. While in his company, she had sat on a wasp and was consequently stung. Neither 'embarrassed or unsure of what to do', Channon 'persuaded [her] to allow him to separate her from her garments' and he gallantly sucked the venom out, thus relieving her of the sting.[35]

The Venetian high jinks reached Castlerosse, and the rest of London, in the following dispatch:

> By day the Lido is equally gay. Mr Duff Cooper strides along the beach – a true outpost of Empire in his khaki shorts and vest. His wife maintains the virgin fairness of her skin against the sun's assault. Lady Castlerosse plays backgammon. The voice of Mr Randolph Churchill – whom Lady Castlerosse calls 'Fuzzy-wuzzy' – goes booming down the canals, presaging at least an audible political career.[36]

Far from shocked by the reports of his wife's behaviour, Castlerosse exerted a cool demeanour, though inside he was seething at a particular anecdote. 'Fuzzy-wuzzy,' he repeated to those who resembled a sympathetic listener. 'Fuzzy-wuzzy, she calls him!'

In London, Doris and Randolph parted due to parental pressure from Winston Churchill and their mutual inability to commit to only one mate, though she remained on good terms with the elder Churchill and continued to correspond with him. It had been a frivolous affair, and Doris moved on from Randolph without a backward glance.

In due course, Doris's time was spent outsmarting Castlerosse, who had set detectives on her in his quest to gather evidence for a divorce. He had since moved into the Hyde Park Hotel in an attempt to lure Doris into her usual trap of bringing men to their home. Hoping to play Castlerosse at his own game, she went to the hotel, learned what room he was staying in, broke in, removed her clothes, climbed into bed, and rang for the valet. When the valet arrived, he had before him the evidence that Castlerosse was not estranged from his wife, and the plot to garner evidence had been thwarted.

It marked a reunion for the couple, and enslaved by Doris and incapable of resisting her charm, Castlerosse took her to the Ritz Hotel in Paris. The detectives telephoned him with the news that Doris was last seen with a man at the Ritz. 'Yes. She had a man with her,' he told them. 'But, you bloody fool, it's me.'

However, during intervals from Castlerosse and their sporadic reunions, Doris continued to see Sir Alfred Beit. It did not go unnoticed by Castlerosse, and the detectives recorded their encounters at the following addresses: 1–12 April 1931, Adlou Hotel, Berlin; June 1931 – September 1932, Blackburn House; 1A Culross Street; 8 Smith Square; 213 Kings Road, Chelsea; Dorchester Hotel; and, August 1932, in Venice.[37]

With this evidence, Castlerosse approached Beaverbrook for guidance and was sent an avuncular letter. 'I am leaving for Canada in the morning,' Beaverbrook wrote, 'and I am leaving you to fix up your difficulty with your wife … I have a greater affection for you outside my own children. It is a real grief to me to see you stumbling over this affair and taking a beating every time.'[38]

In September 1932, Castlerosse filed a petition for divorce against Doris, citing adultery as the cause of the breakdown of their marriage. The suit was labelled Browne versus Browne and Beit, and he was determined to name Sir Alfred Beit as the co-respondent. In his pursuit of targeting Sir Alfred, he did not consider naming Randolph Churchill in the proceedings, though there was a discrepancy in his evidence as it was Randolph, and not Sir Alfred, with whom Doris holidayed in Venice. This deliberate oversight could have been done out of loyalty to Winston Churchill, who was not only a close ally of Beaverbrook but a friend of Lord and Lady Kenmare.

A month later, on 26 October, the Press Association released the following notice to its subscribers:

> A petition has been filed in the Divorce Court by Valentine Charles Browne,
> Viscount Castlerosse, for the dissolution of his marriage with Jessica* Doris,
> Viscountess Castlerosse, formerly Delavigne, a co-respondent being cited.

---

* Doris was incorrectly cited as Jessica rather than her birth-name of Jessie in the divorce papers. Her modified spelling of her surname was also used.

Lady Kenmare's words, 'the terrible thing is done', came back to haunt Castlerosse and, upon releasing the news of his divorce petition, he was filled with 'a certain consciousness of shame and failure'. His mother came to London from Killarney to plead with him not to act impulsively, as he had done in marrying Doris. It was not her son's well-being that prompted her to offer maternal guidance, but the thought of shaming the family and the Catholic Church. His male relatives, namely his uncle Maurice Baring, and his father, offered their advice, whether it was wanted or not. A priest had a sherry with him, and asked him to reconsider what he was doing. The Prince of Wales telephoned and told him not to be a 'bloody fool', and that the Duke of Norfolk was worried about him. To each individual, Castlerosse repeated: 'I have had enough. She has gone too far. I don't even care if the Pope objects. I shall go through with it.'[39]

Doris remained pragmatic about the divorce. It was a bravado that slowly withered as each of her friends shook their heads with disapproval and warned that her reputation would be ruined. Doris herself was the first to admit that she did not have much of a reputation to begin with, and certainly not one that was under threat. 'Imagine what people may think if all the evidence about you comes out,' her friends said.

'About me?' replied Doris. 'I don't mind what they say about me. But does Valentine – or rather, do his friends, mind what tales are told about him?'[40]

Before Doris could inform on such tales, Castlerosse had already confessed to his readers the reasons behind his filing for divorce. 'In Society as I knew it as a boy, certain things could not be done,' he wrote in the Londoner's Log. 'A woman's fair name for fidelity to her husband, her purity as a woman, a man's honour mattered greatly. These moral codes exist no longer in the West End. A woman can do what she likes provided always she can afford food and drink for her friends.'[41]

While Castlerosse's family were reeling from the news, and Beaverbrook was encouraging him to press on with the divorce, Doris's mother's reaction was, presumably, that of disappointment. But what else could she expect from her wayward daughter? She was not the first in her family to divorce; in 1934 her brother, Dudley, had married Countess Felicia Gizycki, the daughter of a minor Polish count and an American heiress whose money came from the *Chicago Tribune*. The marriage was short-lived, for Felicia's overprotective[42] mother accused Dudley of being a fortune hunter, and dispatched her lawyer to London to begin divorce proceedings. The farce was not lost on Doris who, having met Felicia the year before in the company of Beaverbrook, had grown fond of her temporary sister-in-law.

Caring little for public scorn, Doris was unconcerned about what the press printed about her. She telephoned Castlerosse and asked to meet him; the reasons for this were unknown, though others believed she had acted out of spite and longed to sabotage the divorce. He agreed, despite his legal advisers warning him against it. As a result, the divorce petition was withdrawn as there was insufficient evidence of adultery, and of the couple living apart and leading separate lives.

Knowing of Castlerosse's keenness to be rid of her, and of Beaverbrook's opinion on the matter, Doris approached the latter. She told Beaverbrook that she would give Castlerosse a divorce and partake in setting up evidence of adultery if he would take him to Canada. The standard practice was to take a hotel room in Brighton, hire a woman (usually a prostitute) as an accomplice, and ensure the hotel staff got the impression of not only a clandestine visit but could also be relied upon to give evidence in court (they were paid for their trouble). Or in Doris's case, as it was rare for the woman to willingly set herself up, she would have openly cavorted with a man and ensured there was evidence of her association with him, such as a newspaper notice or photographs. Lying under oath would not have troubled her and, thinking her plan was foolproof, she did not consider any potential obstacles she would have to face. But Beaverbrook refused to go along with her suggestion, as Castlerosse did not want to go to Canada, and thus Doris remained a significant presence in her husband's life.

But, as much as Doris thought the charade a great joke, things were becoming strained between her and her friends, many of whom were fond of Castlerosse and pitied his dilemma. Once, she would have enjoyed the disapproving whispers from her contemporaries and elders. However, as her status altered from that of scandalous socialite to social pariah, she realised that life, for a woman in her position, came with a price. With her circle diminishing, she did what she knew best. She moved on to something and someone new. It would be, in many ways, the beginning of the end.

♭EATEN BY ♭EATON

———◆———

If in 1932 Doris had one ally, it was Gerald Tyrwhitt-Wilson, the eccentric 14th Baron Berners, who was seventeen years her senior. She had first met Gerald through Diana Guinness, whose parties at her former home on Cheyne Walk attracted a myriad of aesthetes from her own generation and the one before her. Although from different backgrounds, their leanings towards nonconformity had established both Doris and Gerald as outsiders in their families, each of which was conventional in its own way.

Like Doris, Gerald was a gifted musician and artist; they adored the arts and, in spite of their rather uninspiring upbringings – or perhaps because of them – they thrived in creative settings. Raised by a severe, religious grandmother and a mother with a limited intellect and many prejudices, Gerald's talents were overlooked in favour of developing his masculinity: a trait which did not come naturally to him. After attending prep school followed by Eton, he claimed to have learned nothing from school except that it made him realise he was a homosexual. And it was where he became romantically involved for the first time with an older schoolfellow, a romance which came to a halt when he vomited on the boy.

Faringdon House, Gerald's estate on the edge of Faringdon in the market town of Oxfordshire, was a haven for social pariahs. With the tension mounting between herself and Castlerosse, Doris came to look on Faringdon as a second home. The enchanting setting of sprawling lawns and a conservatory filled with pigeons and fantailed doves dyed in hues of pink, blue and purple, and the 100ft folly built by Gerald with the warning: 'Members of the public committing suicide from this tower do so at their own risk', agreed with her flamboyance. It was not an unusual sight for Penelope Betjeman to bring her white horse into the house for tea, or to see Gerald's dogs bounding through the rooms wearing faux pearl necklaces bought from Woolworths.

Although a depressive by nature, Gerald appeared to treat his surroundings as a joke, and his guests loved him for it. The unconventionality of the house extended to his love life, and residing at Faringdon was his long-term lover and heir, Robert Heber-Percy, known as 'Mad Boy', who was thirty years his junior. Mad Boy was not in the least effeminate or camp, and Doris thought he was entirely heterosexual and, when they were formally introduced, she asked with total sincerity whether or not they had slept together, as she could not seem to remember.

Carrying a torch for Doris, Gerald was ready to leap to her defence when others spoke badly of her latest high jinks. Taking her place on the sofa and with Gerald behind the piano, it was the custom for Doris to say, 'Let's dish the dirt!' and he 'would listen fascinated by her tales of rascality and violence, striking an occasional chord and making some puckish suggestion for a happy solution to her marital dramas'.[1] After exchanging society gossip, she spoke of her dwindling finances and he offered his financial support. Acknowledging his kindness, she kissed him on the lips and said: 'Dear Gerald, anything you could do wouldn't last me two days.'[2] It was the kiss, and not her statement, which drew horrified gasps, as Gerald was known to detest kisses.

Gerald would later use Doris as an inspiration for his farcical play, *The Furies*, which had its debut in Oxford in 1942. The plot centred around Alfred Eversly, a writer, who flees the Mayfair social scene for Cornwall and, when that fails, he escapes to Haiti. The three Furies were based on Gerald's three great friends: Sybil, Lady Colefax; Emerald, Lady Cunard; and, of course, Doris. The character inspired by Doris was the socially unacceptable Vera – 'a tart' – who craves jewellery and rich men, and who marries Eversly, in the same vein as Doris when she had settled for Castlerosse. And, unlike Doris,

Vera is desperate to hold on to her husband and, when she realises he is going to leave her, she drugs and kidnaps him for his own good. As Gerald intended, her character was 'ruthless but with a heart of gold'.

In the meantime, Doris, Cecil Beaton and Oliver Messel served as creative muses for Gerald's book, *The Girls of Radcliff Hall*.[3] Written under the pseudonym Adela Quebec, the title was influenced by the author Radclyffe Hall, whose lesbian novel *The Well of Loneliness* had caused a sensation when it was published in 1928. Gerald cast himself as Miss Carfax, the headmistress of a girls' school, with the main characters, the female pupils, modelled after his male friends. The cast of characters was as follows: Cecily Seymour (Cecil Beaton), Lizzie Johnson (Peter Watson), Olive Mason (Oliver Messel), Mary Peabody (Robin Thomas), Daisy Montgomery (David Herbert), and Helena de Troy (Jack Wilson). Doris was the only female to feature in the story and, ironically, her character was a male. She was the dancing master, Mr Vivian Dorrick, an oversexed gentleman who was 'no novice in the art of lovemaking … his personality was veiled, to a certain extent, in mystery'.[4] Mr Dorrick has a fling with the heroine, Cecily (Beaton), who is in love with Lizzie (Peter Watson). Gerald wrote the novel while staying at his Roman villa with Diana Guinness, and it was privately published for his friends. Doris laughed at the portrayal, but Beaton did not, and he succeeded in destroying almost every copy. Noel Coward, whose former boyfriend Jack Wilson was included in the tease, wrote: 'I absolutely adored Les Girls! What a beastly little book.'

When Cecil Beaton had been initiated into Gerald's circle, the latter had dismissed him in his usual waspish manner, as 'a very odd character with very little heart'.[5] But the socially ambitious Beaton was delighted to be invited to Faringdon, and he overlooked Gerald's assessment. It was at Faringdon that he first met Doris, who arrived in her chauffeur-driven Phantom Rolls-Royce with several trunks bearing a viscountess's coronet. She carried with her a heavy box containing the precious Cartier jewels she had collected from her various rich lovers over the years. With his spectacular eye for detail, Beaton noticed Doris's slender legs and he admired her 'Giselle-like ankles'; her exquisite clothes – suits and dresses – were from Worth and Reville, and she continued to shun skirts in favour of tailored shorts – a daring choice – to display her best features.

A Bright Young Thing, Beaton moved at the centre of this set, photographing mischievous young aristocrats dressed in elaborate costumes or stripped down to a head and bare shoulders. Most notable was the simplistic study of the flaxen-haired society sisters, Teresa and Baby Jungmann, whom Beaton posed against a sheet of wet plastic, with their Marcel-waved heads touching and their eyes closed, as though they were paraffin angels. As the 1930s advanced, his status was further elevated when he photographed Queen Elizabeth. But Beaton did not confine his lens to the Court; he worked for *Vogue*, photographing models and film stars – Greta Garbo became his favourite – and New York socialites, which ultimately boosted his standing across the Atlantic. His professional merits were many, but his love life stalled. Peter Watson, a wealthy young man who, along with Cyril Connolly, would later co-found the literary magazine *Horizon*, was the subject of his infatuation. However he was not attainable to Beaton, for he was in love with Oliver Messel. And, moving on from Messel, he attached himself to Mad Boy. In an attempt to avert Beaton's passion, Watson dismissively told him: 'I'd be delighted if you had an affair.' Beaton took this advice but, surprisingly, it was not another young man to whom he diverted his attention.

In August, Doris travelled to Venice where she stayed for a fortnight at the Villa Foscari, known as 'La Malcontenta', its name derived from the spouse of one of the Foscaris who was imprisoned in the house because she would not fulfil her conjugal duty. The villa was owned by the Baroness d'Erlanger, whose guests for the fortnight included Sir Oswald Mosley, who had since founded the British Union of Fascists, and his wife, Cimmie; Emerald Cunard and her lover, Sir Thomas Beecham; Lady Diana and Duff Cooper; Randolph Churchill; Brendan Bracken; and Tilly Losch, who was estranged from her husband, Edward James.

It was a louche circle of wealthy revellers who were interconnected by society marriages and, more than anything, illicit love affairs. Diana and Bryan Guinness joined this set on the Lido, verifying the truth behind the rumours sweeping through high society that she was having an affair with Mosley. Their clandestine meetings at his London flat transferred to the tiny huts along the lido, where guests cast sympathetic looks in Bryan and Cimmie's direction, and yet they were enthralled by the scandal. And there was the equally promiscuous Tilly Losch, a friend of Doris, but foe of Diana due to her loyalty towards Edward James – she had once been in love with him as a young debutante. Doris and Tilly's old flame Tom Mitford joined the party, and the women's romantic feelings towards him had since mellowed into an agreeable friendship.

In Venice, Peter Watson's suggestion of an affair came to fruition when Beaton looked to Doris with the hope of making him jealous. But it was not Beaton who made the first move. And perhaps, owing to his homosexuality, he never would have approached Doris in the first place. She took the initiative and, planning her seduction of Beaton, she scattered tuberoses – 'the most carnal of scents' – on his bed. Beaton adored attention, and he responded to the flattery she paid him. Doris herself refused to believe his sexual orientation would pose a problem, and she told him: 'There's no such thing as an impotent man, just an incompetent woman.'[6] To ease Beaton's reluctance towards going to bed with her, she assured him he 'wouldn't have to do a thing', and she advised him to 'think of your sister's wedding'.[7]

The affair was not confined to Venice, and when they returned to London, Doris and Beaton often stayed at Faringdon. Guests, eager to judge if the affair had been farce, crept to the lovers' bedroom door and were further astonished when they overheard Beaton squealing: 'Oh goody, goody, goody!'[8]

The droll antics continued when Beaton threw a party, and the guests were ordered to dress as their opposite. For this, Doris came as a nun. There was also a circus-themed party which Doris and Beaton attended with Lady Diana and Duff Cooper, Chips Channon, Nancy Mitford and Daphne Weymouth. Doris – along with Nancy, Daphne and Beaton – dressed as an eighteenth-century equestrian, and Beaton chased her with a whip. They were photographed for *Tatler*, and Doris commented: 'We all look very drunk, I think.'[9]

Doris joined Beaton at Ashcombe, his Georgian manor house in Wiltshire which he had taken a fifteen-year lease on in 1930. Gerald had helped him decorate the bedroom walls of the circus room: he painted a columbine flower and performing dogs, amongst them an ugly mastiff jumping through a paper hoop. Later, Gerald obliged Beaton when he dressed up as the fictional King Boris to be photographed for his satirical book, *My Royal Past*, which featured a tableaux of his friends dressed as fictional members of a royal Court.

But the reception at Ashcombe was not as welcoming as it had been at Faringdon, and Doris was shunned by Beaton's friend, the ageing writer Edith Olivier, who was enraged by this 'common little demi-mondaine'[10] attaching herself to him. Edith recalled how she and Lady Ottoline Morrell were invited to lunch by Beaton, who claimed he was 'alone with Gerald'. When they arrived they found him sitting in the courtyard, with Gerald painting a portrait of Doris, who was sitting on a mattress, her legs on show in a pair of shorts. This confirmed to Edith that the rumours she had heard were true. 'It is a liaison between the two. "<u>We</u>" always includes her. It makes me feel I can never go there again,' she wrote in her diary. 'Why should one put oneself out for her?'[11] Lady Ottoline acidly noted that Mrs Keppel, at least, was 'on the grand scale – a king's mistress'. Doris, Edith bemoaned, 'is nothing but a woman with a physical attraction which she exploits in a mercenary way'.[12]

Doris defended her affair with Beaton, though she did not admit to the financial rewards which she hoped he would lavish her with – his salary from

Doris at Faringdon, surrounded by Gerald Berners, Daphne Weymouth and Mad Boy.

Condé Nast alone was $12,000 per annum. She was far more forthright in her confession: she claimed she was sleeping with Beaton for his own benefit. In an age when homosexuality was illegal, Doris maintained that she was merely trying to cure him of his sexual persuasion.[13] But, in truth, this ran deeper than money; she had developed a deep and complex passion for him, and in turn he repeatedly warned her that he was 'terribly homosexualist'.

In his diary, Beaton wrote: 'Peter loves people that are not in love with him and I in my turn am now worshipped and adored by Doritizins [his pet name for Doris] for whom I hold no emotion whatsoever. It seems so terribly unfair that there cannot be a great straightening out and saving of waste.'[14] In person, however, he played along with her, 'if only to soothe the ache produced by years of rejection' by Peter Watson. He went to bed with her 'in desperation', and he chastised himself when he realised he 'could be so celestial with the bedfellow I love'.[15] Although Watson had encouraged Beaton to have an affair, he did not imagine that it would have been with Doris, whom he loathed. It backfired on Beaton, and Peter, 'so incensed' by his 'relationship with Doritizins,' became 'so bitter' and refused to see him.

The affair between Doris and Beaton might have been founded on deceit, but their personalities and backgrounds were markedly similar. Born four years after Doris, in 1904, Beaton was firmly middle-class, his parents having risen from working-class origins (his grandfather had been a blacksmith; the other ran a chemist's shop in Kilburn); and like Doris, his father was in trade. Like her own brother, Dudley, Beaton was afforded an education befitting an upper-class boy, though at the prep school which he attended with Evelyn Waugh, he was acutely aware of his lowly status in comparison to his schoolfellows. Waugh, the son of a publisher, overlooked his mutual rank with Beaton, and stuck pins in him. The inferiority he felt intensified at Harrow and he masked his feelings of inadequacy by dressing in silk pyjamas and rouging his face. And terrified of having to do an army drill, he bought a pair of boots with irons in them so he could masquerade as a cripple. Surprisingly, his schoolfellows left him alone because they admired his individuality.

Devoting himself to raising his rank in society, Beaton was determined to ignore his father's profession in the timber trade – there was nothing he could change about that – but he made up his mind to turn his mother into a society lady. This *Pygmalion* experiment began when, at the age of 19 and at Cambridge, he began to send details of his mother's engagements to the social editor of *The Times*, and following up on his initial contact, he sent along a box of cigars as a sort of bribe. It paid off when *Tatler* telephoned to ask if they could photograph his mother, and Beaton was so excited that he dressed up too, on the off-chance they might include him in the shot. It was in *Tatler's* studio, with the backdrop of magenta curtains and lighting, that he discovered his vocation. However this curiosity for photography was founded in the nursery when his nanny, an amateur photographer, would lay her prints on the windowsill with a young Beaton helping her. His nanny then assisted him, when he began to take his own photographs, by developing the prints in the bath. Beaton would send his self-portraits to newspapers and magazines and, when that failed, he dressed up his sisters, Nancy and Baba, and sent in photographs of them. His photograph of Nancy and Baba, dressed as angels, appeared in *Vogue*, thus establishing a lengthy association with the magazine.

This, Doris could admire, for she herself had been as ruthless as Beaton in her own quest for social mobility. Although she had used different tactics to enter the aristocratic circles of London, they both shared a canny sense of self-promotion and were shrewd in their exploitation of people for their own advantage. It was those qualities they immediately recognised in one another, and it was those very traits which brought them together.

News of Doris and Beaton's affair reached Castlerosse, and adopting the view of their contemporaries, he thought it a joke. On one of his outings to a London restaurant, Castlerosse spied his wife dining with Beaton and, turning to his companion, he quipped: 'I never knew Doris was a lesbian.'[16] This extramarital affair did little to provoke him, but he added Beaton's name to his growing list of evidence for his much-sought-after divorce.

In March 1933, a deed of separation was entered into between Doris and Castlerosse, with no financial clauses. They had, for some time, maintained separate abodes, and the legal confirmation of their status was of little consequence to either of them. A month prior, a man had arrived to subpoena Cecil Beaton, who had been listed as evidence in their divorce petition. But he was in New York and thus narrowly avoided being drawn into the lengthy saga.

Lady Kenmare continued to nurture a belief that her son and Doris's marriage, as it had taken place in a register office, was not valid. Further incensed by Castlerosse shaming the family and making a mockery of the Catholic Church, she feared the social repercussions divorce would bring, especially in religious Ireland where it was taboo. The disgrace her daughter-in-law had brought on herself paled in comparison to the feelings of hatred simmering beneath her aloof exterior. Lady Kenmare, 'like a sinister black crow',[17] loathed human contact, and to her own son she was 'an ice-cold skeletal figure'[18] who refrained from exerting warmth. Furthermore, she was reluctant to speak kindly of her son, who thrived on praise and affection. She would never admit that the marriage between the viscount and the courtesan had been her own folly.

Castlerosse's emotional state was in turmoil, although it was hidden under a bushel of ferocity and bad-tempered outbursts; his enormous bulk increased to over 300lb and he was eating and drinking more than usual. His appearance inspired jokes and teasing,[19] and stories circulated that he had sat on a small dog and crushed it to death. His contemporaries found this amusing and cartoon sketches began to appear in magazines and newspapers. One such parody titled 'Entering the Embassy' was published in *Tatler*, and it displayed Doris as a wasp-waisted figure next to a perfectly round Castlerosse with his clothes bursting at the seams. Nancy Astor singled him out at a party by announcing: 'Lord Castlerosse, if that stomach was on a woman I would say she was pregnant.' Relying on his wit, he retorted: 'Madame, half an hour ago it was, and she is.'[20] But as much as Castlerosse laughed it off, he was hurt by the mockery.

In the summer of 1933, Doris was the subject of a painting by Sir John Lavery R.A., the Irish artist who was a friend of the Kenmare family. A dignified portrait of a viscountess at home, Doris was dressed in an afternoon frock with wisps hanging from an indeterminate hemline, and her blonde hair hidden by a black hat with ribbons dangling from its brim. The portrait was to hang in the Royal Academy, and Doris was worried that she, as its subject, would hinder its chances of it being exhibited there. 'If I were divorced,' she asked Lavery, 'it would not make any difference, would it, Sir John?' He assured her it would not, even though Doris herself thought getting into the Royal Academy was on a par with being presented at Buckingham Palace, and would adhere to the rule that divorced women could not attend Court. Lavery eased her concerns, though Lady Lavery, who held Castlerosse in esteem, took a dim view of Doris. She had, Lady Lavery said, the same qualities as Ramsay MacDonald: 'the gift of endurance or permanence! They survive everything, rebuffs, unpopularity, plague etc.'[21]

When it was exhibited, the *Sketch* called Lavery's portrait 'a delightful example of the art of the President of the Royal Academy'. Castlerosse, however, took one look at the portrait and remarked: 'It may be art, which I doubt, but it isn't Doris.'

The estranged couple were destined to meet once more over the subject of art. That September, Doris departed for the south of France to stay at Maxine Elliott's villa, Château de l'Horizon, in Golfe-Juan, and Castlerosse went on a yachting cruise of the Mediterranean. Arriving at the villa, he found Doris being painted by Winston Churchill who, along with his wife Clementine, was also a guest. Castlerosse thought it a favourable likeness, due to Churchill portraying Doris wearing her signature shorts. In 1930, the year they had met, Churchill had first painted a head and shoulders study of Doris wearing a green blouse, her arms folded across her chest, with her lantern jaw, sly eyes and pursed lips radiating an air of defiance. The *Daily Express* took note of the latter painting, and wrote:

> Mr Winston Churchill is challenging the achievement of Sir John Lavery. He is painting a portrait of Lady Castlerosse. Lady Castlerosse was one of the few noteworthy features of this year's academy. Mr and Mrs Churchill are among the guests at Miss Maxine Elliott's villa, at Golfe Juan, between Cannes and Juan les Pins. It is there that Lady Castlerosse has been sitting for the portrait.[22]

Although legally separated, Castlerosse appeared chivalrous towards Doris and they were photographed, hand in hand, with him gallantly leading her down the steps into a swimming pool. But in spite of Doris being on her best behaviour in front of the Churchills, Castlerosse could tolerate his wife's company no longer, and he departed for Paris.

On the train, Castlerosse was taken severely ill and was carried by stretcher from the Gare St Lazare to the Ritz Hotel. He was overweight and over-wrought, and for several days he suffered from anxiety attacks. Beaverbrook was telephoned and, concerned for his friend, he sent a specialist to treat the problem. The illness swiftly departed without a formal diagnosis, and Castlerosse announced that he was going to Biarritz to convalesce. It was not a coincidence that Doris was also there, and she had telegrammed him to join her. Only then did the mysterious ailment become apparent to Beaverbrook: Castlerosse was simply missing Doris.

But Castlerosse had misjudged Doris's benevolence, and the trip which had previously appealed to him would end in failure. He attended a bullfight with Doris, and hated every moment of it. From Biarritz he worked on the Londoner's Log, and he reported on the bullfight, claiming that the spectacle could have been improved if a picador was selected from the audience and instructed to fight the raging bull with a spear. Writing had restored him mentally and he was beginning to feel stronger, physically.

Later in the evening, having filed his Log, Castlerosse went to a casino. The visit would end abruptly, and before he could place his bets, he had witnessed a Spanish nobleman putting his arm around Doris. Approaching the Spaniard, Castlerosse threw a glass of sherry in his face and said: 'This is a barbarous country, sir. You should be reported to the RSPCA for the way you treat your horses.'[23] Doris screamed with laughter and the nobleman had Castlerosse ejected from the casino, whereupon she abandoned her Spanish admirer to join her husband. She was prepared to forgive him, and he was aware that no other man in the world could insult her and receive an amused response.

However, by the end of the trip, they could not stand to be in one another's company and Castlerosse realised that, as fond as they were of one another, they just could not live with each other. It would be their fate to separate once again.

With Cecil Beaton in New York, Doris was briefly reunited with Sir Alfred Beit, but she was more than he could handle and he broke off the affair. He was looking for the stability of marriage and someone with whom he could share his passion for art and philanthropy, and although Doris was in the process of divorcing Castlerosse, she was not the type of wife he sought. He would later marry Clementine Freeman-Mitford, a first cousin of the Mitford girls.

Castlerosse helps Doris into a swimming pool in the south of France.

To escape Doris he fled to South Africa 'to cool down', for it was only with a great distance between them that he felt safe from her preying clutches. Diana Vreeland, who ran a lingerie shop near Berkeley Square, was friendly with both Doris and Beaton, and she repeated the familiar *bon mot* that circulated London society at the time: 'Beaten by Beaton and bitten by Beit.'

Beaton returned from America, and they restored their old routine of lunching at the Ritz Hotel. On one occasion, he and Doris dined with Elsie Mendl and her companion, Johnnie McMullin, the social columnist and fashion editor of *Vogue*, who proclaimed: 'A complete jewellery kit is a most important part of a well-dressed man's wardrobe.' A lively conversationalist and a woman of many trades, the American-born Elsie (née de Wolfe) began her career as a stage actress where she was neither on the brink of stardom nor a total failure. She left the theatre to reinvent herself as an interior decorator, and was said to have invented the occupation. Following the 1913 publication of her book, *The House in Good Taste*, she established a list of clients made up of aristocrats, celebrities and American socialites. During their luncheon, Elsie exclaimed, 'I love whores!'

Doris responded by yelling, 'What about homosexuality?' The question was a veiled jibe at Beaton, whose diary she had read. She was still reeling from the shock of learning about his love for Peter Watson.

After lunch they went their separate ways, with Doris going shopping and Beaton feigning an excuse to visit an art gallery, when in fact he had visited Daisy Fellowes. Later that evening, Doris and Beaton went to see Harlem dancers accompanied by a Hungarian band at the Crillon.

However, aside from the Peter Watson confession in his diary, Beaton harboured another secret which he kept from Doris. He had met a rich American, William Odom, who had 'a smile like a snarl',[24] and he invited Beaton on a European tour, all expenses paid. 'The big day of explanation is still afar,' he wrote in his diary. This balancing act of a faux romance with Doris and attaching himself to Odom for self-gain was an 'exciting game' to him, and he admitted: 'I am always fond of anyone who is fond of me.'[25] Gradually, as she realised the true nature of Beaton's feelings, Doris detached herself from him, though she continued to enjoy his company and appeared good-natured about his departure with Odom.

In his absence, Doris busied herself with Diana Guinness, whose complicated love affair with Sir Oswald Mosley was on the rocks. Months before, in November, she had found herself an unlikely player in the break-up of Diana and Bryan Guinness's marriage. And, along with Tom Mitford and Randolph Churchill, she attempted to stop Diana from leaving her husband to set herself up in a townhouse in Eaton Square as Mosley's mistress.[26] Diana had taken that step, in spite of Doris's wise counsel – could her words have disguised a tinge of envy? – that she was leaving a good life with a devoted husband who not only worshipped her, but had not, as so many men of his class were apt to do, taken a mistress. Doris ought to have known: she was often the other woman. But Diana longed for passion and excitement, and Doris could, at least, identify with that.

It was through the Guinnesses that Doris had met her great friend, Phyllis de Janzé. In 1931, while Diana convalesced from the birth of her second child at her country house, Biddesden, she befriended Phyllis through their mutual friend Dora Carrington, as they had both studied at the Slade School of Art in London. In those days, Carrington had fallen in love with Phyllis, and she thought her 'dazzling ... like a Persian whore with a scarlet mouth'.[27] Like Doris, Phyllis was an ambitious woman who sought a rich husband and protector, and she was said to have a violent temper.[28] In 1922, she had married Henri de Janzé, a titled but penniless man who was eight years her junior, and unlike Doris, she came from an aristocratic background; her mother was Lady Lillian Boyd and her grandfather was the 2nd Earl of Munster. Phyllis was also the great-great granddaughter of Dorothea Bland, who had been the long-standing mistress of King William IV.

Under ordinary circumstances Doris and Phyllis would have been viewed as rivals. But Doris appreciated Phyllis's forthright attitude, and in time she became a trusted confidante. Far from threatened by Phyllis's habit of seducing rich men for money and presents, Doris would go along to her tiny house on Chapel Street, the bedroom of which she called 'the office'. Together they called at Eaton Square to visit Diana, whose days were spent waiting for Mosley to call, to show off their baubles from Cartier. In Phyllis, Doris had found an uncritical friend.

But it was in Cecil Beaton's absence that Doris's place in the affair between Diana and Mosley had become a poignant one. Continuing his travels around Europe with William Odom in his open Duesenberg motor car, the two men stopped at Aix-en-Provence, Genoa, La Spezia and Florence. They visited Lady Ida Sitwell in Montegufoni before going to Rome to stay with Princess Jane, the American wife of Principe di San Faustino. It was in Rome that Doris's letter reached Beaton; she had written to tell him that their friend Cimmie Mosley had died from peritonitis following an emergency appendectomy. 'Poor darling Cimmie died at 5.30 this afternoon,'[29] she said.

Doris had been at Diana's townhouse that evening while she waited for news on Cimmie, and she fretted about the status of her relationship with

Mosley. Diana, who was described as being 'off her head',[30] thought their future hinged on Cimmie, and whether or not she would make a recovery. Peter Watson was with Doris, and their mutual friend Robert Byron arrived, bringing with him the news that Cimmie had just died. However, in her letter to Beaton, Doris wrote that she and Watson heard the news just as they left for the nursing home to visit her. 'We have certainly lost a divine friend,' she remarked, 'and none of my holidays will be the same without her.'[31]

Beaton was devastated, and he wrote: 'I am so upset I could cry ... I owe my happiness and success to her appreciation and friendliness.' Doris told him to enjoy himself in Rome, and she urged him to 'come back the same sweet Cecil you were before you went to New York'.[32]

Doris met Beaton in Paris, where he had callously abandoned his American admirer on the grounds that he was not cultured enough for his cultivated tastes. They went to the ballet with Daisy Fellowes, who was working for the French *Harper's Bazaar* in her short-lived position as editor of the magazine. And they mingled with the artist Pavel Tchelitchew, famous in Paris but relatively unknown in London, the poet Edith Sitwell, and the photographer Horst P. Horst, whom Beaton viewed as a rival.

With Doris's arrival, Beaton declared he had become the 'envy of the city'; her appearance marked a 'great sex interlude' in which he became 'a peacock and felt so self-assured and even beautiful'.[33] The revelation in Beaton's diary and, now, the belief that she had become a pawn in his game for self-promotion, conspired to upset Doris. He felt sad that she had suffered for his vanity, but he was not sorry because 'being the loved one does me good morally'. Doris returned to London and Peter Watson arrived in Paris, and she found herself usurped by the object of Beaton's affection. But Watson did not reciprocate his feelings, and Beaton wept 'in a taxi' and 'in the bright sunlight of the Ritz bar'.[34]

Although Beaton and Watson experienced something of a reunion at Ashcombe and had attempted to mend their friendship, Watson did not invite him on his summer holiday. Doris wrote to Beaton, asking him to join her at Maxine Elliott's villa. He came and things were pleasant between the two until a telegram arrived from Watson, who was in Salzburg, and Beaton impulsively abandoned Doris to join him in Austria. It was a miscalculation, for Watson spent the day on the Alps, and Beaton was stranded at the railway station without an explanation or a token apology from him. When Beaton reached his hotel room, his vanity was wounded when Watson dropped in sporadically, claiming that he had little time for him, and Beaton on his behalf sulked in the solitude of the hotel room whilst Doris sunbathed in Cannes.

When they returned to England, Beaton maintained an aloof distance from Doris. His brother, Reggie, died on 18 October after he was hit by a Tube train at Piccadilly Circus underground station. The train driver told the inquest that Reggie had held out his hands in front of him and dived under the approaching train. It was believed to be suicide. Beaton heard the news after he had dropped Doris home from a dinner party given by Sybil Colefax for the American socialite, Mona Harrison Williams. His friends were sympathetic, though Beaton remained oddly unmoved by the death. Doris invited him to dinner at Ciros, but he felt it was too soon to be seen socially after Reggie's demise.

The affair with Beaton fizzled out when he abandoned Doris after realising Peter Watson was not jealous and had become friends with her. They both formed a close bond after Beaton had 'shoved them away', though Watson did not shirk from firing the occasional acid remark in her direction.

As Doris had displayed with her attachment to Beaton, she did not believe a person's sexuality stood in the way of romantic love, regardless if they were compatible or not. She had no scruples when it came to sex, for she used it as a ploy to get what she wanted. It was, to her, a means of survival and a way to fund a lifestyle that had become such a way of life that she saw no alternative. To live within her means was foreign to her, and without her material things she felt lost and without a purpose.

So, when Castlerosse commented, 'I never knew Doris was a lesbian,' he was honest in his observation. However, as time would tell, there was more than a fragment of truth in his statement.

A TANGLED WEB

'What we have to do, what at any rate it is our duty to do, is to revive the old art of lying.'

Oscar Wilde

———————•◆•———————

In September 1935, Doris went to Dr Dengler's sanatorium in Baden Baden for ten days' rest – 'it was needed, too'.[1] Having parted from Cecil Beaton and no further along in divorcing Castlerosse, she returned to the old, familiar pattern of informing on her contemporaries to Beaverbrook.

However, on this occasion Doris used such social gossip to appear, as she hoped, to be doing Beaverbrook a good turn. Beaverbrook's great friend from his youth Sir James 'Jimmy' Dunn's wife, Irene, was staying at the sanatorium and Doris often sat at her table for meals. She wrote to Beaverbrook to tell him that Lady Dunn was a 'loadful' of news, the content of which amused her. But her main priority was to gauge whether or not she planned to divorce Sir James and, as it stood, Doris understood she would not. The subject of Sir James and Lady Dunn's divorce was a personal matter for Beaverbrook, for his friend had fallen into a deep and lasting depression after the death of his daughter, Mona (Lord Birkenhead's mistress), from peritonitis in 1928. She offered to influence Lady Dunn, and asked Beaverbrook to let her know how to proceed, as she had been asking Doris for advice. Lady Dunn was unaware that Doris was writing to Beaverbrook and, hoping to be of use to him, she told him she would be in London on 25 September and would telephone him in due course. She wrote to say she had lots of news.[2] Veering away from the Dunns' divorce, she also wrote to him about Lord Rothermere, who had been staying at Dr Dengler's sanatorium. She claimed he had one girl at the Stephanie Hotel, and two 'hanging around' at the sanatorium.

In response to Doris's letter, Beaverbrook sent her a telegram. After thanking her for the letter, he wrote: 'I do not know and cannot gather Sir James's attitude.'[3] That was all he divulged on the matter, and Doris quickly dropped the subject. And her additional piece of information on Lord Rothermere, proprietor of the *Daily Mail* and his close friend, also vexed him.

When she returned to London, Doris moved out of the flat on Culross Street and into Claridge's Hotel, where Castlerosse was also residing, though in a separate suite. During periods when she felt bored or neglected or in the mood to toy with his feelings, she would telephone her husband's suite and demand to be taken to luncheon or dinner.

Castlerosse would respond that he was unavailable and then, taken in by Doris's charm, he proceeded to cancel any engagements he had. Each time he realised he had been manipulated, and each time he would fly into a rage that provoked him to hurl chairs across the room or tear the telephone cable from the wall. 'How can I be such a bloody, bloody, bloody fool!'[4] he would say. The convenience with which Doris rang him up mirrored his unfavourable opinion of the telephone and its impact on relationships. This, he wrote in the Londoner's Log:

> The value of routine in married life is immense. I know a woman who had held the affection of a wayward man by simply ringing him up at the same time every day. By now it has become such a habit that he cannot do without.[5]

Revelling in the power she held over Castlerosse, Doris continued to berate him when he refused her requests for luncheon or dinner, or when she sensed he was trying to renege on his commitments. When tormenting him over the telephone ceased to satisfy her, she would walk along the corridor and come into his suite unannounced. If his valet or chauffeur were there, she would dismiss them with a flippant gesture of her hand. Sometimes Castlerosse's new secretary, Miss Marjorie Cowell,[6] would be present and she, too, would attempt to leave the room before a quarrel began. He would beg of Miss Cowell: 'Don't go. You must improve your education by talking to my charming wife.'

The remark struck a nerve in Doris and, looking in Miss Cowell's direction, she would snap: 'Don't think your bloody Sunday school mistress is going to stop me!'[7]

After this they began to row, and it ended as it always did: in physical violence. They threw pillows and telephone books at one another, and Castlerosse would chase Doris out of the room and along the corridor. It was a bizarre sight for residents to behold: the elephantine Castlerosse dressed in his pyjamas or, more than often, in only his pyjama top, running after his tiny wife. It was a familiar ritual for the two, until one day Doris stopped him and, as bemused residents passed, she said: 'Careful, darling. You're in your pyjamas. Think what your respectable Miss C.[8] will imagine!' Satisfied that he had been humiliated enough, she walked away.

But Doris did not stop communicating with Castlerosse, and driven by an incessant need to torture him, she, as she had done all those years ago, attacked his weaknesses. When mocking his appearance, weight and finances ceased to infuriate him, she attacked his beloved Killarney and his recent scheme to transform the estate into a golf club.[9] It was an unwise move on Doris's part, for as much as Castlerosse still held a degree of affection for her, his love was waning.

With Doris's presence at Claridge's, Castlerosse's behaviour grew increasingly unreasonable, and everyday trivialities triggered a violent outburst. He liked to show off his skill as a carver in spite of his lame arm, and he specifically asked the chef at the Dorchester to serve the chicken uncarved. During a luncheon for his show business friends,[10] Douglas Fairbanks, Frances Day and Ina Claire, he was enraged to find their food already carved and cunningly put back together again. Castlerosse picked up the chicken and threw it at the waiters, before fleeing the room. Accustomed to his temper, his guests continued to drink and converse as though nothing had happened.

During this period his temperament had become unpredictable, and he directed it at his valet, Welch, and chauffeur, Godfrey. He complained about the specks of dust on the car, or the crease in his trousers. 'He would sometimes get wedged in the back seat of the car and go into a panic,' recalled Godfrey. 'He would scream for me to stop, and if I was slow in pulling up he would get into an absolute frenzy, and swear I was trying to murder him.'[11] On another occasion – because of his stomach he could not bend over to tie his shoelaces – he became impatient with Welch,[12] to whom he offered a tirade of abuse before kicking out and sending him flying towards the wardrobe, against which he hit his head.

Aware of his unreasonable behaviour and, as he was apt to do, Castlerosse made a mockery of the predicament. 'It is good news that jealousy can be cured,' he wrote in his book, *Valentine's Days*, which was published in 1934. He referred to a doctor in Rome 'who undertakes to cure this painful malady'. The methods were 'quite simple', Castlerosse explained: 'He uses no anti-love potion but concentrates on reduction of food, increase of exercise and certain medicines.' The outcome was, he said: 'Whereas Fascism has given Italy a new backbone, this Roman doctor has given Italians new livers.'[13]

However, no amount of remedies could cure Castlerosse. It was only in Doris's absence that he could relax. But this frame of mind was not to last, for his thoughts were fixated on her, and any effort to exorcise her from his life were to be in vain.

In February 1936[14] Doris went to Paris with Mad Boy where, for three days, they took a room at the Ritz Hotel. The occasion was his twenty-fifth birthday and, as a present, she paid for a prostitute to join them in their hotel room. Upon presenting her to Mad Boy, Doris handed him a whip and ordered him to beat the terrified woman to death. Taking the whip, he issued a few gentle taps before an impatient Doris snatched it from his hand and left a welt on the prostitute's body. 'I haven't wasted my money for this,' she said.

'Doris,' muttered a disapproving Mad Boy, 'any more of this and I'll be sick.'[15]

The display of sadism was a step too far, even for Mad Boy, and the camaraderie between the two cooled. They did, however, sail together on the SS *Strathaird* from Marseilles to Port Said.[16]

As was the case with Cecil Beaton, Doris believed she could 'cure' Mad Boy of his homosexuality, though, unlike Beaton, he was not entirely devoted to the male sex. When questioned why he had strayed from Gerald Berners and into Doris's bed, Mad Boy cited her sexual trick known as 'Cleopatra's grip' as the reason. 'If you come across one of those,' he said, 'you sign away your kingdom.'[17]

Whether or not Doris and Mad Boy sailed to Port Said can be disputed given the false evidence reported in the divorce petition. Not only was Castlerosse grasping at any morsel of evidence he could pin on Doris to prove she had committed adultery, he had convinced William Rootes, the motor-car agent, to be listed in the petition. But Doris was not entirely oblivious to Castlerosse's dealings and, to advance the divorce proceedings, she agreed to make it appear as though she and Rootes were having an affair.

The divorce petition was re-filed in November 1936, three years after it had been dismissed due to lack of evidence, with Browne versus Browne and Rootes and Percy.[18] In the file, Castlerosse stated that Doris and William Rootes had committed adultery on the 15, 16 and 17 March 1936,[19] at the Galle Face Hotel Colombo in Ceylon. Their affair continued, Castlerosse said, on 17, 18, 19, 20 and 21 March 1936, aboard the steamship *Aeneas*, on their voyage from Ceylon to Penang. Then, in Penang, Doris and Rootes were said to have spent an illicit three days at the Runnymede Hotel in the Federated Malay States.[20]

Little evidence exists to support Castlerosse's claim of Doris and Rootes's adultery. As Castlerosse was a long-standing client of Rootes's, and the two men shared something of a friendship (though at times it was tested due to Castlerosse's unpaid bills), it appears he was doing his friend a favour. Further evidence suggests that Doris had merely crossed paths with Rootes, who was travelling with his son, Geoffrey, and they socialised for the remainder of the trip.

Before her departure on 23 February, Doris told a newspaper:[21] 'London was very dull when I left. Naturally the death of King George made the city very gloomy.' The newspaper reported that Doris would be staying at the Raffles Hotel in Singapore with the Hon. Mrs Hubert Parker (formerly Miss Loryn Bowser of Kentucky), who was accompanying her on a tour of the Orient, stopping at Java, Bali, the Philippines, China and Japan.

The two women had come to Singapore by way of Kuala Lumpur, where it appears Doris was among the party who were invited to stay at King's House, the residence of the British High Commissioner. This warranted a mention in *The Straits Times*, in which Doris was noted as arriving on 24 March, and she and Rootes were recorded as leaving the next day without the others.

However, Rootes and Geoffrey had been conducting their own tour of the Orient, the purpose of which was to visit the company's distributors and dealers. As they left Madras to go to Ceylon, Rootes informed his son that two women would be joining them for the remainder of their trip. He made no secret, to Geoffrey, that Doris 'was his mistress and that he was very much in love with her'.[22] Rootes also told his son that Doris had brought along a friend to entertain him when they wished to be alone. In Kuala Lumpur, Geoffrey's new friend fulfilled her promise of entertaining him using her 'nymphomaniacal tendencies', which had 'enriched [his] carnal knowledge'.[23]

It appears that, while Rootes was aware that he was participating in a farce, there was nothing platonic about his travelling with Doris. Nor did Doris shirk from living up to her reputation as an adulteress. As for Castlerosse, jealous as he was, he held a realistic view that his friend had made use of the services of his wife. After all, as the terms suggested, it was merely a business transaction.

On the ship home from Hong Kong, Doris was greeted with the 'staggering news' that Charlie Chaplin and his new wife Paulette Goddard, who had recently starred together in *Modern Times* and had been married on their trip, were also on board. She had met Chaplin several years before, in 1931, at a luncheon given by Sybil Colefax whose guests included Lady Diana Cooper, H.G. Wells, George Lloyd, Sir Oswald Mosley and Harold Nicolson. During this first meeting, they had discussed fame, and Doris agreed it would be nice to be famous but not to be instantly recognisable.[24]

Doris and Rootes socialised with the Hollywood couple who had befriended their fellow passenger, the French writer and filmmaker, Jean Cocteau. They met often, to drink and to dine, and to talk shop and appraise the places they had visited as the ship breezed past Egypt, India, Burma, Malaya and Singapore. A photograph of the party, taken on board the ship, was printed. Doris was seated between Rootes and Paulette Goddard, and they were joined by Geoffrey, Chaplin, Mrs Hubert Parker and Jean Cocteau. Glasses of champagne lined the table, and a crying child was seated on Doris's lap, with Rootes leaning across, close to her, to entertain the child. The photograph, probably harmless, was intimate enough to suggest adultery between Doris and Rootes. It was exactly the sort of evidence Castlerosse longed for.

However, a shrewd businessman who was not only married but had established a respectable business with royalty amongst its clientele, it seems Rootes felt out of his depth. In a letter to Winston Churchill, Doris told him she would have let Rootes out of the arrangement.[25] In the same letter she complained about having to give Castlerosse further and better evidence, which she thought ridiculous, and ironic, when she had obtained sworn statements of his indiscretions with three different women. But, as she pointed out, it would have meant a 'beastly fought' case.[26] She accepted responsibility for the failure of their marriage, and the case continued without being defended on her behalf. Rootes was removed from the petition, and Mad Boy's name was listed as the only co-respondent.

In March 1936, Doris met Margot Flick Hoffman, the wife of the writer Richard Sanford Hoffman, whose fiction stories had been published in magazines. The daughter of a wealthy New York businessman, R. Jay Flick, she had lived a privileged life at the family's Fifth Avenue apartment. A maverick socialite, quite unlike anyone Doris had encountered before, Margot was the

Doris on the voyage home from the Orient. Among her friends are Geoffrey and William Rootes, Paulette Goddard, Charlie Chaplin, Jean Cocteau and Mrs Hubert Parker.

only female member of the Pittsfield, Massachusetts polo team; she flew her own aeroplane; and was the owner of Knollton kennels, where she bred prize-winning pedigree dogs. A closet lesbian and of androgynous appearance, her style was often the subject of fashion critique in newspapers and magazines, with the term 'mannish'[27] used to describe her preference for masculine tailoring and fedora hats.

The year before she had met Doris, in May 1935, Margot was embroiled in a much-publicised court case. Her former butler, William Lawrence Graham, was suing her for slander and damages totalling to $10,000. He accused Margot of having said that 'he wanted to linger in her room when she was in pyjamas', a statement which 'cost him his job and his bride'.[28] Driven to drink due to the accusations, Graham argued that it was 'a class war between the rich and the poor … what could I do against multimillionaires?'[29] He lost the case[30] but threatened to appeal, which he never did. During the court case, Margot's sexuality and relationship with a Boston socialite, Mrs Louise Shaw, came under scrutiny. Graham's lawyer questioned the nature of their friendship, and he was asked about a past incident in which he saw them sitting on a sofa before a fire, showing 'a marked affection' for one another. He also observed them 'exchanging kisses on occasion'. Speaking of the incident, Margot said she had entertained Mrs Shaw and her husband, and had 'abandoned her room which contained only one bed and spent the night with Mrs Shaw in a guest room, where there were two beds'.[31]

As the relationship between Doris and Margot advanced, the American newspapers chronicled the 'friendship' between the viscountess and the society girl. It was reported that they had met in Singapore during Margot's honeymoon, part of which she had spent in the Orient and then in England before sailing back to New York. The information coincides with Castlerosse's evidence that Doris and William Rootes had sailed to the Federated Malay States during that period. Given that Doris's visit to Malay was brief, though significant enough to warrant a mention in the newspaper society columns, it is plausible that she met and befriended Margot in England, as opposed to Singapore.

There is no evidence to suggest that Doris had been romantically involved with a woman before, although with the incident surrounding Mad Boy and the prostitute having been met with disapproval from her contemporaries, as well as male admirers, Doris was eager to form an attachment to someone who could afford her lavish tastes. At the time, Margot fitted the bill, and perhaps sensing that she was attracted to her, Doris exploited the situation for her own gain.

Although he had joked of her being a lesbian during her affair with Beaton, Castlerosse was no longer laughing. He reacted to the news that Doris was romantically involved with a woman by banning her from the Royal Enclosure at Ascot, which he had access to. As she had got into the races at Newmarket, despite Castlerosse forbidding her to go, she thought she 'might have a shot at Ascot'.[32] To gain entry, Doris would have had to obtain a sponsorship form and have it signed by someone who had attended the Royal Enclosure for four years.[33] She wrote to Winston Churchill and asked him for his help in securing her a pass.

However, Churchill was reluctant to involve himself with 'the warring Castlerosses', and he told Beaverbrook about her approaching him. Beaverbrook was furious, and Doris wrote to him to defend her actions. In the letter she apologised profusely, but explained that if Castlerosse had been willing to help her, she would not have written to Churchill.[34]

Castlerosse's reaction was prompted by 'the whole world' knowing about Doris and Margot, regarding which they would 'jeer at him'. Underestimating, or rather ignoring, the efficiency in which gossip was spread through Mayfair, Doris dismissed his qualms. She wrote to Beaverbrook with the view that nobody needed to know, unless Castlerosse chose to tell them.[35]

The Ascot incident confirmed to Doris that she had been somewhat ostracised from British society. A month later, in June, she joined Noel Coward in Venice and they went aboard Sir Dudley Pound's boat, where they were joined by Ivor Novello, Douglas Fairbanks and his new wife Sylvia Ashley. As Sir Dudley and Lady Pound's guests, Doris and Coward were given an open guest-list for a party. Doris confided: 'Noel, I have a dreadful feeling we've asked too many queer people.'

Coward reassured her: 'If we take care of the pansies, the Pounds will take care of themselves.'[36]

Since Coward was one of the few who still appreciated Doris's behaviour and outspoken nature, she became a frequent weekend guest at his home. Arriving in her Rolls-Royce with her maid in tow, she brought with her her own monogrammed crêpe de Chine sheets and pillowcases, which her maid ironed every day. With the rooms occupied by Coward's theatrical friends, the maid and chauffeur had to take lodgings at a nearby hotel and travel to Doris whenever their services were required. Among the guests was the theatrical manager and producer Binkie Beaumont. Observing that he looked younger than his years, Doris, upon meeting the 29-year-old Beaumont, nicknamed him 'Baby-Face Killer'.[37]

As much as Doris's latest affair troubled Castlerosse, he was beginning to think of a future without her in it. Enid Cameron, as he had known her, had been living in Mayfair with her second husband Caviar Cavendish, the man she married after a brief affair with Castlerosse in Paris during the war. After the war, Caviar was given command of the 9th Lancers in Cairo, and Enid and her son followed him to Egypt. As she had done in Paris, she caused a sensation amongst her husband's comrades in Cairo and, as a dare, she reportedly slept with his entire regiment. By day she schooled her husband's polo ponies, and by night she dressed as a man to play with the band in the officers' mess hall. Cairo suited Enid's flamboyant tastes: there were picnics by the Nile, parties in sandstone mansions, and rides by moonlight in the Sahara. She met Lord Carnarvon (another of her lovers) on his famous dig of King Tutankhamun's tomb, and was one of the first to be taken down to the discovery. Disapproving of this hedonistic lifestyle, Caviar moved his wife and stepson to London, where their two children were born.

In 1931, though, Enid found herself once again widowed after Caviar died from a cerebral haemorrhage at their apartment in Paris. In the short years that Enid was without a husband, and in the early years of Castlerosse and Doris's marital woes, he had re-established contact with her. He was attracted to Enid; she was a striking woman who stood 6ft tall, with 'cold, cruel eyes',[38] and whose red hair had prematurely turned white in her twenties. As with Doris, she lacked the ability to remain faithful to her husband, yet unlike Doris she did not flaunt her affairs so openly. She was accustomed to wealth, having had a privileged childhood in Australia, but her second husband was not rich and when he died she found herself short of money with three children[39] to care for. Fond as she was of Castlerosse, he did not have the means to support her and, although she enjoyed his company, she looked to another man to provide for her.

This was in 1932, when Castlerosse first petitioned for divorce and, thinking it would be granted because of Doris's adultery, he hoped to marry Enid. As their paths crossed sporadically throughout the years, with Enid in Paris and Cairo and Castlerosse in London, they contemplated marriage several times but, as she put it: 'His wife or my husband got in the way.'[40] With the divorce dragging on and the case finally dismissed in April 1933, Castlerosse realised there was no hope of marrying Enid, and she accepted another viscount's proposal of marriage. Enid and Marmaduke Furness, the 1st Viscount Furness, were married in 1933 following the divorce from his second wife Thelma, the mistress of the Aly Khan and the Prince of Wales. Although he was the sixth richest man in the world, it was a daring move, even for Enid, as Furness had been accused of murdering his first wife,[41] who had died on his yacht while on a pleasure cruise to Monte Carlo, and was buried at sea. Had he been found guilty he would have been hanged by the neck but, as he was a peer of the realm, it would have been from a silken rope.

Castlerosse continued to think of a life without Doris, and although Enid's marriage to Furness was plagued by misery due to his violent temper and dislike of her children, she loved him for his immense wealth and would never divorce him. With this in mind, Castlerosse decided his future wife should be a wealthy widow, whose millions he could fritter away.

However, in the meantime he remained married to Doris and sought distractions from his own unhappiness. Perhaps to relieve him of the hopelessness of his love life, and to remind Doris and his naysayers that he was of social relevance, he agreed to be painted by Walter Sickert. Exhibited at the Royal Academy, the study showed Castlerosse dressed in a lavender- and chocolate-coloured suit with 'tricksy elfish buttons'. It was hailed as 'the portrait of the year',[42] with the *Evening Post* offering the following appraisal:

Mr [Walter] Sickert has a nebulous full-length portrait of Lord Castlerosse. The nebulosity consists in features that are not visible and an indecision in the lines of the figure. It is a man, as it were, seen through a mist.[43]

The public's response to the painting was enthusiastic, and Castlerosse was delighted by the fuss. He collected notices on Sickert's study with reference to himself and carefully pasted them into a scrapbook, next to the negative response of Sir John Lavery's painting of Doris. Also exhibited at the Royal Academy was Enid, now the Viscountess Furness, who was painted by Sir John Lavery wearing a gown of clinging brown chiffon with a dark fur cape draped across her shoulders, and a string of pearls and several diamond bracelets. It was hailed as 'one of the really outstanding portraits of the year'.[44] Castlerosse and Enid's portraits, hanging side by side at the exhibition, was a prophecy of what was yet to come. Perhaps even Castlerosse, a superstitious man himself, thought so too.

Both Doris and Margot were exasperated by their husbands. After only weeks of marriage and having met Doris during that period, Margot realised she had made a mistake.[45] As her feelings for Doris intensified, and admitting that she was in love with her, Margot separated from Richard Hoffman. Accompanied by Doris, the women travelled to Reno, Nevada – 'the divorce capital of the United States' – where she awaited a divorce from Hoffman. Unlike New York, for example, where divorce would only be granted if one spouse had committed adultery, Reno offered nine grounds for divorce: impotency, adultery, desertion, conviction of a felony, habitual drunkenness, neglect to provide the common necessities of life, insanity, living apart for three years, and extreme cruelty entirely mental in nature. Better still, in Reno no proof of misconduct was necessary, and there was no waiting period provided that one of the spouses had been a resident of Nevada for at least six weeks.

With the exception of a brief stopover in Hollywood, where Doris visited her friend Tilly Losch[46] who was starring in *The Garden of Allah* with Marlene Dietrich, she spent a much-publicised six-week stay on a dude ranch in Nevada. 'Lady Castlerosse,' reported one newspaper, 'is en route to Reno to comfort Margot Flick, who is melting from her groom.'[47] She was photographed in her signature shorts, sitting around a barbecue with Margot and her fellow soon-to-be divorcées.

But Doris was still a married woman with no hope of 'melting' from Castlerosse, and he made plans to visit her on the dude ranch. He had gone to Phoenix, Arizona – 'where fellars go when their chest starts operating like a brass band' – with Beaverbrook, in an attempt to restore their health: the former cited his liver as the trouble, the latter his asthma.

Visiting the neighbouring state, Castlerosse's recollection of the ranch was reminiscent of Clare Boothe's Broadway play, *The Women*:

> The place was full of females, a regular mares' nest. Female horses and female humans. It was hard to tell t'other from which, except that some had four legs, couldn't talk and didn't bite you. It was the two-legged kind you had to watch. They could be divided into two classes, those who bit your ear off with too much gossip, and those who scratched your eyes out with too much spite.[48]

He had come to tell Doris in person that he intended to proceed with the divorce. Some months earlier he had issued a writ to William Rootes which, according to Doris's letters and the divorce file, was withdrawn from the evidence. Now he made plans to issue a writ to Mad Boy, naming him as the sole co-respondent in the case.

Although candid with his readers, Castlerosse was hesitant to write about his pending divorce. Doris herself had no such reservations, and she spoke openly about her husband's intentions. The information was circulated in various American newspapers, with the well-known New York gossip columnist, Cholly Knickerbocker, writing:

> The noble and journalistic Viscount Castlerosse is again divorcing his viscountess. I say 'again' advisedly. For I recall that Valentine Castlerosse instituted divorce proceedings against Lady Castlerosse in London, back in 1932, when the young and rich Sir Alfred Beit was named co-respondent.

It would seem something happened to that divorce action of four years ago – perhaps it was 'shelved' or forgotten.[49]

Doris was laughing at Castlerosse from across the Atlantic, and having been accustomed to wielding the poison pen at his foes, he must have felt powerless and ill at ease. The abdication scandal, which had been brewing for months, had come to a conclusion in December 1936, just as Doris was preparing to leave Reno and sail back to London with Margot. Before they left, Cecil Beaton had photographed the two women for a series of formal portraits but the prints went missing in the post, much to Doris's regret.[50]

Had the British newspapers caught a hint of gossip regarding the divorce it would have been overshadowed by the news that King Edward VIII, formerly the Prince of Wales, had given up the throne for Mrs Simpson. As insiders to the scandal, Castlerosse and Beaverbrook returned from Arizona by request of the King, who had asked Beaverbrook to come home and give his advice. Although irritated by the informal royal summons interrupting his holiday, Castlerosse used it as a distraction from Doris, and he turned his attention to the constitutional crisis. In the Londoner's Log, he informed his readers not only of his friendship with Edward but of his opinions of him as a king, whom he had once praised as 'a modernist' and whose 'reign will become famous as a go-ahead period … King Edward will be the king of youth, and his followers will be those who believe that the world can and must be improved.'[51]

However, in light of the situation, Castlerosse could not resist taking a swipe at Doris. He wrote: 'Mrs Simpson built up her man. She cured him of his inferiority complex by telling him: "My boy, you're not the fool you think you are."'[52] Doris, by contrast, did not shirk from reminding Castlerosse that he was not only a fool but a failure, too.

The subject of other people's love affairs also weighed heavily on Doris's mind. As she had done with Beaverbrook, Doris offered her services to Winston Churchill when his daughter Sarah, an actress, eloped with Vic Oliver, an Austrian comedian seventeen years her senior. For three months, beginning in September 1936, she followed the progress of Sarah's affair with Oliver, and reported the news to Churchill.

Writing from Capri, in September, Doris told Churchill that she 'can catch' Sarah, and she wondered if she ought to 'go after her'. Aware of the mounting tension between Sarah and her family, Doris suggested that she could handle the situation better than Randolph[53] (who had intervened), and express their ill-feelings to Vic Oliver accordingly. Churchill wrote to Doris to thank her for her kind offer, but assured her that everything was being taken care of.[54]

For an ambitious woman like Doris it must have seemed as though her connections to rich and powerful men were floundering. But she was not prepared to give up so easily and, like the predator that she was, she waited for an opening before swooping in. Ironically, this opportunity would also involve Castlerosse.

The coronation of King George VI finally gave Doris a purpose at the centre of London society. Reunited with Castlerosse, if only for the sake of appearances, she donned her viscountess coronet to attend the coronation at Westminster Abbey on 12 May 1937. In preparation for the event, she rented the Duchess of Westminster's house at 8 Little College Street, Westminster, for the season, though Castlerosse stayed elsewhere. *The Times* took inventory of her guests which included: the Hon. Mrs Edwin Montagu, the Earl of Warwick, Prince Charles D'Arenberg, Margot Hoffman and her father, Mr Jay Flick. Perhaps it was Margot who was paying the rent, and although not directly involved as Doris was with the coronation, she was at her side for the various parties and balls given that summer. In hindsight, although she was not aware of it at the time, it was to become Doris's last hurrah on the London social scene.

Feigning uninterest in Doris, Castlerosse was intrigued by her social life, and he followed her various engagements which were mentioned in the newspapers. In what had become a habit of his, he cut and pasted the references of Doris into his scrapbook. Before the end of the summer, Sir John Lavery held an exhibition of his paintings at Wimborne House, and included his portrait of her. Waiting until after the opening day to attend the exhibition, Castlerosse could not resist Doris, even in still life.

Although obsessed by her and still in love with her, though from afar, he continued with the divorce. On 10 August 1937, Castlerosse issued the pending writ to Mad Boy, naming him as co-respondent in the divorce petition, after which he publicly announced his intention to divorce Doris.

As Doris had told Winston Churchill in an earlier letter, she had lost interest in the divorce and she hoped Castlerosse could produce sufficient evidence before the judge. The subject of evidence was further simplified for Castlerosse when Mad Boy failed to appear in person or to be represented by a solicitor at the Divorce Registry of the High Court of Justice. Thus, the charges of adultery against Mad Boy went undefended and, as the writ advised him: 'the Court will proceed to hear the said charges proved and pronounce Judgement your absence notwithstanding.'[55]

Finally, on 17 December 1937, Doris and Castlerosse were granted a decree *nisi* due to her adultery with Mad Boy. They were advised that it would take six months for their decree *nisi* to become absolute,[56] thus they were still legally married. The following day, *The Times* reported:

> Browne (Viscount Castlerosse) and Browne (Viscountess Castlerosse) and Percy. Before Mr Justice Bucknill. In this undefended suit, Lord Castlerosse, of Rainbozend, Tadworth, sought the dissolution of his marriage with Lady Castlerosse, née Delavigne, on the ground of her adultery at an hotel in Paris and on the liner *Straithaird* in 1936. According to the case for Lord Castlerosse, there was a good deal of unpleasantness during their married life owing to his wife's extravagance. A deed of separation was entered into in March 1933. Mr Justice Bucknill granted the petitioner a decree *nisi*, with costs against the co-respondent.

Doris's response to the press was characteristically carefree; she was in Venice when the news broke and she swung her famous legs over the balustrade of a mansion on the Grand Canal as she posed for photographers. Now a free woman, she was making plans for her future and how to spend Margot's money.

Castlerosse, by comparison, did not share her optimism. Months before, during the period of the legal separation from Doris and her moving into Claridge's and his moving out, he had bought a house. It was a spacious white bungalow called Frazer's Heath, on the brow of North Downs in Surrey not far from Box Hill. Upon moving in, he changed its name to the romantic-sounding Rainbozend, and left strict orders with his secretary, Miss Cowell, as to how it should be decorated. The renovation, having taken place while he was in America with Beaverbrook, almost bankrupted him: the rooms were painted white with coloured ceilings, and he ordered additional bathrooms to be installed with stars painted on the walls of the lavatories. He gave several parties to 'warm' the house and one big party to celebrate his decree *nisi*, which would not become absolute until June 1938.

To pay for the food and drinks which entertained 'the waifs and strays of Claridge's', Castlerosse turned once again to moneylenders, and he ordered Miss Cowell to go to Oxford to collect money from the 'the boys' – his nickname for them. Although he had attempted to hide this from Beaverbrook, his deception did not go unnoticed. It evoked a similar ill-feeling in Beaverbrook, which he had felt when Castlerosse had married Doris, and owing to his fury he sent him a reproachful letter. He blamed his secretary[57] for divulging the secret to Beaverbrook, but she pleaded her innocence. Months later, while recalling the 'waifs and strays' at his party, he discovered the identity of the traitor. It was, in fact, Doris who had used her connections to inform on him from afar.

But months had passed since Beaverbrook's letter, and Castlerosse was ready to forgive her anything. Doris, however, was not prepared to jeopardise the finalising of their divorce and she declined his offer of a reconciliation. She was too busy sipping champagne and spending Margot's millions to give her husband a second thought.

Tired of London society, she planned to become the toast of Venice and her latest scheme was to build a palace on the Grand Canal. And Margot, besotted with Doris, agreed to fund her wish. 'I much prefer the life I am leading,' she said to a lonely Castlerosse. 'Takes half the effort and earns twice the money.'[58]

PLAYING TO THE GALLERY

'I'll go through life either first class or third, but never in second.'

Noel Coward

———————•◆•———————

It was as though Doris was purposely trying to shock London society, to play up to the role of social pariah which her peers had proclaimed her to be. Her latest high jinks were committed, not because of her careless attitude, which in part was true, but due to her loyalty to Diana Guinness. She had been present at Diana's Eaton Square townhouse when tensions ran high due to Unity Mitford, Diana's younger sister, flaunting the fascist badge that Sir Oswald Mosley had given her. A self-proclaimed National Socialist and fixated with 'the Leader', as Mosley's comrades called him, Unity was known to give impromptu pro-fascist speeches in Hyde Park, offer the Nazi salute to passers-by, and to storm Communist meetings at Speakers' Corner. Caught up in a scuffle and beaten by anti-fascists because of her badge, she returned to Eaton Square and refused luncheon. Doris was having tea with Diana and Nancy Mitford when Unity arrived and, sensing they wished to discuss their sister's perilous behaviour, she left them alone.

In the evenings, Doris and Diana would go along to Mosley's British Union of Fascists (BUF) meetings, where they sat at the front amongst his 'Blackshirts' – as his uniformed men were nicknamed. On the opposite side, Mosley's sisters-in-law, Lady Irene Curzon and Lady Alexandra 'Baba' Metcalfe (the latter a friend of Castlerosse's), would stare in their general direction, disapproving of Diana's presence. All three women had had an affair with him at some point, with the passion between Baba and Mosley ongoing, which Diana was aware of.[1]

As for Doris, there is no evidence to suggest she had slept with Mosley, though he was renowned for having affairs with all of his wife's friends. However, an interesting paradox relating to Doris's character was her loyalty towards her few female friends, which in turn inspired affection. This might explain Diana's enthusiasm for having Doris by her side, as opposed to her friend Georgia Sitwell (one of her few remaining friends after she left Bryan), who had been seeing Mosley in the early days of his affair with Diana. It was also interesting that, although acquainted with Sir Oswald Mosley, it was with his late wife Cimmie whom Doris shared a close friendship. It was an ironic stance, given her fondness for Diana – the woman responsible for Cimmie's misery before her untimely death in 1933.

This bold move of allying herself with Diana and showing what appeared to be public support for fascism brought Doris much criticism from those who viewed Mosley and his BUF as a band of thugs. Prior to her unintentional endorsement of far right politics, she had been the target of the *Daily Worker*, a communist publication. Their attack on her extravagance was printed in 1932, a period during which they criticised socialites and those who had access to wealth. They wrote:

A comrade sends us this cutting from Modern Weekly:

Of all the luxury-loving young women in London today I suppose Lady Castlerosse is easily the first and foremost. I know nobody who can spend so much money with such an easy grace, nor who displays such perfect taste in the matter of clothes and home decoration.

Lady Castlerosse's stockings, which are always much finer than anybody else's, are all marked in the weave with her name, and she never wears one pair more than once. Her shoes, the slimmest of all perfect things, are usually discarded after the second or third time of wearing, and when she travels or stays with friends she takes her own crepe de Chine sheets and pillowcases with her all embroidered with the monogram and coronet![2]

The retaliation of Doris's actions came in 1937 when Mosley's BUF (now renamed the British Union of Fascists and National Socialists), which had previously risen in glory, had begun to decline following the riots between the Blackshirts and communists at the Olympia in 1934, and his ill-fated march down Cable Street in 1936 in which anti-fascist organisers protested against it. Violence had become the norm at his meetings, an element which Mosley thrived on 'like a silly schoolboy only proud of some silly scuffles and rows'. Or, as Lady Irene Curzon said: 'All the swagger and vanity to Mrs Bryan Guinness and Doris Castlerosse.'[3]

Unlike Diana, Doris was far from political and she viewed attending Mosley's rallies merely as a social outing. But as the murmurs of war with Nazi Germany became a reality, Doris's actions as a casual spectator were seen as provocative and, by some, treacherous. As the wife of a peer, her behaviour was no longer amusing.

As was the norm during their long absences from one another, Doris weighed heavily on Castlerosse's mind. He was inspired to change his lifestyle of heavy drinking and excessive eating, and to lose weight for the sake of his health. This was due in part to the teasing he endured from his contemporaries and the press. One incident, in particular, served to infuriate him. Beaverbrook's little granddaughter, Lady Jeanne Campbell, would visit Rainbozend, and while Castlerosse worked on the Londoner's Log in his sun-room, the child would dance and shout: 'Ooh, look at the fat man!'[4] Privy to the unflattering comments made about Castlerosse's weight, Doris became an unlikely ally and she defended his physique. She remarked to a friend: 'I don't think it's fair of you to call Valentine a pig. I do admit he guzzles a lot. But who am I to complain of excess?'[5]

Having attempted a diet which consisted entirely of herrings, and feeling nauseated as a result, Castlerosse took Beaverbrook's advice and became tee-total. He lost one stone and 'felt all right – but low. *I could do with a drink.*'[6] But as his health improved his work deteriorated, and the editor of the *Sunday Express*, John Gordon, was becoming exasperated by the quality of the Londoner's Log. Gone were the witty anecdotes and social observations, and in their place were quotations from books and magazines. One magazine in particular, *Lilliput*, pursued legal action when Castlerosse extracted a story without permission. Refusing to take the case seriously and accept he had committed plagiarism, he challenged the editor of *Lilliput* to a duel[7] and was consequently turned down.

Doris continued to ignore Castlerosse, and his efforts to reform his health and character had gone to waste. He was increasingly lonely for female attention, though careful not to jeopardise his divorce during the interval between the decree *nisi* and decree absolute. However, female friends would often visit Rainbozend for dinner or drinks. On one such occasion, a friend kissed him goodbye on the doorstep and was astonished when Castlerosse broke away and dived into the shrubbery. 'Sorry my dear,' he said as he returned. 'Thought I saw one of those chaps in bowler hats skulking around. Bloody menaces. Would have thrashed him within an inch of his life.'[8]

It was an unnecessary gesture, for as much as Doris had once enjoyed manipulating and torturing Castlerosse, she had moved on with her life. There were no spies set upon him, as he had done to her during his pursuit of evidence, and she, too, welcomed the divorce.

Given his disapproval of Doris as a suitable wife for Castlerosse, Beaverbrook seemed to enjoy spreading the rumour that she had approached him and implored him not to let Castlerosse remarry. Certainly, she had visited Cherkley Court during that period, entering with a group of 'smarties' and resembling 'a picture in *Vogue*', dressed in a white satin dress over which she wore a coat made from wolf fur. Guests observed that she 'whispered in a corner'[9] with Beaverbrook, and whether or not she asked this of Beaverbrook or meant what she said is debatable. Could she have been making mischief for Castlerosse before they were to finally part?

In the spring of 1938, Doris went to Venice with Margot Hoffman where they searched for a palazzo to fulfil Doris's dream of owning a palace on the Grand Canal. In the meantime, while she shopped for clothes and a suitable Venetian property, the two women set up home in the Grand Hotel, its bill paid for by Margot. Doris was, once again, a kept woman, though in those days she was merely described by the press as Margot's 'protégée' and no hint of romance was ever touched upon. Her friends, however, knew the truth, and many thought it bad form for her to exploit Margot. And with the exception of Margot, nobody was fooled by Doris's involvement with her.

With Margot's money and connections, Doris had begun to forge a new life for herself away from London society, and she looked to America to re-establish herself as a socialite. She was still known as Lady Castlerosse, and as far as American newspapers and waspish, transatlantic socialites were concerned, she was just another high-born English woman. There were mentions of her background, but not of her origins in Beckenham. And the American press wrote of her past romance with Laddie Sanford, who had since married Mary Duncan, a former actress who was known as 'Queen Mary', a title derived from her social standing. Her dominion was North Ocean Boulevard, a hub of millionaires' mansions along the 16-mile radius of Palm Beach, Florida.

Much was made of Doris and Laddie's association with one another and the press waxed lyrical about his love for her and wrote that many believed she would have become Mrs Laddie Sanford, had he not met Mary. Nothing could have been further from the truth but Doris appeared to revel in this new image, a world away from her reputation in London. She was lamented as a friend of Winston Churchill, an intimate of the Duke of Windsor (formerly King Edward VIII), and a witty and charming Mayfair hostess.

Although she usually went to Maxine Elliott's villa in Golfe-Juan, Doris was reluctant to visit due to Castlerosse being there.[10] It was not a risk she was willing to take, as their divorce had not yet been finalised. Her previous visits to the Château de l'Horizon had been unpleasant. Over luncheon, one day, she complained bitterly that her newest evening dress had been covered with smuts that had drifted through her bedroom window. On another occasion, Maxine's temperamental monkey bit Doris on the ankle, a painful nip that was provoked because the monkey's tray of strawberries[11] rested on the floor, too close to her legs. She was further put out when Maxine claimed there was not a drop of iodine in the house to clean the wound.

Instead, Doris went with Margot to Palm Beach, Florida, where the Hoffmans owned a house on Via Del Lago in the area of South Ocean Boulevard, neighbouring Laddie and Mary Sanford's mansion, Los Lucas. Given her current status as an almost divorcée, Doris fitted in with this social set described as 'a rudderless ship, an untethered balloon'. Lawsuits were the topic of conversation, and love affairs and divorces were rife, yet glamorous. Detectives were a common sight, set on philandering spouses,[12] as they were on Doris in London, to speed divorce proceedings along. Many went to Reno for a 'quickie divorce', but others battled through the long and arduous process, especially if money and property were involved. Although Doris was undertaking a similar path, her situation differed from the American women she met in Palm Beach, for Castlerosse had no money to give her. She envied their lives, many of which were the product of marrying into families who had made their money during the Gilded Age. In turn, they coveted her title.

After a fortnight in Palm Beach, Doris and Margot headed west to Palm Springs, a desert city in southern California. Popular with Hollywood stars, it was a resort constructed from mansions and luxurious hotels, many of which were owned by retired silent film stars; there were tennis clubs, golf clubs, and secluded ranches marketed towards health tourists who went to Palm Springs for the healing properties of its dry heat. Doris and Margot stayed at El Mirado, where it was noted by the local press that Doris and her fellow English guests inspired the hotel to serve tea at four o'clock.

Using her influence as a viscountess, Doris obtained an invitation to the world premiere of *Camille*, starring Greta Garbo and Robert Taylor, at the gala opening of the Plaza Theatre in Palm Springs. She mingled in the foyer of the theatre with Barbara Stanwyck, Tyrone Power, Amelia Earhart, Jeanette MacDonald and Shirley Temple. Her presence there, alongside the Earl of Warwick and Viscountess Tredegar, warranted a mention by the Hollywood gossip columnist Louella Parsons. This association with the Hollywood elite was not a chance encounter, for Doris was consciously forming a new circle away from the aristocratic set in London. Her new show-business friends, she hoped, would become useful in the future.

However, while in Palm Springs she was content to associate with figures from the past. One such acquaintance was Sir John Lavery, who was staying as the guest of the tubercular artist Gordon Coutts and his wife Gertrude at their home, Dar Marroc. Modelled on the castles Coutts had seen in Tangier, Dar Marroc was at the centre of Palm Springs culture, an oasis of bohemianism amid the desert landscape. It was here that Doris was painted for the second time by Lavery.

Unlike Lavery's previous effort, in which he portrayed her in a sombre Victorian riding habit, this later attempt was to be a contemporary study. Doris posed on a diving board dressed in white shorts, with her famous legs dangling over the edge. She looked less like a viscountess and instead resembled an all American girl. Her bare feet hovered over the water of the swimming pool and, adding to Lavery's exotic approach, there were citrus trees in the background. Another pair of female legs were featured off to the edge of the frame, but the owner's torso and head were missing from the painting.[13] Doris, with her golden head tilted, looks in their general direction. Perhaps the woman was Margot.

She was also photographed in a similar setting with Lavery. A suntanned Doris, dressed in a sunsuit, was perched on a diving board with her legs crossed at the ankle. Lavery, aged 81 at the time, hovered behind her, a picture of formality in his three-piece tweed suit and hat, holding his paintbrushes. He looked in the direction of the camera, uncertain about being photographed, while she glanced over her shoulder, sporting a bemused grin. It was a prophetic expression towards all she had left behind, given her current arrangement consisting of Margot's millions, year-round sunshine, palm trees and seafront mansions. Castlerosse, on the other hand, was spending an English winter semi-estranged from Beaverbrook, succumbing to debt, and facing the reality that he had to sell Rainbozend.

The painting, titled 'Viscountess Castlerosse in Palm Springs',[14] was exhibited at Wimborne House in July 1938. Incidentally, July was also the month in which Doris and Castlerosse's divorce became final. 'I do not know whether you noticed it or not, but last week my divorce was made absolute,' wrote Castlerosse in the Londoner's Log. It was a solemn announcement, appealing to those female readers who had once thought him a catch. In that pithy sentence he had announced he was free, but the once jolly, corpulent gossip columnist had lost his appeal.

Doris, less of a romantic than Castlerosse, took a pragmatic approach. 'We were married for ten years. We lived together for one,' she said. She also bore the responsibility of paying Castlerosse's legal fees, as it was stated in the decree absolute that costs were to be covered by the co-respondent. But, Doris could not grumble: she was enjoying her freedom, and she continued to use the courtesy title of Viscountess Castlerosse.

If Doris had any regrets about her failed marriage she did not say, and her behaviour belied any remorse she might have felt. She was living the sort of life she thought she deserved, and one that Castlerosse could not give her. Her days were spent sailing along the Grand Canal in Venice, with gondoliers dressed in liveries. But as privileged as she was, there was one element she missed from her life, and that was men. Her male friends, many of whom were past lovers, had kept

Such eccentricities were common for Doris. Here she is at Deauville, coming out of the sea wearing her shoes and a hairnet over her face.

their distance from Doris during the divorce proceedings. This was due to Castlerosse's willingness to pin evidence of adultery on to those men she associated with and her acceptance of their being used as pawns in a bid to speed up the divorce. Margot did not help matters, as her possessiveness towards Doris was well known. And not in love with Margot, Doris treated it as a joke.

One such man who kept his distance was Winston Churchill. The Ascot incident had left him cold, and with his criticism of Neville Chamberlain's appeasement of Hitler a prominent subject in modern politics, perhaps Churchill was reluctant to attract further negative press from his association with Doris. It was Doris who made the first move and initiated contact. In her letter she expressed her wish to see him, and she wrote details of her travel itinerary. At the end of the letter she told him that she was not dangerous any more, now the divorce had been granted.[15] Churchill must have agreed with her sentiment, for the two revived their correspondence. But his letters were to remain cordial while Doris was as candid as before, and in the near future she would turn to him for advice.

After a year of searching for the perfect Venetian property, Margot bought Doris the Palazzo Venier dei Leoni,[16] located on the Dorsoduro bank of the Grand Canal just below the Accademia Bridge. An eighteenth-century waterside palace designed by the Venetian architect Lorenzo Boschetti for the dynastic Venier family, its name was derived from the eighteen lion heads decorating the base of the façade, or the rumour that a pet lion had once been kept in a cage in the garden.

The palazzo, designed to be the grandest palace on the canal, had remained unfinished since its construction in 1759, and never progressed further than the first storey.[17] Its recent custodian, Marchesa Luisa Casati, an Italian noblewoman, was given the palazzo in 1910 by one of her lovers, Gabriele d'Annuzio. With her pale face, heavily made-up eyes and dyed orange hair, the Marchesa was renowned for her eccentric behaviour. At her dining table sat wax mannequins; the drawing room was filled with monkeys; snakes slithered in the hall and were worn (alive, though drugged) as necklaces; albino blackbirds hovered overhead; and she walked a tranquillised leopard on a lead – the same pet leopard which had previously attacked several guests at a party. Although slightly reclusive, she could be tempted to visit those she liked best, and she travelled everywhere with her half-naked African servant who held a feathered parasol over his mistress's head. Doris had met the Marchesa on occasion at Faringdon, where Gerald Berners had entertained her as a guest, alongside Diana Guinness, and Gladys, the Duchess of Marlborough.[18]

Perhaps Doris should have viewed the Marchesa as a cautionary tale. Her outrageous parties, hosted at the palazzo, led to her downfall. The final party turned out to be one that included nude men gilded in gold leaf, and legend has it that one man was asphyxiated by the toxic paint. But a hint of scandal never deterred Doris, and her plans for the Palazzo Venier dei Leoni were ambitious.

When Doris acquired the palazzo it was practically a ruin due to the marchesa squandering her entire fortune (by 1930 she had accumulated a personal debt of $25 million), and she invested a large sum of Margot's money into renovating it. She fixed the roof, installed six new bathrooms in black, pink and green marble, replaced the floors with mosaic tiles inlaid with mother of pearl, and covered the walls with Liberty *stucchi*. A terrace was created on the flat roof for Doris to sunbathe on, and from there she could watch the traffic on the Grand Canal. There were gondolas placed on either side of the house, with liveried gondoliers, two to a gondola, who were employed as her private staff.

The exclusivity of Venetian society did not pose a problem for Doris and, with Margot's connections, she befriended rich Americans who had settled in Venice, at the American bar, Harry's. She threw parties at the palazzo; its dilapidated state did not deter its hostess or her guests, as old friends from London – those accustomed to her shocking ways – and new friends from Venice, spilled from the gondolas. The rebirth of Doris as a Venetian society hostess was an ambitious one, for the palazzo was far from comfortable for daily living, and the romantic vision of dancing amongst its ruined pillars and columns was not to last. Still, it was memorable enough for Cole Porter to reference it in his song, *Where is the Life that Late I Led,*[19] with the lyrics: 'Where is Venetia who loved to chat so? Could still she be drinking in her stinking pink palazzo?'

Tension between Britain and Italy had become increasingly fraught due to Italy's ongoing conflict with Abyssinia, as the Empire of Ethiopia was then commonly known in Europe. This, in part, was to undermine the credibility of the League of Nations and to encourage Fascist Italy to ally itself with Nazi Germany. Consequently it brought an end to peace in Europe, and by 1937 it was evident there were two defining ideologies on the continent. Britain, who had formerly supported Ethiopia and invited the old Emperor of Abyssinia to the coronation in 1937,[20] cleared its warships from the Mediterranean and, along with its ally France, did not impose sanctions on Italy. With Hitler's invasion of the Rhineland in March 1936, and France's desperate attempts to ally itself with Italy against Germany, it was clear that the threat of war was imminent.

Doris, in Venice, was all too aware of the Abyssinian Crisis. Although not troubled by its threat towards her homeland or what war would mean for her as an individual, she was perplexed by the potential disturbance it might spell for the palazzo. She wrote to Winston Churchill to confide her fears, and to ask his advice. She was worried she would lose the house, and in the same letter she asked Churchill if there would be a war with the Italians. It was the last thing she wanted, she said, and, as she thought, the last thing all of her friends wanted.[21]

With the latest political developments causing 'a lot of trouble with the Italians',[22] Doris left Venice as the renovation of the palazzo continued and went to Monte Carlo, and then on to Paris where she and Margot stayed at the Ritz Hotel. She implored Churchill to write to her at the Ritz Hotel, Paris,[23] or at the Berkeley in London, where she would be staying the following month. In her absence, she lent the palazzo to Douglas Fairbanks and his wife, Sylvia Ashley.

The stay in London was to be brief, and with the palazzo in the Fairbanks' custody, Doris sailed to America. She was already plotting her next venture.

ĐORIS ĐREAMS OF STARDOM

'I could have had a part in *Gone with the Wind* … but I could not be there at the time.'[1]

– Doris Delevingne

In 1937, Doris met the Hollywood film director George Cukor on an ocean liner going to New York. This was according to Doris herself, who was not above embellishing such connections. She also maintained that she stayed at Pickfair, the 18-acre Beverly Hills estate of Douglas Fairbanks and Mary Pickford, during a Hollywood visit that same year. She was an ironic guest given that Fairbanks, who had divorced Pickford in 1936, was staying at the Palazzo Venier dei Leoni with his new wife, Sylvia Ashley. Mary Pickford, Doris told the press, was 'a great friend' – she also happened to be the best friend of Mrs Laddie Sanford.

On her outward journey, Doris told a London correspondent that she intended to become a film actress. George Cukor had, according to Doris, offered her a part in a film he was to direct and it was possible that she might make her debut in a Greta Garbo picture.[2] 'I could have had a part in *Gone with the Wind*, now being made in Hollywood, but I could not be there at the time,' she said. 'As yet I have agreed to act in only one film because I want to return to Europe in December to furnish a villa I am building in Venice. I intend to spend three or four months there every year. If I find, however, that I like making pictures I may return to Hollywood later on and appear in several.'[3] Her comments did not conjure an image of a determined thespian, but of an individual who believed she could flit in and out of films, and on and off the screen, as she saw fit.

It appears such claims were invented by Doris, who had not stayed at Pickfair but at the Beverly Hills Hotel.[4] Likewise, her comments to the press about appearing in *Gone with the Wind* are conflicting. A best-seller when published in 1936 and whose film rights were purchased that same year by David O. Selznick, *Gone with the Wind* did not begin production until 1938,[5] with principal photography beginning in January 1939. Although George Cukor had been involved in the picture's pre-production for two years, and was hired as director before being replaced by Victor Fleming, it seemed far-fetched that he would have offered Doris a part. Famous actresses who had been considered for and were subsequently refused roles included Bette Davis, Katharine Hepburn and Norma Shearer. Tallulah Bankhead, an old friend of Doris's from the 1920s, was said to have been promised the part of Scarlett O'Hara only to be offered the smaller role of Belle Watling, a former prostitute and owner of a brothel. With the leading parts filled by well-known actresses, it is difficult to know which part Doris might have been offered, if her statement was true. Cukor was renowned for his sense of humour and association with actresses and socialites, and with this in mind could he have envisioned Doris as Belle Watling, a self-made woman with (dyed) golden hair,[6] who had slept her way to the top?

Interestingly, around this time Doris had rekindled her friendship with Paulette Goddard, who was the strongest contender for the part of Scarlett in *Gone with the Wind*. Although Doris was a decade older than Paulette, the two women shared a similar background. Like Doris, Paulette, as a young woman, was determined to escape her family and make her own way in the world. At the age of 17 she married Edgar James, the much older president of the Southern Lumber Company, and after two years of marriage the couple divorced with Paulette receiving a divorce settlement of $375,000. With her beauty and money, Paulette thrived where Doris had failed. But, aside from Paulette maintaining the momentum of her success, Doris was not jealous and she admired her young friend's gumption.

It appears Doris and Paulette had become reacquainted in Hawaii in December 1937, where Doris was spending Christmas with Margot at the Royal Hawaiian Hotel in Honolulu, and they were photographed at a festive party wearing traditional leis. Doris and Margot had come from a visit to the Federated Malay States, where they stayed with Sir Shenton Thomas,[7] the former Governor of Nyasaland, at his country residence in Kuala Lumpur.

That same year, Doris's brother Dudley had married Angela Greenwood, the beautiful daughter of the 1st Viscount Greenwood, who, at the age of 7, had narrowly avoided being kidnapped by the IRA.[8] Dudley and Angela honeymooned in Hollywood and had met Paulette Goddard and Charlie Chaplin, and the couple became friends with Clark Gable. According to Angela herself, she was also offered a part in *Gone with the Wind* by David O. Selznick, but had to decline as she was pregnant when filming commenced. So it would appear that both Doris and her sister-in-law narrowly missed being part of Hollywood history.

During the Hawaiian trip Doris encountered Peter Watson, who had sailed alone from Hong Kong. The former foes, who had been used by Cecil Beaton in a bid to spark jealousy in a love-triangle of his invention, restored their friendship in Hawaii. Nursing a broken heart and feeling lonely, perhaps Watson had turned to Doris because she was the only familiar face at the time. Likewise, for Doris, the two-week trip was a welcomed departure from Venice and the ongoing, and costly, renovation of the Palazzo Veneir de Leoni, the political tension caused by the Abyssinian Crisis, and the frosty reception she had received from her acquaintances in London. For both Doris and Watson, Hawaii was the perfect blend of American hospitality, agreeable weather and good-looking young men. There were 'flowers everywhere and everyone gay and singing with ukuleles'.[9]

Inviting Watson to join her party made up of Margot and the film crowd, they dined with Hollywood producer Samuel Goldwyn and the Broadway lyricist and MGM publicist, Howard Dietz. Watson knew Dietz's wife, Tanis, and Doris introduced him to the two men. They discussed films, which depressed him, and he wrote in his diary: 'I have realised the hopelessness of expecting a really intelligent film coming out of Hollywood.'[10]

In the second week of January 1938, Doris, Margot and Peter Watson sailed together from Hawaii to Los Angeles. Doris took an adobe villa on Roxbury Drive in Beverly Hills, the rent costing $1,000[11] for the month she lived there. Watson stayed with her for a brief period, but grew tired of the superficial trappings of Hollywood and, more importantly, of Doris's infuriating self-belief that she, at the age of almost 40, would find fame as a film star.

Doris's dream of becoming a screen actress was not a new one. As early as 1933 she 'fancied herself as a film star' and she would go to Elstree Studios for screen tests. 'My God, Cecil, isn't she unnerving,' Peter Watson had remarked to Cecil Beaton at the time. 'I go nearly mad at her sometimes.'[12] According to Watson, the screen tests were 'flops', but undeterred she would approach the studio and ask to have a job dressing the cast. Both of her ambitions to act and to serve in the costume department – she retained an interest in clothing and dressing actresses since her days in the rag trade – amounted to nothing.

In those days, Doris had her gaze fixed on British pictures when, regardless of Watson's objections, aristocratic women and various high-born beauties were appearing on the stage and screen. Diana Guinness had been asked by C.B. Cochran to appear in the stage production of *The Winter's Tale* – it was his vision to cast a new face in his productions, known by reputation and not talent – and Pamela Stanley (Diana's distant cousin), daughter of the 5th Baron Stanley of Alderley, made her stage debut in 1932. Although Diana had considered the idea and then declined, Doris was further motivated by her friend's appeal to casting directors and producers. And she, too, wanted to be a part of it. There was to be no success for Doris in the British film industry, but as time progressed she began to consider Hollywood, even if it was not her first choice.

The idea of going to Hollywood was inspired by her old friend and former love interest, Charles Greville, the 7th Earl of Warwick. In 1936, he became the first British aristocrat to be offered a contract by MGM, and was nicknamed the Duke of Hollywood by the American press. Using the stage name Michael Brooke, his once promising career was not to last. Referring to his £10,000 per year salary as 'pocket money', and stating that his accepting a contract was motivated by sex, he was dropped by MGM and a long court battle ensued. But, as a celebrity aristocrat in Hollywood, he socialised within the inner circle of Hollywood's elite and had an affair with Paulette Goddard. Predicting the Earl of Warwick was a useful connection to have, Doris sought to attach herself to him as she attempted to negotiate the studio system. However, with his bad behaviour counting against him in an era when American cinema was governed by The Motion Picture Production Code, she was, from a studio executive's point of view, more trouble than an aristocratic name on the screen credits was worth.

Castlerosse, too, had dabbled in show business on and off since 1932, around the same time Doris fostered her dream of becoming a film star. In 1932 he wrote the screenplay *Diamond Cut Diamond* (also titled *Blame the Woman*), a

Doris and Paulette Goddard at a Christmas party in Honolulu, Hawaii.

quota quickie[13] starring Adolphe Menjou and Benita Hume. The plot had been suggested by Doris,[14] based on conmen, the art of pickpocketing and jewel thieves. It was a period that saw him becoming significantly productive, with his anecdotal memoir, *Valentine's Days*,[15] being published to commercial and critical acclaim in 1934.[16] His writing credentials were impressive, though his finances and spiritual integrity remained poor.

With success on his mind, Castlerosse's thoughts turned to the subject of publicity and what it meant for an individual. 'Good publicity is valuable,' he wrote. 'Some people recognise this and become rich ... This fact is surely obvious and in keeping with human nature, the simple reason being that we are all vain in varying degrees.'[17]

While Doris was acting on her ex-husband's earlier musings by attending film premieres, socialising with the Hollywood crowd at the El Morocco,[18] and dreaming of a studio contract, Castlerosse was lying low. In 1938 he complained of ill-health – his usual cry of feeling lethargic – and this was attributed to his over-indulgent lifestyle and the recent stress of selling Rainbozend to pay off his creditors. It was not a surprise to Beaverbrook or those closest to him when Castlerosse suffered a mild heart attack, as his doctor had predicted he would. Having already lost a son, it caused Lady Kenmare considerable worry – even if it was expressed through her usual icy reserve. The doctor advised Castlerosse to go to a European spa, preferably Dr Dengler's sanatorium in Baden Baden, where he could 'take a cure'. But he was reluctant to follow his doctor's advice, thinking he would run into tempting friends,[19] most notably Doris, who frequented the Bavarian retreat.

Castlerosse opted to go to Karlsbad, in Czechoslovakia. His decision to stay away from the spas on the continent might have been made with a level head, but his choice of location was an unfortunate one. It was the summer of 1938 and Karlsbad, the capital of the Sudetenland, was under threat from Hitler. The English, especially his own class, thought little of the threat and did not warn him otherwise. And, unlike Doris who thought war plausible, Castlerosse overlooked the issue entirely, though he did sympathise with the Jews of Germany, and he commented:

> I do not think the ordinary German understands the ordinary Briton's attitude towards the persecution of the Jews which is being carried out in Germany. I sometimes wonder whether the heart of England has not changed. It whelms my heart with a flood of shame to think that this little minority of men and women, with hearts, souls and feelings just like you and me, are being trodden down like the muck of the road.[20]

But, as with Doris when she was in Italy, as soon as Castlerosse arrived in Karlsbad he sensed the political tension. 'I am having the worst of both worlds here,'[21] he said, and he considered fleeing to the safety of the Balkans. Instead he learned that Neville Chamberlain was going to Munich to see Hitler, and he abandoned Karlsbad for the White Cliffs of Dover.

In late 1938, Doris and Margot returned to the Palazzo Venier dei Leoni. Hostility was in the air, more so than when Doris had departed for America. Mussolini's *Manifesto della razza*, or Manifesto of Race, a series of racial laws inspired by Hitler's Nuremberg Laws in which Jews were stripped of their Italian citizenship, had been drawn up in July 1938 and implemented in October of that same year. Having previously expressed her concerns about a war to Winston Churchill, she was beginning to take the threats seriously. As Fascist Italy allied itself with Nazi Germany, and with the significance of Hitler's state visit to Italy concluding in Venice, her dream of reigning over the palazzo was beginning to fade. She was now an enemy in the country where she had hoped to make her home. Her friends remained blasé: Elsa Schiaparelli claimed she knew there would be no war 'just by instinct', and Diana Vreeland said it was all chemical and that Hitler only became a madman during a full moon.[22]

In the wake of a war, and consumed by feelings of displacement and with her thoughts turning to the future – she had no immediate plans to return to England – she surrounded herself with familiarity. She turned to her brother, Dudley, whose new wife Angela's social connections rivalled her own (she was a close friend of Prince Philip of Greece and Denmark, later the Duke of Edinburgh), and as they travelled on an extended honeymoon, she invited them to stay with her in Venice. Arriving to find the palazzo[23] empty, they went to bed only to be awoken at 4 a.m. by a Venetian orchestra playing at their bedside. Doris arranged it all, thinking they 'might appreciate the welcome', and had brought the orchestra from a party she had attended.

But the frivolous atmosphere was not to last. There was political tension amongst the Venetians as another world war brewed in the background, and there was domestic tension between Doris and Margot at home. Blinded by love or infatuation, Margot did not, or perhaps chose not, to see Doris's faults. She had squandered a great deal of Margot's money in the renovation of the Palazzo Venier dei Leoni; it had escalated from a home for the two women to a status symbol on a par with Doris's ego. She boasted it was the only house in Venice in which every bedroom had its own bathroom.

Doris's celebrity in Venice could be measured against the grandeur of her parties. One evening, towards the end of 1938, she gave a party at the palazzo. A dance floor was built in the garden – one of the largest gardens in Venice, shaded by ancient cedar, elm, magnolia and acacia trees – and the exterior lights were turned around to reflect off the surface of the canal. The Venetian aristocracy came, and Prince Philip, who was staying with his uncle Prince Christopher of Greece, was also in attendance. It was a memorable evening, and the memory of the party lived on and embedded itself in Venetian lore – a distraction from the topic of war.

However, at two o'clock in the morning, as Doris and her guests waltzed amongst the ruins of the palazzo, a report arrived of the imminence of war over Czechoslovakia, and that Duff Cooper, the First Lord of the Admiralty, had mobilised the British fleet.[24] Fearing the frontiers would be closed and that

153

they would all be stranded in Venice, the guests fled the party and immediately made arrangements to return to England, and the women boarded trains, boats and aeroplanes still wearing their ball gowns.

Although Doris had previously expressed concerns about a potential war raging through Europe, Margot acted on those qualms and suggested they leave Venice. London, in wartime, was no place for Doris, and she decided the austere conditions that were certain to prevail were not to her liking. But Margot convinced her to go by suggesting it would be a temporary solution, during which time they could ponder their next move. While peace reigned, they packed up the palazzo and left for London, where they took a suite at Claridge's.

New York was on the horizon for Doris, and influenced by Margot – who promised her a gilded life in Manhattan and an equally rich social life amongst the east coast socialites – she made arrangements to cross the Atlantic. Doris placed her furniture in storage in London and made plans to bring with her the portraits painted by Winston Churchill, and her Rolls-Royce.

The dream of stardom continued to linger in her mind, and such was her arrogance (or naivety) that she believed she would see her face on the silver screen. With her ego fanning the flames of ambition, Doris did not sense that she was flying too close to the light. Her star, which had flickered with a second wind, was already beginning to wane.

A LAST RESORT

'If you're going through hell, keep going.'

Winston Churchill

London on the eve of the Second World War was a cold and inhospitable place to those who showed little interest in patriotism. More than ever, Doris found the city to be a world away from the place where she had thrived and carved a life for herself, as debauched as it was. Friends who were once welcoming to her, and amused by her excessive tastes, were preoccupied by their own worries; it was no longer a question of *if* there would be a war but, rather, *when*. Doris continued to drink and to dine at the Embassy Club and the Café de Paris, and to act on impulse with the gregarious spirit of her youth. She encountered Castlerosse one evening, as the former husband and wife frequented the same night spots, and Doris herself felt no bitterness towards him and greeted him warmly. As for Castlerosse, he was less than charitable when he said afterwards: 'I caught sight of [Doris] the other day. I bowed politely. The truth is, I thought it was her mother.'[1] In his opinion, she was losing her looks, and he did not shirk from telling their mutual friends that he thought so.

Since their divorce and during their absence from one another, Doris had begun to think about a reconciliation. It was not a coincidence that she chose to live at Claridge's, when Castlerosse himself occupied a suite on the top floor, though in recent days he had decamped to Beaverbrook's home in Surrey. As much as Castlerosse infuriated her, and had squandered her money and, materialistically speaking, had little to offer her, Doris gravitated towards the rambunctious man who shared the same personality traits as she did. His wit and humour and disregard for responsibility had become all the more attractive to her, though from afar, in comparison to Margot's serious nature. But beholden to Margot, as she provided money and, more importantly, a roof over her head, Doris perceived Castlerosse's churlish comments as hatred. Whereas, in reality, he was pining after her and lashing out to disguise his feelings for her. Some believed that Doris was the great love of his life.[2]

Before Doris left for New York she remained in London for the summer, and under the shadow of war, the social events of 1939 would become known as 'the last season'. Margot – whose former husband Richard Hoffman had lived in relative poverty since their Reno divorce, and had committed suicide by means of carbon monoxide poisoning – sailed to New York without Doris.

Alone in London, it was a bittersweet period for her. Although her old friends were 'doing' the season, they had become preoccupied by what their role in wartime would be. Many of her male acquaintances could guess what their fate would entail: young men such as Tom Mitford and Randolph Churchill would see battle, and her older friends would take desk jobs at various ministries. Adding to this feeling of isolation and uncertainty, Castlerosse had been taken ill and remained hospitalised for the duration of the summer, leaving Doris with little opportunity to see him socially.

Since his mild heart attack the year before, Castlerosse's health had come under scrutiny by those closest to him. This latest bout of illness – cirrhosis of the liver was one of the ailments – caused enough concern for Beaverbrook to ask his son, Max Aitken, to write a full-page article on Castlerosse's condition and recuperation.

In his suite at Claridge's, Castlerosse was propped up by twenty pillows and attended by Sir Charles Wilson (later, Lord Moran, Churchill's personal doctor), nurses, a secretary, and his chauffeur. He was surrounded by flowers, which overflowed down the corridor. Receiving over fifty telephone calls each morning, he filled his days correcting the names and titles mispronounced by the overworked operators. He also insisted on practising his golf swing with a walking stick, naked,[3] in front of an open window; he drank too much champagne and ate too much food, and entertained his many visitors until his energy was spent. All the while he had a soaring temperature of 103 and was prone to hallucinations, much to his guests' amusement.

Beaverbrook, who was footing the bill, ordered Castlerosse to be moved across the road to the London Clinic. But determined to outsmart its stricter regime, he managed to have his meals delivered from Claridge's restaurant and his bed brought over too. Regardless of Beaverbrook and the doctor's orders to limit his guests, pretty women continued to be allowed into his room, with a window of ten minutes between each visitor. Castlerosse had got around the rules by telling the clinic that his female visitors were faith healers sent on Beaverbrook's instructions. 'What charming disciples they have in this order,' said the matron.

Lady Kenmare arrived from Killarney with her Irish priest, the sight of which inspired Castlerosse to send a message to the *Cork Examiner* to inform the anxious people of southern Ireland that he had been given the last rites. But sensing that his joke had gone too far, he tried to stop the telegram in its tracks. 'Down home,' he told Beaverbrook who perceived the telegram as a ploy to trick the creditors, 'people take the Last Sacrament devilish seriously. I was frightened they might think I was putting a swift one over them.'[4]

The topic of death was on his mind, prompting him to question: 'Am I going to die slowly or swiftly? Is my heart all bust up? I cannot clean my teeth without the damned thing giving an imitation of an airplane engine. Doctors won't tell … Death means nothing to me. The only living thing I possess is a dog and she is a bitch.'[5] The truth was, Castlerosse was tempting death with his eating and drinking, or as his doctor put it: 'You will die unless you keep your stomach away from food and drink, your eyes away from books, your thoughts away from women – and, furthermore, you must eschew eroticism in your dreams.'[6]

To the relief of his readers, Castlerosse recovered from a 'long and tiresome illness', though his overall health would remain precarious, as a result of the five stone he had gained that year. He remarked: 'It is years since I have had so much kindness, especially from women. Most of the ones I know appear to have been born with "no" on their lips.'[7] He went to Paris to convalesce and to resume work on the Londoner's Log. And, in a macabre frame of mind, he wondered if he ought to write his own obituary. 'I hope you will explain with crystal lucidity to Doris that, if I do kick the bucket, I died entirely as the result of an attack of streptococcus,' he wrote to Beaverbrook. 'I don't want her swaggering about saying she broke my heart.'

When war was declared on 3 September 1939, it did not come as a surprise, but it still fell like a lead balloon as the season came to a close. The remainder of the year would prove to be a sedate one for Doris, though her social life would experience something of a renaissance over the Christmas period. Accompanied by Venetia Montagu, she spent Christmas without Margot at Madresfield Court, the ancestral home of the Earls of Beauchamp which served as the inspiration for Evelyn Waugh's novel, *Brideshead Revisited*.

For years she had been an acquaintance of the four Lygon girls, particularly Lady Sibell, who had recently married a bigamist. The entertainment, provided unwittingly by Lygons, was a tonic for Doris, and a reminder of the foolishness from her youth. Especially poignant was the presence of Lady Mary Lygon and her husband, Prince Vsevolod Ivanovich of Russia, for the quarrelling couple rivalled the fights between Doris and Castlerosse, and were prone to hurl cups of scalding tea over one another when irate. Another interesting anecdote, given that Doris and her contemporaries' love lives often came full circle, was that Lady Dorothy Lygon would marry Mad Boy, decades later, in 1985.

After her stay at Madresfield, Doris wrote in a letter to Winston Churchill that Venetia had been trying to marry her off again.[8] If she was lonely she did not say, and her letter brimmed with friendly chatter as though she were trying to find some common ground with him, or to evoke the devilish personality that he had known from their encounters at grandiose villas dotted around the continent.

Symbolising the end of the lifestyle Doris had known, her great friend Maxine Elliott had suffered a stroke and was gravely ill. She wrote to Churchill to tell him that she would be leaving for Vaynol, Sir Michael Duff's estate in Wales, on 28 December, to collect Maxine and bring her to London on 2 January. Her concern for Maxine's convalescence and how she took it upon herself to fetch her to London was a testament to Doris's loyalty towards her friends, and the generosity she was renowned for even though it was often clouded by her wrongdoings. She found Maxine a 'lovely' eighth-floor flat at Grosvenor House, and engaged a full-time nurse who was to provide treatment all day. In the letter to Churchill, Doris explained that Maxine's blood was 'rotten all through' and that she was at risk of having another stroke. Had she not been in ill health, Doris told Churchill that she would have taken Maxine with her to America and then to the Caribbean, where they could have visited Montego Bay ('really lovely') in Jamaica.[9] Maxine died two months later at the age of 71.

Doris continued to live at Claridge's and she found this to be a nerve-racking experience. During air-raid warnings, the hotel insisted that its guests go to the shelter, which meant the lifts stopped working and she had to negotiate the back stairs. Sometimes, she would reach the bottom as the 'all clear' signal sounded. The bombing of London would begin in earnest in September 1940.

In the meantime, an opportunity to leave for New York presented itself in June, when the American government issued a statement informing all Americans and refugees that it was their final opportunity to leave wartime Europe on the SS *Washington*. Britons also viewed America's warning as a last chance to scurry to safety. There was no question of Doris returning to Venice, for Italy had declared war on the United Kingdom and France, and furthermore the Palazzo Venier dei Leoni would soon be occupied by a succession of German, British and American troops. With the German occupation of Paris, and German U-boats sweeping the Channel, it would have been impossible for Doris to return to her old haunts.

Aside from the death of Maxine Elliott, adding to Doris's loneliness was her friend Diana Guinness's – who had since married Sir Oswald Mosley – imprisonment without trial at Holloway jail under Regulation 18B (a defence regulation used to imprison those suspected of being Nazi sympathisers). With her male friends off at war, and Winston Churchill now Prime Minister, Doris must have felt that there was no one in London to whom she could turn.

Owing to such feelings of isolation and thinking there was nowhere else she could go, Doris booked her passage on the SS *Washington*. With her Rolls-Royce in the hold of the ship, she set sail to join Margot in New York, before stopping at Galway to collect the remaining Americans wishing to return home.

In a cruel twist of fate, Castlerosse had been living at Killarney, and his mind was on two things: his beloved golf club and his former wife. Like Doris, he took little interest in the war effort and with Beaverbrook taking an appointment at the Ministry of Aircraft Production, he felt like an outsider due to his lack of responsibility. Before flying to Ireland, he managed to convince his elderly parents to leave their London home for Hertfordshire, explaining that he should 'hate for them to die in a cellar'. And, as was his wont, he managed to disappoint the patriotic Kenmares when he spoke openly about his approval of southern Ireland's neutrality in the war. His father called him a 'coward' and a 'traitor', and his mother reminded him that she was an Englishwoman by birth and would not desert her country in wartime. Castlerosse responded by fleeing to Ireland where he played golf and avoided news broadcasts over the wireless. 'We don't want to bother with that nonsense,'[10] he would say. But the moment of irony came when he went to Galway with the intention of visiting a group of American friends on the SS *Washington*, unaware that Doris was on the same ship.

Although it was a luxury liner of the United States Lines, life on board the SS *Washington* was a world away from the ocean liners that Doris had sailed on in the past. It was a chaotic scene: all of the 1,130 cabins (580 in cabin class, 400 in tourist and 150 third class) were filled, and passengers resorted to sleeping in the corridors, and on cots in the Grand Salon, Palm Court, library, post office and in the empty swimming pool. Those who did not have cots slept in chairs and on tables, and infants slept in baskets. Doris had access to a first class cabin but without the privileges it usually afforded: she slept with a lifejacket under her pillow, and her food and bathwater were rationed – a reminder of wartime England, something she wished to forget.

There was an anxious moment at five o'clock in the morning when a German U-boat had stopped the ship as it made its voyage to Galway with a warning, in English, that it would be torpedoed and every passenger had 'ten minutes to abandon ship'. There were 1,020 passengers (this increased to 1,787 including 700 child evacuees after its stop in Galway) and 540 crew on board, and the wartime tragedies of the SS *Athenia* and *Lusitania* were not far from its captain's mind. The ship's watertight doors were closed and the general alarm was sounded, whereupon passengers were ordered to get into lifeboats. While the evacuation commenced, the captain attempted to reason with the U-boat: 'American, Washington,' he radioed. Eventually, the German crew came aboard and checked the papers, and the SS *Washington*, a case of mistaken identity,[11] was permitted to proceed with its journey into the harbour. However, it continued to encounter U-boats as it did so.

As a consequence of this disturbance, the passengers were not allowed to go ashore and visitors were not permitted on board. Castlerosse was disappointed that he could not bid his friends *bon voyage* in person, and was reduced to waving goodbye from the railside. He would have felt further anguish had he known that Doris was amongst the passengers.

While Doris was on her way to New York, Castlerosse made plans to return to London. He moved into his old suite at Claridge's where, to his sorrow and disappointment, he discovered she was no longer in residence at the hotel. They had missed an opportunity for a reunion, though Doris did try to engage Castlerosse's attention and, nursing a broken heart and harbouring years of pent-up resentment, he ignored her. As the first bomb dropped on London, and aware of his own mortality, he missed her more than ever. With

Doris's permanent absence and the vast distance between them, Castlerosse's love grew deeper and, ironically, without her there to needle and torment him, the cycle of regret and recrimination from their married days was reignited. He realised that only Doris had the flippancy to care about something other than the war.

Doris was met by Margot on 21 June when the SS *Washington* docked in New York harbour. Aside from her Rolls-Royce, paintings by Winston Churchill, and collection of jewellery, there was little hope of reverting to the life she had led before the war. Even Margot's money and former promise of hospitality could not distract from the political tension that lingered over the city. Everyday civilians, largely made up of immigrants and the recent influx of refugees, voiced their opinions on war and whether or not the United States should intervene. With war a dominant subject, Doris must have felt as though she could not escape it entirely. Furthermore the blockades across the Atlantic meant there was little chance of returning to England, or indeed leaving America should it enter the conflict. And, because of this, there was a sense of entrapment to her new venture, which had once seemed so promising.

It appears that either Doris herself felt self-conscious about her arrival in New York while her country was at war – she told the *New York Times* that she planned to stay for two months – or that she was treated with contempt by others who could not fathom her desertion. Many ex-patriots failed to return to England when war was declared, preferring to remain in neutral America, but Doris's circumstances were unique in that her timing was off. In short, her arrival was not viewed as patriotic.

Still referred to as Viscountess Castlerosse by the New York newspapers – they frequently used the term 'England's Lady Castlerosse' when writing about her – and like many American socialites whose sympathies lay with Britain, Doris took up work for the war effort. Perhaps seeing her courtesy title as a pillar for the British in New York, she hosted and attended lunches for charitable purposes. Her name appeared in newspaper notices, notably the *New York Times*, amongst prominent families such as the Astors and Vanderbilts. And she was mentioned alongside various socialites who were reported to have given 'prefatory dinner parties' ahead of patriotic functions, such as the Star-Spangled Fete for which 2,000 tickets were sold with the monies aiding America's allies. She attended a Christmas bazaar, given by the Ambulance Corps for boys and girls, where she manned a stall alongside her friend Tilly Losch, who had married the 6th Earl of Carnavon in 1939, and Princess Kyril Scherbatow, an American socialite who had married into Russian nobility.

However, Doris's contemporaries back home remained unconvinced that she was in any way beneficial to the British war effort. English society women were providing vital services to the British government: Gertrude Lawrence, unlike Doris, went to great efforts to return to Britain from Massachusetts to accept an invitation from the Entertainment National Service Association to perform for troops; Edwina Mountbatten worked tirelessly to relieve the suffering of refugees, Jews and the wounded; Nancy Mitford took on various roles from fire-watching to running her family's London townhouse as a home for Jewish refugees from the East End; and Sylvia Ashley, widowed by Douglas Fairbanks and living in Los Angeles, would establish the British Distressed Areas Fund in 1941. Doris's efforts, by comparison, were viewed as frivolous and insignificant.

Ignoring female criticism, she formed a social circle made up of handsome young men in their twenties. An early friend from her New York days came in the form of Wayne Lonergan, who would rise to infamy in 1943 for murdering his wife, the Burton-Bernheimer beer heiress, Patricia 'Patsy' Burton.[12] Another was John Galliher, known to his friends as 'Johnny', a young man not unlike Doris with his charisma and talent for forming friendships with the rich[13] and famous – in his teens he was a favourite of Evalyn Walsh McLean, a Washington hostess and owner of the Hope Diamond. These new friends, in particular the young men, were on the fringes of café society, and although they came from humble beginnings, they had managed to charm the moneyed families of New York.

For a woman like Doris, this was not viewed as vulgar or a step backward from the social advancement she had previously enjoyed – she took her money, and attention, where she could find it. She became involved with Johnny Galliher, aged 25 to her 40 (though by then she removed a year or two off her age), but his sexual attitude matched her own and they began a casual affair. The dynamic was more friendship than romance, and he made a willing and decorative escort for Doris when she was invited to social events.

But with America joining the war on the horizon, not even Doris's male companions were assured permanency in her life. Margot was still on the scene, paying for everything and, as the years advanced, she had grown less besotted and more irritated by her behaviour. Margot struck an amusing parallel to Castlerosse, whose jealousy she could not rival but, unlike Castlerosse, her response proved far more detrimental to Doris's future.

OUT OF LUCK

'In her they instinctively sensed an outlaw.'

Radclyffe Hall, *The Well of Loneliness*

———◆———

The love affair between Doris and Margot was destined to end badly, even before it began. Aside from its social implications – not only was homosexuality illegal – such novels as Radclyffe Hall's *The Well of Loneliness* with its lesbian plot were deemed 'gravely detrimental to the public interest', and its publisher, Jonathan Cape, was warned to suppress the book or face legal action.[1] Thus, their union was shrouded in secrecy, though from the beginning Doris treated the relationship as a joke, and her friends were aware that she had 'taken up with an American lady' and nobody except for Margot took it very seriously. Margot, however, was reluctant to have her sexuality revealed. This was apparent when her involvement with Mrs Louise Shaw was questioned during the court case involving her former butler in 1935, and she played along with this thin disguise of friendship. Doris herself was, perhaps, entirely heterosexual, and she never loved Margot or considered her feelings.

Described as 'formidably rich, formidably tough',[2] Margot was an overbearing figure when around Doris, and her friends who were high camp, outrageous and living for pleasure could not warm to this humourless American. Not only did Margot lack appreciation for their high jinks, she resented their presence in Doris's life.

In a way, she had filled the void Laddie Sanford had left in Doris's life: like Laddie, Margot came from old American money, and Doris was attracted to lavish displays of wealth – something that was frowned upon among the British upper classes; even Beaverbrook's money was considered vulgar by some. Coincidentally, Margot was also a celebrated polo player and as such was connected to the same circles as Laddie, not only socially but through their mutual love of sport. Although Laddie had broken Doris's heart when he left her for Edwina Mountbatten – it was this rejection which had hardened her heart against future relationships and, to a degree, marriage – it was Margot who, after breaking off their relationship, would cast a shadow over her life.

Castlerosse was in a romantic limbo when it came to resolving his issues with Doris and restoring his old romance with Enid, then Viscountess Furness, who found herself in a familiar predicament. Her third husband, the hard-drinking Marmaduke Furness, died of cirrhosis of the liver in October 1940, and for the first time since their wartime affair in Paris, both Castlerosse and Enid were free from the ties of matrimony.

However, as was the obstacle during their long, drawn-out courtship – most of which happened in one another's absence – Enid was not readily available. With the exception of widowhood and observing a respectable period of mourning, she was trapped at her villa in the south of France, where she had presided over Furness's deathbed. Furthermore, she had since become entangled in a much-publicised court case with his former wife, Thelma, for his millions. The dying Furness had changed his will so that Enid, and not his son Anthony (his son with Thelma, whose paternity he questioned and whom he called 'the bastard'), would inherit £10 million from his estate. He made another pledge before he took his last breath, so feeble his signature was a mere scrawl, in which he left Enid £100,000 to allow her to purchase the villa where they resided, at Cap Ferrat.

The money and Enid's alleged motives came under scrutiny. Furness's yacht *Sister Ann* was to ferry him back to England where he wished to die, but Enid dismissed his dying wish on the grounds that the yacht would be at risk from bombs – it was the last ship to escape from France. Another issue was the money left to Enid to buy the villa, as the property was rendered worthless since France had fallen to Hitler. Not only was Furness on his deathbed but, a drug addict, he had suffered violent hallucinations and was haunted by an

Doris and Margot in Deauville.

invisible presence (believed to be his dead daughter) in his bedchamber, whom he begged 'not to throw herself away on a mere groom'.

But the war had stalled Enid's return to London, and the court case's status remained inconclusive due to complications regarding Furness's inheritance, owing to his eldest son, Richard, being declared missing in action. All Castlerosse could do was wait: he pined for Doris, though in acid moments he thought of his love for her as 'purgatory on earth', and he followed Enid's news with interest. After all, he needed the money.

In the summer of 1941 Doris was, in theory, a single woman. Although she no longer had access to Margot's money she must have felt optimistic that she would find another benefactor, for she took a lease on a furnished apartment at Sutton Place,[3] overlooking the East River, an enclave for heiresses and celebrities. Her neighbours included the widow of William K. Vanderbilt; J.P. Morgan's daughter, Anne; the silent film star Lillian Gish; and her friend from her halcyon days in London and Paris, Elsie Mendl.

For the first time in her life, since she had befriended Gertie all those years ago, Doris now had to fend for herself. She began to sell some of her jewellery to pay the rent, as she had done several times in the past, but it was something that would have dire repercussions in the near future. Among her assets were her paintings by Winston Churchill, which she flaunted as a status symbol and as proof that she was, perhaps, someone important. There was also the Palazzo Venier dei Leoni, since occupied by troops, and impossible to not only get to, but to sell. And the remainder of the jewellery which she had not sold.

However, not only was Doris struggling to afford a lifestyle that was no longer attainable to her, her timing could not have been worse. The month was June, and Manhattan was devoid of anyone worth knowing during the summer, as the rich and famous had absconded to their mansions on Long Island and Palm Beach. Johnny Galliher was still in her life and willing to escort her to various engagements but he, too, was scouring the social scene for his own benefit. With the exception of sex and having a much younger, handsome man on her arm, there was little else Doris could get from him. And time was running out.

This feeling of isolation[4] was intensified when America declared war on Japan following its attack on Pearl Harbor in December 1941, and in retaliation Japan's allies Germany and Italy declared war on America, beginning its direct involvement in the Second World War. With America at war, Doris's circle of young men was decreasing, with the exception of Wayne Lonergan who was called up twice for the American army but was rejected each time because of his homosexuality – a fact he had shared when attempting to enlist. Having already taken a trip down the primrose path with Cecil Beaton, it is assumed that Doris was reluctant to proposition Lonergan in spite of his access to Patsy's millions. For not only was his temperament erratic, he only liked rich women, and Doris was broke. Johnny Galliher, who had enlisted in the navy, remained in New York but his time was spent on a ship dry-docked at the Brooklyn Navy Yard before his posting to Europe.

Castlerosse experienced similar upheaval in his private life. In November 1941, his father died at the age of 81. He went to his grave harbouring contempt for his fellow Irishmen due to their ideology regarding the Second World War, and disappointment towards his prodigal son – not only was Castlerosse a wastrel, in his father's eyes he was also a traitor. At Killarney, Castlerosse might have managed to bury his head in the sand and avoid the war, but with his inherited earldom and responsibilities to the realm, he could not languish indefinitely. War also marked the end of the Londoner's Log; with the pages of newspapers needed for war news there was little room for a gossip column. It was a cruel blow for him, for as much as he loved to be idle, he had lost a sense of purpose and his yearly salary from the *Sunday Express*.

More than ever, Castlerosse longed for Doris to be by his side, to behave badly with and, as was his wont, to behave badly towards. His elevation in the peerage was bittersweet: nobody paid much attention to his new rank of earl or addressed him as Lord Kenmare – they continued to refer to him as Castlerosse – and, in a way, it made him feel as though his old lifestyle was still within his grasp. Only Doris could add to his fool's idea of stability.

There were reminders of Doris's life with Castlerosse everywhere she looked and she found herself reminiscing about their marriage, as tempestuous as it was, and it struck her with a sense of regret. Instigating such feelings were Wayne and Patsy Lonergan, a couple whose arguments had become a spectator sport in the nightclubs and supper clubs of New York. They loathed one another, unlike Doris and Castlerosse – who in spite of their differences felt bonded together – and as Castlerosse had done when he married Doris, Patsy had eloped with Lonergan because he was considered by her family to be a poor match. Doris made a curious onlooker to the couple's fights, and her sympathy lay with Patsy who wished to divorce Lonergan but, due to her wealth, he refused to co-operate.

Although their backgrounds were significantly different, Doris was aware of the similarities between herself and Patsy. Like Doris, Patsy was socially ferocious and she thrived on her engagement diary being filled with dates; she went out every night and was always happy in nightclubs. Patsy's outrageous behaviour did not shock Doris, but onlookers at the country club were appalled when Doris's young friend played a game of tennis without wearing any underwear beneath her tennis dress. It was as though Doris was observing a younger version of herself, and as unnerving as it was, Patsy proved useful, for she could wrangle invitations to parties to which she had not been asked. She had nymphomaniac tendencies and juggled several men at once. Her friends were rich and, even more appealing to Doris, lacked self-control. It was a louche circle, as indulgent and reckless as Doris's youth in London, and Patsy had what was known as a hollow leg – she could drink copious amounts of alcohol without getting drunk while her suitors grew more intoxicated and loose with not only their morals but their money, too.

Through Patsy, Doris met John Harjes, a member of the banking family whose mansion was at Tuxedo Park, an exclusive area not far from the city. He held a special affection for Wayne Lonergan, and showered him with expensive gifts, something which Patsy told the guests at a dinner party Harjes gave at Le Pavillon during the Christmas period. Doris, accustomed to candour, was not shocked by Patsy using her husband's homosexuality as a dinner table anecdote. She was faced with her own precarious situation when Johnny Galliher, whom she had invited, arrived late from the navy yard as the last course was being served. As he bent down to kiss Doris, he knocked over a glass of red wine, to which Harjes complained: 'Your friend is not only late, but clumsy.' To ease Johnny's embarrassment, Doris stood up and took her glass of crème de menthe, and announced: 'Merry Christmas, everybody.'[5] Pouring the green liqueur over the spilled red wine on the tablecloth, she turned the awkward situation into a joke, and the mood lightened. As the evening progressed, Harjes telephoned his butler to bring his dogs to the restaurant, the Lonergans continued to bicker, and Doris was confronted with the fact Galliher and her male friends would be sent overseas in the New Year.

As the year petered out, Doris was grateful for Patsy's company and connections. She was lonely and feeling less confident,[6] and in this frame of mind she wrote to Castlerosse, who busied himself in London by writing screenplays – that same year he appeared on-screen, credited as Man in Bath Chair, in *The Remarkable Mr Kipps*. Unknown to Doris, he had been following her movements in New York and pasting the newspaper clippings into his scrapbook, and to her surprise he broke his long silence and replied,[7] imploring her to return to London. With her confidence bolstered by his unexpected response, she asked: 'If I come home will you marry me again?' to which he cabled, 'Yes.'[8] With civilian travel on ocean liners halted due to the blockades on the Atlantic and commercial air travel reserved for the war effort, the only obstacle was how to get home.

In the New Year of 1942, Doris could no longer afford the rent on her Sutton Place apartment and she moved into the Hotel Delmonico on Park Avenue. She pawned her diamonds to cover her expenses but her tastes were not simple and although she viewed her present living arrangements as somewhat reduced – from a spacious apartment to a room in a luxury hotel – she was still living beyond her means. It was a situation which caused her embarrassment: she had lost her home, was running out of money, and was losing her looks. In comparison to the delicate beauty of her aristocratic contemporaries, Doris was described as having 'a hard, blonde beauty' (as photographs of her can attest), and approaching middle age she began to look haggard, even bitter. The consequence of losing the very things her life had been built upon – her face, her figure, her unnerving self-belief – came as a cruel blow. Adding to her personal woes, she experienced ill-health – possibly a nervous breakdown – and the result was that her nerves were on edge and she could not sleep.[9]

Although she did not care for hard work, her time was spent serving in a milk bar for the British War Relief on East 57th Street and selling badges in aid of the USO 'until all hours at night' for Mrs Dwight Morrow, the wife of the former United States Senator. With each passing day she grew more desperate,[10] and she scoured the newspapers for mentions of the powerful men she knew, hoping they might come to her rescue. She was enthused when she learned from Winston Churchill's godson, Winston Guest, that Churchill would be paying the first of his historical wartime visits to President Roosevelt in Washington.

According to Doris herself, Churchill came to America in January and invited her to a private dinner party at his Washington hotel. She assumed that her friend wished nothing more than to visit with her, and to dine and gossip, as they had done in the old days before the war. It appears her judgement was wrong on this occasion. Churchill had heard, falsely, from various sources that Doris was decrying the Allied cause amongst her American friends and he wished to stop her. And, as she told the story, he insisted that she come back to Britain immediately.

Doris's story is conflicting for several reasons. Churchill's first wartime visit to Roosevelt occurred in December after he had undertaken a dangerous crossing on the HMS *Duke of York*; he arrived in Washington on the 22nd to spend Christmas at the White House. The crossing, combined with the speech he gave to the Congress in an attempt to win support for his concept of the war, took a toll on his health and he suffered a mild heart attack. And, apart from being one of the most powerful men in the world, he could have summoned her home if he had felt the need to do so. He did not, and after his first visit to Washington, Doris remained in New York, a place she did not want to be. So, why did Doris not act on Churchill's stern advice that she ought to leave at once?

Another story, possibly invented by Doris herself, was that she had approached Harry Hopkins, Roosevelt's closest adviser, who took her to see the President in person, whereupon she told him that a high member of the British government wished her to return to England. The result of their exchange was that Roosevelt was reported to have given her a priority passage to England. But the circumstances which saw Doris leave America did not coincide with her version of events.

In March, Doris discovered through John Foster, the First Secretary and legal adviser to the British Embassy, that Beaverbrook was in America. She confided to Beaverbrook that she wanted to go back to London and that he was the only person who could have helped her. Telling him that she had 'no reason and no money' to remain in America, she added that she could meet the expense of her fare if only he could use his authority to approve her travel. She pleaded with him and, hoping to convince him of her plan, she agreed to undertake any war work that she was given.[11] She was willing to embrace austerity and discipline, and the life she had once run from was growing more appealing by the day. Beaverbrook, however, chose to ignore her.

In May, she wrote to her brother, Dudley: 'I have been trying to get home but it seems impossible. I am so homesick and miserable being away from England.'[12] Although Dudley sympathised with Doris, he was serving with the Royal Fusiliers in North Africa and there was little he could do to help. All she could do was wait.

A month later, in June, Doris received a telephone call from Winston Churchill. During their exchange she told him of her ambition to fly back to England by Clipper, after she had settled her debts. 'Could you ring me up again?'[13] she asked him.

The truth was that Doris had written to Churchill from her Park Avenue hotel, telling him of her homesickness and repeating much of what they had spoken about on the telephone. The letter arrived at Churchill's hotel in Washington after he had left for an engagement, and Harry Hopkins snaffled it. It is unknown whether or not Churchill read the letter, the contents of which describe to him her bad health and homesickness. She told him that her 'present situation here is most difficult' and, having confided that she was suffering a breakdown in health and the possibility that he might not believe her, she explained that she could produce a doctor's note. Perhaps to maintain her pride, she wrote that she could have gone to Bermuda or Nassau to recuperate (a lie as she had no money) but could not as she would have been stranded there without a hope of returning – a consequence of her visitor's visa which had a no entry permit. Hoping to appeal to him, she drew on the war effort and how she could help. She thought her work in New York was insignificant and she asked him to arrange it so she could find a job helping the war effort in London, where she felt she would be of greater use. In the event that he did not want to bring her home with him, she took the opportunity to ask who she could send her 'five papers' to in the State Department, adding that such information 'would be wonderful'.[14]

However, the letter and appeal were to prove unsuccessful. Having no influential contacts in Washington to whom she could turn, Doris realised she would have to remain in America.

During the years Doris and Castlerosse spent together and apart, she never imagined she would be competing with another woman for his attention. While Doris's plan to return to London was thwarted, Enid, who had been living in France for a year, managed to escape to Lisbon where she used her influence to secure passage on a flying boat to England. Back in London, she took a suite at Claridge's, where Castlerosse was also residing.

As she had felt about Edwina Mountbatten, Doris knew she could not compete with Enid. She was accomplished in ways Doris was not: she rode, she shot, she fished, she was a gifted painter and sculptress, she did exquisite needlework, and she was a talented cook and did not shirk from domesticity when it came to mothering her children, though the staff dealt with everything else. Over the years her beauty had become renowned and her physical appearance had become something of a fable. Tall, fair and with a patrician face, she looked ethereal. She carried herself like a queen;[15] some say she did not walk but floated into a room, turning heads with her emeralds and flowing gowns. She was a gambler like Castlerosse, and frequented the casinos of Monte Carlo and Beaulieu, carrying a stash of pound notes in her handbag for such recreation. She never showed emotion if she won or lost, and her opponents were too mesmerised by her looks to take notice of her reaction. By the time Castlerosse had reunited with Enid she had become such a celebrated character that people began to invent stories about her and, enjoying the attention, she inflamed the rumours about herself. Accused of being a 'mythomaniac', her acquaintances thought her stories were dangerous to her reputation. 'You don't know why those people lie,' said a friend, 'but they do.'[16]

Starved of female attention – all the young women were helping in the war effort – Castlerosse was struck by Enid's unchanged appearance when their paths crossed. She had not aged since their last meeting on Le Touquet golf course when she broke the news to a furious Castlerosse that she was going to marry Viscount Furness. Enid maintained her beauty by undergoing face-lifting operations; the story goes that she wrote to Furness before he was dying and threatened to commit suicide by shooting herself in a taxi. She was located at a hospital and indeed she had a wound, but it was from the secret plastic surgery.

Perhaps the most attractive thing about Enid to Castlerosse was the maternal side of her personality, a trait which Doris lacked. She was devoted to her three children, especially her oldest son Rory, who was born when she was 21. To outsiders they appeared to be close friends rather than mother and son, and they attended parties together and lived as a couple with Enid guiding Rory's life, though he concealed from her that he was gay,[17] and she never suspected. She nurtured and encouraged Castlerosse, a feeling that was provoked by pity for him, and she shared his fondness for golf and for animals. At one time she had 'a mangy pack' of twenty miniature poodles who followed her everywhere. Another permanent feature was a parrot, which she carried on her shoulder and taught to mimic her voice so that it could yell, 'Pat, the telephone,' prompting her daughter to answer it. During her marriage to Viscount Furness she had a pet (rescued) cheetah that she walked on a lead through Hyde Park, and which had its own collection of jewelled Molyneux collars. She also kept a pet hyrax which she fed from her own fork, and when out in public onlookers were astonished to see Enid retrieving lettuce leaves from the bodice of her dress to feed it. The hyrax was trained to use the lavatory, and sometimes Enid would allow her guests to spy through the bathroom window, out of sight, for it was terribly shy.

But there were similarities between the two women which Castlerosse undoubtedly found attractive, and could he have viewed Enid as a distraction while he missed Doris? Like Doris, Enid had magnificent eyes and a much-admired figure. However, unlike Doris, she possessed a steely self-control which had inspired Emerald Cunard to nickname her 'the stucco Venus'. This could be attributed to the belief that she 'lived in a haze of drugs' and drank

Coca-Cola (its original recipe contained cocaine) 'the way most people drink water'. She also had a peculiar speaking voice, entirely her own invention, and her Australian accent was replaced with a slight American tone. Doris, however, spoke in a loud voice which grew more aggressive when she was in a bad temper. But the two women shared a penchant for swearing, and Enid's vocabulary was as colourful as Doris's. She loved to shock, as did Doris, and she gave exaggerated responses to ordinary questions – a female friend once asked her what Castlerosse's first name was, and was told: 'Fucked if I know.'[18] Of course she knew, and she liked to call him Val. As with Doris, Enid was motivated by money and in the past she had counted the Duke of Westminster and one of the Selfridges (of the department store family) as her benefactors. 'Some women can only go to bed with handsome men,' remarked a mutual friend of both women, 'with Enid it didn't matter.' The same could be said about Doris.

Regardless of the duplicity of Enid's nature, Castlerosse appreciated her serenity and, under her spell, it put Doris out of his head and, temporarily, out of his heart.

ꟼHE JIꟼ IS ꟼP

'I have laughed with people and slept with despair.'

Viscount Castlerosse

———◆———

With Doris feeling as though she was trapped in New York indefinitely, she began to make plans about how she would support herself financially. With nothing left to pawn by way of jewellery, she turned to the paintings Winston Churchill had done of her. Although she did not aspire to sell them or indeed to have them valued, she knew the American press would be intrigued by such works of art by their Allied statesman.

Churchill himself must have predicted the lengths Doris would go to, and unconcerned about his artistic talents being open for scrutiny, he was far more worried about the subject of his paintings and, perhaps, the interest they might garner. The Prime Minister and the courtesan was not a topic he relished. Churchill pondered the idea of buying the portraits back from Doris but this plan did not succeed, possibly because he realised the underhand power it would give to her. There is no evidence to suggest she was manipulating Churchill with the paintings, but one thing was certain: her self-sufficiency and survival instincts were admirable and, as she had displayed in her youth, she would go to any lengths to preserve them. Churchill knew this, and Beaverbrook did too but, unlike his friend, the latter had nothing to lose.

Thus it was Churchill who came to Doris's rescue, though it was a gesture carried out to protect his own interests.[1] Eventually, by one means or another, she obtained a priority air passage to England in early December 1942, something which, at the height of wartime, was exceptionally rare. The journey, made by Clipper, was a dangerous undertaking, and for the duration of the eighteen-hour flight there was a risk of being shot down by the Luftwaffe.

Before she had left New York, Doris sent Castlerosse a telegram with the news of her arrival. She planned to take a room at the Dorchester, and had invited him to dine with her. Although he was overjoyed by the news – there was a time when he had thought of little else – his reunion with Enid had made him reluctant to commit to Doris. His opinion of her behaviour, through time, had mellowed and he thought only of her physical appearance. To his new friend and confidant, the film director Carol Reed, he spoke often of Doris, and noticing a vase of yellow daffodils, he said: 'Ah, how pretty they are. Doris always liked yellow.' Such remembrances struck him daily.

When Doris's train got into Waterloo station, Castlerosse was waiting for her on the platform. The years that had passed since their last meeting induced in him a nervousness, and he fretted about disappointing her. The bouts of illness and his increasing weight had taken a toll on his appearance, but he dressed himself carefully and went happily to the station.

On that particular evening, the blackout was in force and Doris exited the train shrouded in darkness. He could not see her face, but her voice and laughter were familiar; he noted the line of her smart clothes (rationing was not imposed in America) and the overpowering scent of her perfume. He understood this as a sign that her life in New York had been glamorous in comparison to the austerity of wartime Britain. Above all else, it inflated his ego when she appeared pleased to see him; this he construed from her eagerness to talk and the over-exaggerated laughter in which she punctuated her speech.

It was not until Doris and Castlerosse entered the Dorchester, and the light revealed her appearance, that his enthusiasm turned to disillusionment. He was confronted with a physical reminder of the years they had spent apart: she had gained weight, her face was etched with lines from the worry and strain of the past year in New York, her mannerisms were erratic, and her speech highly charged. The laughter, Castlerosse realised, was not provoked by gaiety but by anxiety. Despite the strange atmosphere between the former spouses, he saw his commitment through and they dined together, as Doris had wanted them to.

There had been an intimacy to their arguments and in their past resentment towards one another; now there was nothing to bond them together. She knew that his earlier telegram, in which he promised to marry her, had been an impulsive response. And she also sensed that his original feelings were beginning to waver. She was, after all, experienced in the behaviour of men. But Doris did not stop to consider that, in her absence, Castlerosse had turned to another woman who was also well-versed on the subject of men.

As they had grown apart, Castlerosse had also grown up, and he sought something different from what Doris could offer him. Although alike in nature, Doris and Enid snared men in remarkably different ways. Whereas Doris expressed her intelligence and wit in their company, Enid remained silent, a picture of still beauty as she underplayed her intelligence to bolster a man's ego. She made it a rule to never show a man how much she was in love with him, and she never displayed any signs of jealousy as she felt that gave a man power. 'A man is a predator,' she would say. 'He enjoys the uncertainty of the chase; so never let him feel sure of his prey.'[2] This gave men confidence, and they spoke more freely in her presence.[3]

Part of Enid's charm was that she was not overly social, despite marrying for money and becoming titled along the way. This appealed to Castlerosse, who was constantly abandoned by Doris in favour of parties, trips abroad with her friends, and the siren call of other men's beds. Enid stayed at home with him as his weight increased, his health declined, and he began to venture from the house less and less. He moved into Lees Place, Enid's townhouse left to her by Furness, though he complained that the stairs would kill him more quickly than any heart attack could, and he often left for Claridge's. After his volatile marriage to Doris, he and Enid appeared to be well suited and to have a good relationship.

However, when she became pregnant, Castlerosse assumed it was by another man and he launched an attack on her reminiscent of his fights with Doris. He called Enid a whore and hurled chairs at her, but unlike Doris she did not retaliate with physical violence. Instead, she remarked: 'I might be a whore but it seems to me that I am the one paying for your servicing!'[4] The pregnancy appeared to be a false alarm or one of Enid's tales – she had tried to conceive a child with Furness but was unsuccessful, a regret that manifested itself during the battle against his legal heir for his millions.

For a man as irresponsible and self-involved as Castlerosse, he revelled in the fatherly roles he inadvertently found himself in throughout the years. Beaverbrook enlisted him to watch over his teenage daughter, Janet, and to keep her out of trouble, but his efforts were resented by his charge. He adored Cynthia Smith, the young daughter of his friend Ben Smith, the American businessman. He called her 'princess' and whisked her off to tea at the Carlton, and bought her a horse and had a set of miniature golf clubs made for Smith's three children so they could join him in a game of golf. To his godchildren he was an indulgent godfather, and he gave them dogs on their birthday along with whimsical notes advising a diet of ice-cream, champagne and frogs, to the delight of the children. Enid's 17-year-old daughter, Patricia, was particularly close to Castlerosse and looked upon him as a father; her own father died when she was an infant and her former stepfather, Viscount Furness, did not like Enid's children. He became a mentor of sorts and took the shy girl under his wing, and for someone who had been at the mercy of others for money and praise, his new paternal role gave him a sense of pride and purpose.

For a woman so eager to marry into the aristocracy, it was surprising that Doris never bore Castlerosse a child. It was something that remained a sensitive topic for his parents, Lady Kenmare in particular; before her second and favourite son, Dermot, was killed during the First World War, she believed he was to be the only hope for the earldom. The future of the earldom remained Castlerosse's responsibility and, given his record for disappointing his family, his non-existent heir added to his list of failures. Doris herself showed no interest in children, and with an estate on the brink of bankruptcy and little by way of financial security, there was no incentive for her to try and produce an heir. In short, there was nothing in it for her. A child, or children, to a penniless man, the weight of whose title was only of significance to a son, was perhaps a symbol of repression to Doris. She was determined not to be tied to the home, albeit a grander one than she was brought up in, like her mother was. It would not have guaranteed her financial support, and with her lifestyle and instinct to hunt rich men (Castlerosse loathed the hunter in her), it would have hindered her future.

For almost a year, Doris had done everything within her power to leave America and to return to Castlerosse, whom she thought would be waiting for her. It was not only lack of money or loneliness that prompted this decision, but his telegram, stating that he would marry her again, had given her the motivation to see her plan through. Their meeting had been rigid and polite, with Doris talking incessantly and Castlerosse saying very little; his silence was attributed to his shock at her appearance. If she felt there was a lack of chemistry between them, she overlooked it. She wanted him to marry her, and she hoped he would see his promise through. After her experience in America, she longed for security and he was one of the few men who had not been called up to war. He was perhaps the only man who matched her temperament, and penchant for irresponsibility and extravagance. In her current frame of mind such things mattered little to Doris; she appeared depressed and in need of reassurance – rare for a woman who, in the past, would take no counsel.

To Doris the world appeared as a dark place and not one in which she had a role. When she stepped off the train at Waterloo station she was met with the dismal sight of bombed buildings and deserted streets, a terrifying reminder that she had returned to a city destroyed by German bombs. Where some had found excitement in the uncertainty of life and death and the influx of American GIs, the London Doris came home to was not the city of her youth and she found little that was familiar in the place where she had once thrived. The blackouts and nightly air raids, the wailing of the sirens and blasts from the naval anti-aircraft guns in Hyde Park, which shook the tray of glasses in her room, played havoc with her nerves. And, having been overseas for two and a half years, there was little sympathy directed at Doris from those who thought such nightly occurrences were the norm.

She was terrified, and the rumour that the Dorchester was the safest building in London did little to settle her nerves. The old underlying fear of money, and how she would get it, continued to haunt her, and having spent sleepless nights since her return she began to take barbiturates to ease her anxiety. It did not help when she telephoned old friends to offer them nylon stockings from America, then unavailable in England due to rationing, only to be rebuffed. 'You have behaved too badly,' she was told, 'deserting Britain at a time like this.'

'What am I supposed to do?' Doris asked.

'You can come help me with my war work,' said the friend.

She cut a lonely figure in the dining room of the Dorchester, sitting at a small table, eating alone. One evening she encountered Winston Churchill's uncle, the Duke of Marlborough, whose snide remark about people deserting their country in wartime had rattled her. His comment was a reflection of how others felt.

It is interesting that Doris did not turn to her mother, who was living comfortably in Kent. Instead, she remained hopeful that Castlerosse would come to her rescue. After the death of his father, he inherited not only

Killarney where he lived in converted stables but the family's London home, and Doris continued to believe that he would remarry her and, in doing so, she would have a roof over her head. Going home to her mother was not an option, and she did all she could to avoid this.

Before she left New York she had pawned the remainder of her valuable jewels, but her departure was so hastily arranged that she came to England without the money. She sent a telegram to the pawnbroker to inquire about her money, unaware that all telegrams were subject to censorship during wartime and that its contents had been read. After the telegram was dispatched, detectives from Scotland Yard arrived at the Dorchester to question her. She was also unaware that selling diamonds was illegal during wartime and she confessed to the detectives and explained her predicament, but still pleaded innocence. When the detectives left, Doris became panic-stricken. She felt as though her luck had run out, and the future was bleak.

With Scotland Yard seizing the telegram and faced with the reality that the money would not reach her, Doris telephoned an old friend who was a bookmaker and asked to borrow £500. Explaining that such a sum of money was difficult to come by, he sent a note containing £200. However, Doris had already said to him over the telephone: 'If I can't borrow £500 from an old friend when I need it, then it really is time I left this vale of tears.'[5]

It was a peculiar thing for Doris to say, as she was no Christian, but she must have believed in the literal meaning of the phrase that life's tribulations are left behind only when one leaves the world and enters Heaven. She had no money of her own, no way of getting money, and no friends. And now her involvement with Scotland Yard would bring grave consequences. There was no leniency shown towards those who stepped out of line during wartime, and Winston Churchill did not shirk from making an example out of individuals who undermined his regulations. The fate of Diana Mosley must have played on Doris's mind, and she was afraid of being sent to prison.

The moments in which Doris pondered her own fate were tense. She had always been clever, always a step ahead of any man and ready to take from him what she could get. Perhaps for the first time she realised that she was, indeed, the one who was at their mercy, for without the money and the jewellery (which she could sell for more money) she had nothing to show for her efforts. At the age of 42, Doris perhaps felt it was too late to begin again. When the messenger arrived with the £200 from the bookmaker, and knocked on her door, there was no answer. After some time the door was forced open and Doris was found unconscious in bed. She had taken an overdose of barbiturates.

Taken to St Mary's hospital in Paddington, Doris was put on the danger list. For days she remained in a comatose state, hovering on the brink of life and death. Castlerosse visited her bedside; he blamed himself for Doris's overdose and thought it was because he had refused to remarry her. Beaverbrook offered him solace at his London flat, where he spoke of Doris and dwelt on the situation. But owing to the Official Secrets Act, Beaverbrook did not tell his friend that it was the police investigation and not his rejection which had provoked her overdose. Castlerosse knew in his heart that he had more than a minor role in her demise. She never regained consciousness, and she died on 12 December. Her mother, whom she had pushed away and whose ideals she rejected, identified the body.

There was an inquest and her doctor confirmed that she had been suffering from insomnia and, due to the nature of the barbiturates which were prescribed, the notion of a deliberate suicide was questioned. The coroner's report stated that she had, indeed, 'died from barbiturate acid poisoning, the drug being self-administered in circumstances not fully disclosed by the evidence'. Those who knew Doris claimed she had been optimistic about her future and that she spoke of a reconciliation with Castlerosse; but such friends were the ones who had turned their back on her in her hour of need.

The truth might have been something far more cynical. From the moment she had embarked on a career as a courtesan, she knew it came with an expiry date. The period in which she had shone was not an age of gilded prostitution – the world was changing too fast – and what was deemed as brave and bold in the aftermath of Edwardian England and the Roaring Twenties was no longer shocking as the Second World War began. A life like Doris's could only end in riches or in tears.

Years before, she had lunched with Phyllis de Janzé, who waxed lyrical about men and money. Doris, whose charms were waning, observed her friend with a cold and menacing look in her eyes. 'You may think it fun to make love,' she warned, 'but if you had to make love to dirty old men as I do, you would think again.'[6]

AFTERWORD

'Before you embark on a journey of revenge, dig two graves.'

Confucius

———•◆•———

Doris's death was the darkest moment of Castlerosse's life and he never did learn the truth of what provoked her to commit suicide. The Official Secrets Act concealed her trouble with Scotland Yard, and his flippant rejection of her on that December night in 1942 kept from him the truth of the desperate measures his former wife had resorted to. She did not confide her woes to him, and he did not ask. Her habit of talking rapidly and the girlish laughter from her heyday was an act she had known well, and she fooled those to whom she had played the part. Castlerosse wrote in a letter to Beaverbrook that he 'loved Doris with a folly and futility that passes belief'. He spoke of her depressed state and how he had not seen the 'crisis' that had arisen. 'I could have lifted Doris up, given her hope, but I did not. I let her die.'[1]

But Castlerosse himself had a role to play and a lifestyle to maintain. Six weeks after Doris's death, he married Enid in the belief that she would soon inherit the money Viscount Furness had left to her. At a low point in her own pursuit of riches, Enid fell for Castlerosse's charm and affection. She was not

181

in love with him but she loved him with 'such a tremendous affection', and was grateful that he had come into her life when she was 'down and out'. He, as she said, 'took all my worries upon his shoulders',[2] and he promised her that if she married him he would pay £3,000 into her bank account and sign Killarney over to her. It was an attractive proposal, and Enid wanted to wait until her inheritance was settled, but Castlerosse announced their engagement and she felt 'rushed' into the marriage. As Lady Kenmare was elderly and ill, Castlerosse also told Enid that their marriage would make his mother happy and she might change her will in their favour.

Surprisingly, Lady Kenmare was fond of Enid, and by marrying her this made Castlerosse feel, in some way, that he had made his mother proud. On the eve of the wedding, Lady Kenmare gave a party at the Dorchester for Castlerosse and Enid, and guests had observed him as 'obese, grasping, dissipated', and she was described as 'chic, vulnerable [and] paper-thin'.[3] They were married at Brompton Oratory on 26 January 1943.

Castlerosse and Enid were married in January 1943.

Money, food and drink continued to be Castlerosse's downfall, and his doctor warned Enid that he would be dead within the year if he continued with his habits. She was advised to not only discourage his gluttonous ways, but was told to withhold sex as his heart could not take the strain. 'It was one of the only pleasures left to him in life,' Enid said, 'so how could I ration him?'[4] She would succeed in planting the final nail in his coffin, 'for which I will never forgive myself'.[5]

Nine months after his marriage to Enid, Castlerosse died of a massive heart attack, as the doctor predicted he would. His death, like his life, was a farce. The estate and earldom were to pass on to his youngest brother, Gerald, but Enid thwarted this plan when, at the age of 51, she claimed to be pregnant with Castlerosse's child. Lady Kenmare was beside herself. 'After all he has done, this,' she said. 'He loses our fortune, he ruins our lives. And now this.'[6] She ordered Enid to terminate the pregnancy, telling her that any child born to a woman of her age was bound to be an idiot. And, according to Enid herself, she followed through with her mother-in-law's demands and had an abortion. The baby, she said, had been a boy. There are those who dismissed Enid's story as a ploy to hold on to Killarney until her inheritance from Furness came through – 'she was up to that sort of thing'[7] – and either way, baby or not, she enjoyed the ridiculousness of the situation. It was the type of scenario Castlerosse himself would have delighted in. In the end there was no baby, and Gerald inherited the earldom. After the sound and fury directed at Castlerosse from his mother, it turned out Gerald would be the last Earl of Kenmare. The title is now extinct.

Doris and Castlerosse died nine months apart having, in their own way, succumbed to their lifestyles. Before his death, he said: 'There is but one tremendous force in the world and that is love, and I loved Doris.'[8]

ꟼOTES

1. Doris Casts a Spell

1–2   Edward Delevingne's profession has been incorrectly described in various biographies as a butter importer. He was a button importer as confirmed by a notice in the *Gazette* archive dated 2 June 1925: 'Notice is hereby given, that the Partnership heretofore subsisting between us, the undersigned, Edward Charles Delevingne, George Edmond Delevingne and Robert Frederick Delevingne, carrying on business as Dealers in Laces, Buttons, Haberdashery and Fancy French Goods, at 4, Hamsell Street, in the City of London under the style of firm of Edward Delevingne, has been dissolved by mutual consent as and from the first day of January, 1925. All debts due to and owing by the said late firm will be received and paid by the said Edward Charles Delevingne. Dated this twenty-sixth day of May, 1925.'

3   Doris was wrongly reported as being the oldest of four children. Historical documents show that only two (surviving) children were born to Edward and Jessie Delevingne.

4   As told to the author by Doris's cousin, Helen Tyrell.

5   Doris was described as working in a fashion house in *Castlerosse* by Leonard Mosley and *Lord Castlerosse: His Life and Times* by George Malcolm Thomson. This is inaccurate. Perhaps, given the biographies were published in 1956 and 1973 respectively, this was written to be flattering to Castlerosse's wife.

6   Daphne du Maurier described Gertrude Lawrence as a 'dyed-haired tart'.

7   '…[Castlerosse] has had an unhappy childhood like mine, and he understands.' Mosley, Leonard, *Castlerosse* (Arthur Baker, London 1956) p. 81.

8   Pugh, Martin, *We Danced All Night: A Social History of Britain Between the Wars* (Vintage, London 2009) p. 217.

9   Working-class girls were viewed as more liberated, with looser morals. 'Servant girls are that way. They kiss first and are proposed to afterward.' Maloney, Alison, *Bright Young Things: Life in the Twenties* (Virgin, London 2012) p. 1.

10 'Gertie was taught everything by Philip, who guided her taste in clothes and everything else and she, "money-quick", picked up everything from him, every trick of behaviour and social jargon until the girl from Brixton emerged during their long relationship as a perfectly polished product of Mayfair.' Quotation by Cole Lesley. Morley, Sheridan, *Gertrude Lawrence* (Weidenfeld and Nicolson, London 1981) p. 34.

11 As said by Doris to Daphne Fielding and published in her book, *The Duchess of Jermyn Street: The Life and Good Times of Rosa Lewis of the Cavendish Hotel* (Penguin, London 1978) p. 170.

12 Daphne Fielding's description of Doris's dual personality. *The Duchess of Jermyn Street: The Life and Good Times of Rosa Lewis of the Cavendish Hotel* (Penguin, London 1978) p.170.

13 'These impetuous creatures were often scorned by their aristocratic peers as *nouveau-riche*.' Malone, Alison, *Bright Young Things: Life in the Roaring Twenties* (Virgin Books, London 2012) p. 10.

14 More accessible in America, the pills were predominantly used by upper-class women who could afford them. They would have been easily available to Doris, who visited America several times a year. Furthermore, she was not short of American connections who could have sourced such pills. I discovered the reference to these pills in *Flappers: Six Women of a Dangerous Generation*, Mackrell, Judith (Sarah Crichton Books, London 2015).

2. Castlerosse is Summoned

1   Mosley, Leonard, *Castlerosse* (Arthur Baker, London 1956) p. 47.

2   Mosley, Leonard, *Castlerosse* (Arthur Baker, London 1956) p. 52.

3   Mosley, Leonard, *Castlerosse* (Arthur Baker, London 1956) p. 27.

4   Thomson, George Malcolm, *Lord Castlerosse: His Life and Times* (Weidenfeld and Nicolson, London 1973) p. 24.

5   Letter from Enid, Lady Kenmare, to Lord Beaverbrook, (day and month unknown) 1944. Parliamentary Archives, BBK_C_19.

6   Mosley, Leonard, *Castlerosse* (Arthur Baker, London 1956) p. 28.

7   Mosley, Leonard, *Castlerosse* (Arthur Baker, London 1956) p. 31.

8   Mosley, Leonard, *Castlerosse* (Arthur Baker, London 1956) p. 26.

9   In late October 1914, Castlerosse had been reported as 'missing and wounded'. *The Catholic Press* reported that he was 'known to be in a hospital in Paris', 5 November 1914. Lady Kenmare also believed that Castlerosse had been killed, and then when found, that his arm had been amputated.

10   Mosley, Leonard, *Castlerosse* (Arthur Baker, London 1956) p. 39.

11   Thomson, George Malcolm, *Lord Castlerosse: His Life and Times* (Weidenfeld and Nicolson, London 1973) p. 51.

12   Lady Kenmare wrote in a letter to Ettie, Lady Desborough: 'My darling, we have died with them [Ettie had lost two sons], but we must not grudge them their glory. I think of his short life full of blessings, full of love and joy, and that was all God wanted him to know.' 2 October 1915. DERV C307/11. Davenport-Hines, Richard, *Ettie: The Intimate Life and Dauntless Spirit of Lady Desborough* (Hachette, London 2012) p. 210.

13   Thomson, George Malcolm, *Lord Castlerosse: His Life and Times* (Weidenfeld and Nicolson, London 1973) p. 57.

14   'Another threw himself under Le Train Bleu ... because he thought my mother would be on it with her new lover. In fact she wasn't ... One besotted young man apparently threw himself overboard as the ship he and my mother were travelling on to Australia went through the heads of Sydney. Mummy had, by the end of the voyage, shown a marked preference for someone else.' Cavendish O'Neill, Pat, *A Lion in the Bedroom* (Jonathan Ball, Cape Town 2004) p. 21.

15   'Legally a heroin addict. She was on the drug list, you know, registered ... she smoked opium certainly, and took heroin.' As told to Dominick Dunne and published in his book, *Fatal Charms and*

Other Tales of Today/The Mansions of Limbo (Crown, New York 1987) p. 306.

16 Mosley, Leonard, *Castlerosse* (Arthur Baker, London 1956) p. 51.

17 *The Duchess of Jermyn Street: The Life and Good Times of Rosa Lewis of the Cavendish Hotel* (Penguin, London 1978) p. 171.

3. Doris the Demi-mondaine

1 John Hayden Halsey (www.phoenixmediaworks.com).

2 As told to the author.

3 John Hayden Halsey (www.phoenixmediaworks.com).

4 A popular phrase used by the Bright Young Things.

5 A quotation attributed to Vanessa Bell.

6 In America, a female smoker lighting up in the street could have been arrested in the early 1900s.

7 A daring fashion statement and a world away from the corsets and long dresses of the Edwardians. Eminent doctor and sociologist, Arabella Kenealy, wrote in 1920: 'Many of our young women have become desexed and masculinised, with short hair and skirts no longer than kilts, narrow hips and insignificant breasts.'

8 'I remember ... the bright gold of Doris's hair, which the years were so sadly to tarnish.' Nichols, Beverley, *A Case of Human Bondage* (Secker and Warburg, London 1966) p. 175.

9 This quotation is often misattributed. It was said by Rosa Lewis to Daphne Fielding, as published in her book, *The Duchess of Jermyn Street: The Life and Good Times of Rosa Lewis of the Cavendish Hotel* (Penguin, London 1978) p. 171.

10 Welham, Mike and Jaqui, *Crabb and the Grey Rabbit* (Welham Books, 2015).

11 $548,802,385 in today's money. Bank of England inflation calculator.

12 Pugh, Martin, *We Danced All Night: A Social History of Britain Between the Wars* (Vintage, London 2009) p. 161.

13 Mosley, Leonard, *Castlerosse* (Arthur Baker, London 1956) p. 80.

14 In 1938 Warner Brothers released a film based on the horse.

15 As told to the author by Katya Anderson, a relative of Laddie Sanford.

16 Morgan, Janet, *Edwina Mountbatten: A Life of Her Own* (HarperCollins, London 1991) p. 190.

17   It has been written that Sir Edward MacKay Edgar bought Doris
     her house on Deanery Street. The sources that I have used to create
     a timeline of Doris's life suggest that it was Laddie Sanford who gave
     her the house.

18   Mitford, Nancy, *The Water Beetle* (Penguin, London 1965) p. 117.

19   '… the Lygon girls who, in their father, the seventh Earl of
     Beauchamp's absence (he lived abroad having been accused of
     homosexuality), while living in the lap of luxury, were always
     short of pin-money and reduced (as Sibell put it) to accepting
     'hand-me-down' stockings from Doris.' *Madresfield: One House, One
     Family, One Thousand Years*. Mulvagh, Jane (Black Swan, London
     2009) p. 29.

20   Mosley, Leonard, *Castlerosse* (Arthur Baker, London 1956) p. 80.

21   Thomson, George Malcolm, *Lord Castlerosse: His Life and Times*
     (Weidenfeld and Nicolson, London 1973) p. 96.

22   Daphne Fielding recalled Doris coming to stay at her husband's
     family seat, Longleat, for the weekend, and that she sat next to
     her father-in-law and charmed him completely. They spoke about
     county councils and hospital management. Fielding, Daphne, *The
     Duchess of Jermyn Street: The Life and Good Times of Rosa Lewis of the
     Cavendish Hotel* (Penguin, London 1978) p. 174.

23   '… girls from nice families took chloroform as a recreational drug.'
     Wallace, Carol, *Dance: A Very Social History* (The Metropolitan
     Museum of Art, New York 1986) p. 46.

24   As described by the press. Dudley Delevingne was actually a
     stockbroker and would later become a successful estate agent.

25   Nichols, Beverley, *A Case of Human Bondage* (Secker and Warburg,
     London 1966) p. 132.

26   'Would Cecil Beaton and Oliver Messel have bothered to champion
     a tasteless vulgarian?' Nichols, Beverley, *A Case of Human Bondage*
     (Secker and Warburg, London 1966) p. 132.

27   Morgan, Janet, *Edwina Mountbatten: A Life of Her Own*
     (HarperCollins, London 1991) p. 165.

28   Morgan, Janet, *Edwina Mountbatten: A Life of Her Own*
     (HarperCollins, London 1991) p. 190.

29   'The most arrogant, temperamental and beautiful woman in
     London.' Mosley, Leonard, *Castlerosse* (Arthur Baker, London 1956)
     p. 77.

30 Fielding, Daphne, *The Duchess of Jermyn Street: The Life and Good Times of Rosa Lewis of the Cavendish Hotel* (Penguin, London 1978) p. 170.

31 *The Argus*, 10 November 1934.

32 *The Argus*, 10 November 1934.

33 James 'Jimmy' White poisoned himself. White and Mike were both struggling to resuscitate their waning fortunes, and they came into conflict over British-controlled oilfields. White had large holdings, but he was desperately in need of money for other projects. Mike, who had seemed to be helping White, changed his tactics. He unloaded nil of his shares, and White could not raise another pound on his own holdings owing to the depreciated price. White went down to his country house and put a pad soaked in chloroform over his face. Mike was foolish enough to boast of his victories to a party of journalists in his flat at Mount Street. "'It was a two years' battle between Jimmy White and myself," he said, "and the one to lose was Jimmy! It was rotten fighting an old friend, but it wasn't my fault. I didn't make the rules of this game."' *The Argus*, 10 November 1934.

34 'It made a lasting change in her character.' Thomson, George Malcolm, *Lord Castlerosse: His Life and Times* (Weidenfeld and Nicolson, London 1973) p. 98.

35 Mosley, Leonard, *Castlerosse* (Arthur Baker, London 1956) p. 79.

4. Castlerosse the Court Jester

1 Mosley, Leonard, *Castlerosse* (Arthur Baker, London 1956) p. 56.

2 £1,085,586 in today's money. Bank of England inflation calculator.

3 Thomson, George Malcolm, *Lord Castlerosse: His Life and Times* (Weidenfeld and Nicolson, London 1973) p. 68.

4 £10,855,866 in today's money. Bank of England inflation calculator.

5 Lady Kenmare wrote in a letter to Ettie, Lady Desborough, that she was thankful to be at Killarney (Dermot's home, as she called it). 'I walk in the golden sunshine and calm peace of lovely autumn days, through his woods, his hills, and tell him he is not forgotten.' Davenport-Hines, Richard, *Ettie: The Intimate Life and Dauntless Spirit of Lady Desborough* (Hachette, London 2012) p. 245.

6 Mosley, Leonard, *Castlerosse* (Arthur Baker, London 1956) p. 29.

7   Mosley, Leonard, *Castlerosse* (Arthur Baker, London 1956) p. 62.

8   Mosley, Leonard, *Castlerosse* (Arthur Baker, London 1956) p. 64.

9   £2,172 in today's money. Bank of England inflation calculator.

10   Mosley, Leonard, *Castlerosse* (Arthur Baker, London 1956) p. 59.

11   'He was the court jester, a diligent gossip whose self-elected role was to know everything that was happening on the political and social scene.' Aitken-Kidd, Janet, *The Beaverbrook Girl* (Collins, London 1987) p. 39.

12   £169,203 in today's money. Bank of England inflation calculator.

13   'An immense, kindly, jovial, witty creature, Falstaffian, funny and boisterous and always grossly overdressed; yet with a kind heart, and was not quite the fraud he pretended to be. [He] made a precedent in writing gossip, and by becoming a journalist when it was still thought extraordinary and in bad taste to do either. He had a garish wit, and was the supreme raconteur.' James, Robert Rhodes (ed.), *Chips: the Diaries of Sir Henry Channon* (Phoenix, London 1993) p. 376.

14   Ziegler, Philip, *Diana Cooper: The Biography of Lady Diana Cooper* (Hamish Hamilton, London 1981) p. 6.

15   Ziegler, Philip, *Diana Cooper: The Biography of Lady Diana Cooper* (Hamish Hamilton, London 1981) p. 169.

16   Mosley, Leonard, *Castlerosse* (Arthur Baker, London 1956) p. 77.

17   Mosley, Leonard, *Castlerosse* (Arthur Baker, London 1956) p. 77.

18   Thomson, George Malcolm, *Lord Castlerosse: His Life and Times* (Weidenfeld and Nicolson, London 1973) p. 83.

5. Meeting at a Disadvantage

1   Anecdote from *Valentine's Days*, Castlerosse, Lord (Methuen, London 1934).

2   Thomson, George Malcolm, *Lord Castlerosse: His Life and Times* (Weidenfeld and Nicolson, London 1973) p. 82.

3   Castlerosse admired the latest fashions that were far more daring and revealing than his mother's generation. But even he had his limits. 'I am prepared to put up with most things, but I really cannot bear the sight of a female garter on the back of a motorbike.'

4   It can be said that Castlerosse was out of his depth with Doris. 'He bit off more than he could chew when he met Doris.' Aitken-Kidd, Janet, *The Beaverbrook Girl* (Collins, London 1987) p. 61.

5   Mosley, Leonard, *Castlerosse* (Arthur Baker, London 1956) p. 81.

6   Mosley, Leonard, *Castlerosse* (Arthur Baker, London 1956) pp. 81–2.

7   Mosley, Leonard, *Castlerosse* (Arthur Baker, London 1956) p. 82.

8   Castlerosse was 'writing open letters *every* week to Doris Delavigne'. A cause of concern for his editor at the *Sunday Express*. Christiansen, Arthur, *Headlines All My Life* (Heinemann, 1961) p. 77.

9   Thomson, George Malcolm, *Lord Castlerosse: His Life and Times* (Weidenfeld and Nicolson, London 1973) p. 92.

10 Mosley, Leonard, *Castlerosse* (Arthur Baker, London 1956) p. 80.

11 Thomson, George Malcolm, *Lord Castlerosse: His Life and Times* (Weidenfeld and Nicolson, London 1973) p. 93.

12 Mosley, Leonard, *Castlerosse* (Arthur Baker, London 1956) p. 89.

13 Young, Kenneth, *The Diaries of Sir Robert Bruce Lockhart: 1915–38* (Macmillan, London 1973) p. 138.

14 Lady Diana Cooper was expected to marry someone of her social standing. Instead she chose Duff Cooper, 'a penniless commoner of whom no one had ever heard'. At the time of their marriage he was, in fact, a rising political star in Conservative politics, but notoriously unfaithful to his wife.

15 Mosley, Leonard, *Castlerosse* (Arthur Baker, London 1956) p. 86.

16 Mosley, Leonard, *Castlerosse* (Arthur Baker, London 1956) p. 87.

17 Mosley, Leonard, *Castlerosse* (Arthur Baker, London 1956) p. 79.

18 Witnesses to the marriage were Dudley Delevingne and Millie Hulton, a former music hall artist and second wife of Sir Edward Hulton. Millie and Sir Edward's daughter, Betty, married Major Charles Greville Bartlett Stewart-Stevens, with whom she had a son, Jocelyn Stevens. Interestingly, Jocelyn's daughter Pandora (née Stevens) married Charles Delevingne, Doris's nephew.

6. Lady Castlerosse

1   Recalled by Lord Donegal.

2   Around £280 in today's money. Bank of England inflation calculator.

3   Castlerosse to Dudley Delevingne, letter circa 1928: 'Doris thinks she pays her own way, yet I can tell you that her casual expenses cost me £100 a week.'

4   Letter to Dudley Delevingne, circa 1928. Thomson, George Malcolm, *Lord Castlerosse: His Life and Times* (Weidenfeld and Nicolson, London 1973) p. 105.

5   Mosley, Leonard, *Castlerosse* (Arthur Baker, London 1956) p. 99.

6   Mosley, Leonard, *Castlerosse* (Arthur Baker, London 1956) p. 89.

7   Fielding, Daphne, *The Duchess of Jermyn Street: The Life and Good Times of Rosa Lewis of the Cavendish Hotel* (Penguin, London 1978) p. 172.

8   Young, Kenneth, *The Diaries of Sir Robert Bruce Lockhart: 1915–38* (Macmillan, London 1973) p. 138.

9   Chisholm, Anne and Davie, Michael, *Beaverbrook: A Life* (Hutchinson, London 1992) p. 499.

10   Mosley, Leonard, *Castlerosse* (Arthur Baker, London 1956) p. 90.

11   'During WWI Lady Massereene had been Commandment of Women's League Canteens, but was dressed so inappropriately that on a day visit to a canteen, some soldiers asked her if she had experienced any luck at Piccadilly the night before.' Vickers, Hugo, *Elizabeth: The Queen Mother* (Hutchinson, London 2005).

12   Aitken-Kidd, Janet, *The Beaverbrook Girl* (Collins, London 1987) p. 61.

13   Mosley, Leonard, *Castlerosse* (Arthur Baker, London 1956) p. 91.

14   Mosley, Leonard, *Castlerosse* (Arthur Baker, London 1956) p. 92.

15   Mosley, Leonard, *Castlerosse* (Arthur Baker, London 1956) p. 92.

16   'Castlerosse is the only man, except royalty, who gets through life without using money, "ready money" I mean. I don't say he doesn't spend money. He spends it like water with a splendid impartiality as to whether the prevailing financial situation is one of flood or drought. But he doesn't so demean himself as to carry the emblems of filthy lucre in his trouser pocket. He puts it on the bill.' Mosley, Leonard, *Castlerosse* (Arthur Baker, London 1956) p. 99.

17   £284 in today's money. Bank of England inflation calculator.

18   'The pretty matrons and girls in the younger set of society who are always willing to take part in pageants and charades have already had their services enlisted for October 31. Lady Ashley, Lady Inverclyde, Lady Plunket, Lady Castlerosse, Miss Baby Jungman and Mrs Peter Thursby are to be some of the thirteen superstitions in a procession

that Mrs Alexander McCorquodale is arranging for the Hallowe'en Ball. Mr Simon Elwes and Mr Oliver Messel have also helped in the arrangements. *Daily Mirror*, 27 August 1930.

19   Lockhart, Sir Robert Bruce, *Friends, Foes and Foreigners* (Putnam, London 1957) p. 255.

20   Fielding, Daphne, *The Duchess of Jermyn Street: The Life and Good Times of Rosa Lewis of the Cavendish Hotel* (Penguin, London 1978) p. 171.

21   Fielding, Daphne, *The Duchess of Jermyn Street: The Life and Good Times of Rosa Lewis of the Cavendish Hotel* (Penguin, London 1978) p. 171.

22   '… his public performance as Gay Lord Castlerosse'. Mosley, Leonard, *Castlerosse* (Arthur Baker, London 1956) p. 94.

23   Fielding, Daphne, *The Duchess of Jermyn Street: The Life and Good Times of Rosa Lewis of the Cavendish Hotel* (Penguin, London 1978) p. 170.

24   Fielding, Daphne, *The Duchess of Jermyn Street: The Life and Good Times of Rosa Lewis of the Cavendish Hotel* (Penguin, London 1978) p. 174.

25   Mosley, Leonard, *Castlerosse* (Arthur Baker, London 1956) p. 93.

26   '[Doris] tried her best, but it just couldn't work.' Mosley, Leonard, *Castlerosse* (Arthur Baker, London 1956) p. 94.

7. Doris Misbehaves

1   Young, Kenneth, *The Diaries of Sir Robert Bruce Lockhart: 1915–38* (Macmillan, London 1973) p. 262.

2   'The truth is that the witty, pretty, hospitable Lady Castlerosse was looked on with black disapproval by parents with susceptible sons, or daughters who might be led from the stricter paths.' *Thomson, George Malcolm, Lord Castlerosse: His Life and Times* (Weidenfeld and Nicolson, London 1973) p. 100.

3   Young, Kenneth, *The Diaries of Sir Robert Bruce Lockhart: 1915–38* (Macmillan, London 1973) p. 264.

4   Letter from Doris to Lord Beaverbrook, 19 May 1929. Doris writes that she pawned several pieces of jewellery including two strings of pearls on 8 November 1928; 28 November 1928; 29 December 1928; 10 April 1929; 22 February 1929. BBK_C_19, Parliamentary Archives.

5   Mosley, Leonard, *Castlerosse* (Arthur Baker, London 1956) p. 100.

6   Kidd-Aitken, Janet, *The Beaverbrook Girl* (Collins, London 1987) p. 134.

7   The story goes that Beaverbrook returned to Josef's some time after the incident, and was greeted by the head waiter, who asked after the health of Lord Beaverbrook. 'Why, who do you think I am?' asked Beaverbrook. 'Lord Castlerosse, of course,' replied the head waiter.

8   Letter from Doris to Lord Beaverbrook, 18 June 1929. BBK_C_19, Parliamentary Archives.

9   £42,556 in today's money. Bank of England inflation calculator.

10 £56,742 in today's money. Bank of England inflation calculator.

11 £204,270 in today's money. Bank of England inflation calculator.

12 Letter from Doris to Lord Beaverbrook, 19 May 1929. BBK_C_19, Parliamentary Archives.

13 £226,966 in today's money. Bank of England inflation calculator.

14 Letter from Doris to Lord Beaverbrook, 18 June 1929. BBK_C_19, Parliamentary Archives.

15 Letter from Doris to Lord Beaverbrook, 18 June 1929. BBK_C_19, Parliamentary Archives.

16 Letter from Doris to Lord Beaverbrook, 18 June 1929. BBK_C_19, Parliamentary Archives.

17 £5,606,586.80 in today's money. Bank of England inflation calculator. The amount has also been listed as £30,000. Chisholm, Anne and Davie Michael, *Beaverbrook: A Life* (Hutchinson, London 1992) p. 273.

18 Letter from Enid Kenmare to Lord Beaverbrook. Letter undated, circa 1942–43. BBK_C_19, Parliamentary Archives.

19 Letter from Enid Kenmare to Lord Beaverbrook. '… Everything I have now and leave, must go to the others.' Undated, circa 1942–43. BBK_C_19, Parliamentary Archives.

20 Chisholm, Anne and Davie, Michael, *Beaverbrook: A Life* (Hutchinson, London 1992) p. 273.

21 Letter from Doris to Lord Beaverbrook, 19 May 1929. BBK_C_19, Parliamentary Archives.

22 The earliest letter existing between Doris and Lord Beaverbrook appears to be 10 November 1928. BBK_C_19, Parliamentary Archives.

23 Letter from Doris to Lord Beaverbrook. '… Can I persuade you to dine here on the 21st? Then they will all be here.' 10 November 1928. BBK_C_19, Parliamentary Archives.

24 £280 in today's money. Bank of England inflation calculator. Letter from Doris to Lord Beaverbrook. 'Five million thanks for the five pounds, and a hundred million thanks for the most enjoyable evening.' 1 December 1928. BBK_C_19, Parliamentary Archives.

25 Letter from Doris to Lord Beaverbrook, 1 December 1928. BBK_C_19, Parliamentary Archives.

26 Fielding, Daphne, *Mercury Presides* (Eyre & Spottiswoode, London 1954).

27 Letter from Doris to Lord Beaverbrook. Arthur Bendir's daughter, Babe Bendir (also known as McGusty), was a prominent member of the Bright Young Things. A friend of Doris's, she caused a variety of scandals in the late 1920s and '30s, and all of her brief marriages ended in divorce. 21 May 1929. BBK_C_19, Parliamentary Archives.

28 Letter from Doris to Lord Beaverbrook, 24 April 1930. BBK_C_19, Parliamentary Archives.

29 Letter from Doris to Lord Beaverbrook. 18 June 1929. BBK_C_19, Parliamentary Archives. Beaverbrook would be appointed godfather to Diana's son, John Julius Cooper, later Viscount Norwich.

30 Letter from Lord Beaverbrook to Lady Diana Cooper. Chisholm, Anne and Davie, Michael, *Beaverbrook: A Life* (Hutchinson, London 1992) p. 267.

31 Hathaway, Sybil Collings, *Dame of Sark: An Autobiography* (William Heinemann, 1961) p. 90.

32 Dimbleby, Josephine, *A Profound Secret: May Gaskell, Her Daughter Amy and Edward Burne-Jones* (Black Swan, London 2005) p. 361.

33 Letter from Doris to Lord Beaverbrook, circa Sept 1929. BBK_C_19, Parliamentary Archives.

34 Letter from Doris to Lord Beaverbrook, circa 1929. BBK_C_19, Parliamentary Archives.

35 Letter from Doris to Lord Beaverbrook, circa 1929. BBK_C_19, Parliamentary Archives.

36 Letter from Doris to Lord Beaverbrook, circa 1929. BBK_C_19, Parliamentary Archives.

37 Mosley, Leonard, *Castlerosse* (Arthur Baker, London 1956) p. 102.

38 £1,148 in today's money. Bank of England inflation calculator.

39 'Do come over and join us.' Letter from Doris to Lord Beaverbrook, circa Sept 1929. BBK_C_19, Parliamentary Archives.

40 Mosley, Leonard, *Castlerosse* (Arthur Baker, London 1956) p. 103.

41 £170 in today's money. Bank of England inflation calculator.

42   Letter from Lord Beaverbrook's secretary to Doris, 6 Sept 1929.
     BBK_C_19, Parliamentary Archives.
43   Approximately £31,492 in today's money. Bank of England inflation
     calculator.
44   Mosley, Leonard, *Castlerosse* (Arthur Baker, London 1956) p. 103.
45   £14,185 in today's money. Bank of England inflation calculator.
46   £25,704 in today's money. Bank of England inflation calculator.
47   £25,700 in today's money. Bank of England inflation calculator.
48   £624 in today's money. Bank of England inflation calculator.
49   £742,053 in today's money. Bank of England inflation calculator.
50   £28,371 in today's money. Bank of England inflation calculator.
51   Mosley, Leonard, *Castlerosse* (Arthur Baker, London 1956) p. 122.
52   Castlerosse liked to tell a story about the time he dined with Doris
     and Beaverbrook. The company was less jovial than usual because
     Max had a pimple on his leg and feared it might be syphilis.
     Doris had a pimple on her breast and thought it might be cancer.
     Beaverbrook, who was a hypochondriac, telephoned his doctor,
     Lord Horder, the most famous physician of the day. Castlerosse said:
     'When Horder came, this is what he saw: Doris was stroking Max's
     leg. Max was stroking Doris's breast. And the only person really ill
     was myself, who had clap.'
53   'His great flaw was his inability to treat his women with dignity,'
     said Beaverbrook's granddaughter, Lady Jeanne Campbell. 'Slowly
     he would turn on them and devastate them. He made them feel
     they had no right to exist.' Chisholm, Anne and Davie Michael,
     Beaverbrook: A Life (Hutchinson, London 1992) p. 500.
54   'The Weymouths realised that their secret had become an
     after-dinner joke among the Beaverbrook circle and that they
     had no choice but to laugh at it themselves; and they continued
     to accept his invitations.' Chisholm, Anne and Davie Michael,
     Beaverbrook: A Life (Hutchinson, London 1992) p. 316.
55   Letter from Doris to Lord Beaverbrook, 9 May 1930. BBK_C_19,
     Parliamentary Archives.
56   Castlerosse wrote in the Londoner's Log that Tom Jones wrote
     speeches for Stanley Baldwin. 'The publication of this paragraph
     made me furiously angry,' Lord Beaverbrook wrote in a letter to
     Winston Churchill, 29 August 1927. CHAR 2/153/34–35, The
     Churchill Papers, Churchill Archives Centre (Cambridge), Churchill
     Archive.

57 'In a battle of wits, Lady Castlerosse could hold her own with the most formidable opponents.' Thomson, George Malcolm, *Lord Castlerosse: His Life and Times* (Weidenfeld and Nicolson, London 1973) p. 106.

58 Thomson, George Malcolm, *Lord Castlerosse: His Life and Times* (Weidenfeld and Nicolson, London 1973) p. 106.

8. Old Habits

1 £704,950 in today's money. Bank of England inflation calculator.

2 Letter from Doris to Lord Beaverbrook, undated but had 11.30 at the top (referring to time it was written). Its place in the chronology of the letters suggests it was written at the beginning of the year. BBK_C_19, Parliamentary Archives.

3 Letter from Doris to Lord Beaverbrook, 23 April (year is not dated but the chronicle order of letters suggests it was circa 1930). BBK_C_19, Parliamentary Archives.

4 Wilkes, Roger, *Scandal: A Scurrilous History of Gossip 1700–2000* (Atlantic Books, London 2002) p. 157.

5 The earliest letter from their volume of correspondence. The Churchill Papers, Churchill Archives Centre (Cambridge), Churchill Archive.

6 Roberts, Brian, *Randolph: A Study of Churchill's Son* (Hamish Hamilton, London 1984) p. 98.

7 Approximately half a million pounds in today's money.

8 'The penetrating screams of Lord Randolph's last days may have contributed to his own rejection of casual sex.' Purnell, Sonia, *First Lady: The Life and Wars of Clementine Churchill* (Aurum Press, London 2015) p. 45.

9 Purnell, Sonia, *First Lady: The Life and Wars of Clementine Churchill* (Aurum Press, London 2015) p. 45.

10 Pearson, John, *The Private Lives of Winston Churchill* (Simon & Schuster, London 1991) p. 292.

11 'This type really depends on the institution of marriage being strict and divorce impossible or rare. Now people marry for a year or two and then pass to the next period of what is really licensed concubinage. Since the so-called upper classes are as corrupt as they can be, these ladies, like Harriet Wilson, are cut out by real

ladies … I think the old way was really the best.' Davenport-Hines, Richard, *An English Affair: Sex, Class and Power in the Age of Profumo* (HarperPress, London 2013) p. 10.

12   'Lunched with Dolly [Castlerosse] and Delly [Adele Astair]. Delly said I don't mind people going off and fucking but I do object to all this free love.' Letter from Nancy Mitford to Diana Guinness, 25 January 1933. Mosley, Charlotte (ed.), *The Mitfords: Letters Between Six Sisters* (Harper Perennial, London 2008) p. 28.

13   Young, Kennedy (ed.), *The Diaries of Sir Robert Lockhart Bruce: 1915–1938* (Macmillan, London 1973) p. 166.

14   *Mosley*, Leonard, Castlerosse (Arthur Baker, London 1956) p. 117.

15   *Reading Eagle*, 5 March 1950.

16   *Reading Eagle*, 5 March 1950.

17   Letter from Doris to Lord Beaverbrook, 29 July 1931. BBK_C_19, Parliamentary Archives.

18   Irene Curzon's diary. de Courcy, Anne, *The Viceroy's Daughters* (Weidenfeld and Nicolson, London 2001) p. 172.

19   'Sybil: But I'm very glad, because if she hadn't been uncontrolled, and wicked, and unfaithful, we shouldn't be here now.' Coward, Noel, *Private Lives* (1930) Act I.

20   Payn, Graham and Day, Barry, *My Life with Noel Coward* (Applause Theatre and Cinema Books, New Jersey 2000) p. 271.

21   Coward, Noel, *Private Lives* (1930) Act II.

22   Coward, Noel, *Private Lives* (1930) Act II.

23   Coward, Noel, *Private Lives* (1930) Act III.

24   Mosley, Leonard, *Castlerosse* (Arthur Baker, London 1956) p. 95.

25   Arlen, Michael, *The Green Hat* (Collins, London 1924) p. 23.

26   Wilson, John Howard, *Evelyn Waugh: 1924–1966* (Fairleigh Dickinson University Press, New Jersey, 2001) p. 92.

27   Wilson, John Howard, *Evelyn Waugh: 1924–1966* (Fairleigh Dickinson University Press, New Jersey, 2001) p. 92.

28   *The Canberra Times*, 25 June 1994.

29   Young, Kenneth (ed.), *The Diaries of Sir Robert Bruce Lockhart*: Vol. I 1915–1938 (Macmillan, London 1973) p. 177.

30   Pearson, John, *The Private Lives of Winston Churchill* (Simon & Schuster, London 1991) p. 292.

31   O'Connor, Anthony, *Clubland: The Wrong Side of the Right People* (Martin Brian & O'Keeffe, Dublin 1976) p. 30.

32 On 3 November 1914, Winston Churchill ordered the first British attack on the Dardanelles following the opening of hostilities between the Ottoman and Russian empires. The attack took place before a formal declaration of war had been made by Britain against the Ottoman Empire.

33 Mosley, Leonard, *Castlerosse* (Arthur Baker, London 1956) p. 109.

34 *Daily Express*, 12 July 1932.

35 '… Suddenly, their pleasant chatter was interrupted by a howl of pain. The Viscountess had sat on a wasp. The sting was not just painful, it was embarrassingly located on the lady's behind. But Chips was neither embarrassed nor unsure about what to do. With the charm and confidence of a man who has spent his life among the rich, he persuaded the lady to allow him to separate her from her garments, applied his mouth to the wound, and sucked away the poison.' The Secret World of Chips Channon, *The Independent*, 13 April 2007.

36 Mosley, Leonard, *Castlerosse* (Arthur Baker, London 1956) p. 113.

37 Divorce Court File: 4678. Appellant: Valentine Edward Charles Browne, Viscount Castlerosse. Respondent: Jessica Doris Browne, Viscountess Castlerosse. Co-respondent: Sir Alfred Lane Beit, baronet. Type: Husband's petition for divorce. J 77/3073/4678, The National Archives, Kew.

38 Mosley, Leonard, *Castlerosse* (Arthur Baker, London 1956) p. 112.

39 Mosley, Leonard, *Castlerosse* (Arthur Baker, London 1956) p. 114.

40 Mosley, Leonard, *Castlerosse* (Arthur Baker, London 1956) p. 114.

41 Mosley, Leonard, *Castlerosse* (Arthur Baker, London 1956) p. 114.

42 In 1906, Felicia had been kidnapped by her father, Count Joseph Gizycki. He snatched Felicia from her pram, fled to Russia with her and was said to have placed her in a convent. A fortune hunter, he demanded a ransom from his estranged wife in exchange for returning the child. Eventually, Tsar Nicholas II intervened and ordered the count to return Felicia to her mother in America.

9. Beaten by Beaton

1 Zinovieff, Sofka, *The Mad Boy, Lord Berners, My Grandmother and Me* (Jonathan Cape, London 2014) p. 109.

2 Zinovieff, Sofka, *The Mad Boy, Lord Berners, My Grandmother and Me* (Jonathan Cape, London 2014) p. 109.

3   Written in forty-eight hours at Gerald's Roman villa while Diana Guinness was staying. It was published in 1932.

4   Berners, Gerald, *The Girls of Radcliff Hall* (privately printed, London 1932).

5   Zinovieff, Sofka, *The Mad Boy, Lord Berners, My Grandmother and Me* (Jonathan Cape, London 2014) p. 107.

6   Vickers, Hugo, *Cecil Beaton: The Authorized Biography* (Weidenfeld and Nicolson, London 1993) p. 162.

7   'Doris instructed him in the arts of love-making. In bed, if he performed too precipitately, she would slow him down by saying: 'Think of your sister's wedding.' Vickers, Hugo, *Cecil Beaton: The Authorized Biography* (Weidenfeld and Nicolson, London 1993) p. 162.

8   Vickers, Hugo, *Cecil Beaton: The Authorized Biography* (Weidenfeld and Nicolson, London 1993) p. 162.

9   Letter from Doris to Cecil Beaton. A1/114, Papers of Sir Cecil Beaton, St John's College Library.

10 Edith Olivier's diary, 21 July 1933. Thomasson, Anna, *A Curious Friendship* (Macmillan, London 2015) p. 265.

11 Edith Olivier's diary, 21 July 1933. Thomasson, Anna, *A Curious Friendship* (Macmillan, London 2015) p. 265.

12 Edith Olivier's diary, 21 July 1933. Thomasson, Anna, *A Curious Friendship* (Macmillan, London 2015) p. 265.

13 'For her part, the viscountess … insists that she has the power to convert poor Cecil from a homosexualist to a much healthier heterosexualist, if only he would give her the chance. I take this to mean that [she] is on a crusade to rescue these men, which is a noble thing.' Boyd, D.K.R., *The Reflecting Man: Volume Two* (Wonderdog Press, 2015) p. 263.

14 Vickers, Hugo, *Cecil Beaton: The Authorized Biography* (Weidenfeld and Nicolson, London 1993) p. 163.

15 Vickers, Hugo, *Cecil Beaton: The Authorized Biography* (Weidenfeld and Nicolson, London 1993) p. 163.

16 Zinovieff, Sofka, *The Mad Boy, Lord Berners, My Grandmother and Me* (Jonathan Cape, London 2014) p. 111.

17 'I could not understand how mummy could bear having her around, she was like a sinister black crow.' Cavendish O'Neill, Pat, *A Lion in the Bedroom* (Jonathan Ball Publishers, Cape Town 2004) p. 160.

18   Cavendish O'Neill, Pat, *A Lion in the Bedroom* (Jonathan Ball Publishers, Cape Town 2004) p. 160.

19   The *Sunday Express* ran a competition in which they asked their readers to fit the following into their appropriate categories: A Mouse is 21 stone; The Queen Mary is three pounds; A Football is three ounces; Viscount Castlerosse is 67,000 tons.

20   Bunbury, Turtle, *The Glorious Madness: Tales of the Irish and the Great War First-hand* (Gill & Macmillan, Dublin 2014). The story also goes that Lady Astor patted Castlerosse's stomach and remarked, 'If that was on a woman we should know what to think,' to which Castlerosse replied, 'Well, it was last night, so what do you think?' Mosley, Oswald, *My Life* (Black House Publishing, London 1968) p. 81.

21   Young, Kennedy (ed.), *The Diaries of Sir Robert Bruce Lockhart: 1915–1938* (Macmillan, London 1973) p. 249.

22   5 September 1933. Mosley, Leonard, *Castlerosse* (Arthur Baker, London 1956) p. 115.

23   Mosley, Leonard, *Castlerosse* (Arthur Baker, London 1956) p. 117.

24   Vickers, Hugo, *Cecil Beaton: The Authorized Biography* (Weidenfeld and Nicolson, London 1993) p. 166.

25   Vickers, Hugo, *Cecil Beaton: The Authorized Biography* (Weidenfeld and Nicolson, London 1993) p. 167.

26   '… in fact everybody that you know will band together and somehow stop it. How, I don't attempt to say.' Letter from Nancy Mitford to Diana Guinness, 29 November 1932. Mosley, Charlotte (ed.), *The Mitfords: Letters Between Six Sisters* (Harper Perennial, London 2008) p. 26.

27   Spicer, Paul, *The Temptress: The Scandalous Life of Alice, Countess de Janzé* (Simon & Schuster, London 2011) p. 46.

28   Barbara Cartland saw Phyllis dancing at the Embassy Club in London in the early 1920s and noted her 'mysterious, haunting beauty, her high cheekbones and pale aquamarine eyes, as well as her violent temper'. Spicer, Paul, *The Temptress: The Scandalous Life of Alice, Countess de Janzé* (Simon & Schuster, London 2011) p. 46.

29   Letter from Doris to Cecil Beaton. A1/114, Papers of Sir Cecil Beaton, St John's College Library.

30   Peter Watson wrote that Diana was 'nearly off her head … poor Diana'. Clark, Adrian and Dronfield, Jeremy, *Queer Saint: The Cultured Life of Peter Watson* (John Blake Publishing, London 2015) p. 73.

31 Letter from Doris to Cecil Beaton. A1/114, Papers of Sir Cecil
    Beaton, St John's College Library.

32 Vickers, Hugo, *Cecil Beaton: The Authorized Biography* (Weidenfeld
    and Nicolson, London 1993) p. 167.

33 Letter from Doris to Cecil Beaton. A1/114, Papers of Sir Cecil
    Beaton, St John's College Library.

34 Vickers, Hugo, *Cecil Beaton: The Authorized Biography* (Weidenfeld
    and Nicolson, London 1993) p. 168.

10. A Tangled Web

1   Letter from Doris to Lord Beaverbrook, 13 Sept 1935. BBK_C_19,
    Parliamentary Archives.

2   Letter from Doris to Lord Beaverbrook, 13 Sept 1935. BBK_C_19,
    Parliamentary Archives.

3   Telegram from Lord Beaverbrook to Doris, 17 Sept 1935.
    BBK_C_19, Parliamentary Archives.

4   Mosley, Leonard, *Castlerosse* (Arthur Baker, London 1956) p. 142.

5   *Central Otage Gazette*, 22 October 1930.

6   'I remember the interview for the job. He was at his suite in
    Claridges wearing a stripy dressing gown which was billowing over
    his enormous belly and he looked like an enormous tent.' Marjorie
    Cowell, *Sunday Express*, 29 May 2011.

7   Mosley, Leonard, *Castlerosse* (Arthur Baker, London 1956) p. 142. In
    Castlerosse by Leonard Mosley the original quote has the secretary
    called Miss B. I changed it to Miss C. for accuracy reasons.

8   Mosley, Leonard, *Castlerosse* (Arthur Baker, London 1956) p. 143.

9   … The Bishop was horrified. 'Do you realise what you are saying,
    my son?' he asked. 'You are suggesting we should turn this lovely,
    lonely place into a bedlam of English people, all equipped with
    smelly motor-bikes and there will be airplanes overhead and girls in
    bathing costumes.' 'My dear Bishop,' said Castlerosse, 'you talk as if
    golf were a cannibalistic orgy.' Mosley, Leonard, *Castlerosse* (Arthur
    Baker, London 1956) p. 138.

10 'My mother,' Castlerosse used to say, 'is always criticising me because
    I have some odd friends. What she doesn't understand is that I lack
    money; these people have money, or have influence with people
    with money. I need money for Killarney, so whether they can

speak the King's English I care not a fig.' Castlerosse said in
response to Lady Kenmare's disapproval towards his show business
friends. Mosley, Leonard, *Castlerosse* (Arthur Baker, London 1956)
p. 141.

11   Mosley, Leonard, *Castlerosse* (Arthur Baker, London 1956) p. 119.

12   'You bloody idiot,' Castlerosse said. 'I'm employing a fucking blind
man.' Cavendish O'Neill, Pat, *A Lion in the Bedroom* (Jonathan Ball,
Cape Town 2004) p. 151.

13   *The World's News*, 11 July 1934.

14   As stated in the divorce petition filed on 3 November 1936. The
date given was 24–26 February 1936. Divorce Court File: 4678.
Appellant: Valentine Edward Charles Browne, Viscount Castlerosse.
Respondent: Jessica Doris Browne, Viscountess Castlerosse.
Co-respondent: Sir Alfred Lane Beit, bart. Type: Husband's petition
for divorce. J 77/3073/4678, The National Archives, Kew.

15   Zinovieff, Sofka, *The Mad Boy, Lord Berners, My Grandmother and Me*
(Jonathan Cape, London 2014) p. 109.

16   As stated in the divorce petition filed on 3 November 1936. Divorce
Court File: 4678. Appellant: Valentine Edward Charles Browne,
Viscount Castlerosse. Respondent: Jessica Doris Browne, Viscountess
Castlerosse. Co-respondent: Sir Alfred Lane Beit, baronet. Type:
Husband's petition for divorce. J 77/3073/4678, The National
Archives, Kew.

17   Mad Boy told this to Hugo Vickers. Zinovieff, Sofka, *The Mad Boy,
Lord Berners, My Grandmother and Me* (Jonathan Cape, London 2014)
p. 110.

18   Divorce Court File: 4678. Appellant: Valentine Edward Charles
Browne, Viscount Castlerosse. Respondent: Jessica Doris Browne,
Viscountess Castlerosse. Co-respondent: Sir Alfred Lane Beit, baronet.
Type: Husband's petition for divorce. J 77/3073/4678, The National
Archives, Kew.

19   Divorce Court File: 4678. Appellant: Valentine Edward Charles
Browne, Viscount Castlerosse. Respondent: Jessica Doris Browne,
Viscountess Castlerosse. Co-respondent: Sir Alfred Lane Beit, baronet.
Type: Husband's petition for divorce. J 77/3073/4678, The National
Archives, Kew.

20   Divorce Court File: 4678. Appellant: Valentine Edward Charles
Browne, Viscount Castlerosse. Respondent: Jessica Doris Browne,
Viscountess Castlerosse. Co-respondent: Sir Alfred Lane Beit, baronet.

Type: Husband's petition for divorce. J 77/3073/4678, The National Archives, Kew.

21 *The Singapore Free Press and Mercantile Advertiser*, 27 March 1936.

22 Bullock, John, *The Rootes Brothers: Story of a Motoring Empire* (Patrick Stephens, London 1993) p. 82.

23 Bullock, John, *The Rootes Brothers: Story of a Motoring Empire* (Patrick Stephens, London 1993) p. 83.

24 Nicolson, Harold, *Diaries and Letters Vol. 1 (1930–1939)* (Faber and Faber, London 2009) p. 87.

25 Letter from Doris to Winston Churchill. [undated] CHAR 1/299/77, The Churchill Papers (CHAR 2/153/34–35), Churchill Archives Centre (Cambridge), Churchill Archive.

26 Letter from Doris to Winston Churchill. [undated] CHAR 1/299/77, The Churchill Papers, Churchill Archives Centre (Cambridge), Churchill Archive.

27 *The Evening Independent*, 19 May 1934. 'If the men think they have a copyright on the oddly mixed costumes for sport wear, they'll get a surprise in this picture. With the poise of a princess, Miss Margot L. Flick, New York society girl in Palm Beach, steps out for a stroll in light trousers and smartly cut checkered coat.'

28 *St Petersburg Times*, 18 May 1935.

29 *Gettysburg Times*, 18 May 1935.

30 'How would a household run unless there is freedom of conversation between the members of the family as to the servants?' Justice Philip McCook asked the jury as he dismissed the suit. *Gettysburg Times*, 18 May 1935.

31 *Pittsburgh Post Gazette*, 17 May 1935.

32 '… he said he could not get me in, I also asked him about Ascot and he said he could not get me in and would not be bothered to either.' Letter from Doris to Lord Beaverbrook [undated]. BBK_C_19, Parliamentary Archives.

33 Convicted criminals and undischarged bankrupts were barred from the Royal Enclosure. Divorcees have been allowed in since 1955. Source: Debrett's.

34 Letter from Doris to Lord Beaverbrook [undated]. BBK_C_19, Parliamentary Archives.

35 Letter from Doris to Lord Beaverbrook [undated]. BBK_C_19, Parliamentary Archives.

36 Hoare, Philip, *Noel Coward* (Sinclair-Stevenson, London 1995) p. 289.

37 Lesley, Cole, *Remembered Laughter: The Life of Noel Coward* (Knopf, New York 1976) p. 194.

38 Fox, James, *White Mischief* (Vintage, London 1998) p. 60.

39 'Before anything else, Enid was a mother. Most of the things she did, marrying all those men, were for the children more than herself.' Related by Yves Vidal to Dominick Dunne for his book, *Fatal Charms and Other Tales of Today / The Mansions of Limbo* (Crown, New York 1987) p. 316.

40 Mosley, Leonard, *Castlerosse* (Arthur Baker, London 1956) p. 184.

41 'I always thought Enid had a lot of courage to marry Lord Furness.' Batsell Herter, Solange, *No More Tiaras: A Memoir of Eight Decades* (Xlibris, Indiana 2011) p. 224.

42 '... Lord Castlerosse has posed for this portrait of the year in a lavender and chocolate suiting whose cut will send the art critic of the *Tailor and Cutter* into anguished fits.' Mosley, Leonard, *Castlerosse* (Arthur Baker, London 1956) p. 125.

43 *Evening Post*, 30 May 1935.

44 *Table Talk*, 23 May 1935.

45 '... Now Margot and Doris will have something in common. For I'm given to understand that Dick Hoffman and [Margot] have decided their union was a mistake.' Cholly Chats of Mayfair Divorces, Cholly Knickerbocker. *Syracuse NY Journal*, 30 December 1936.

46 'Dorus [*sic*] Castlerosse is arriving tomorrow.' 15 November 1936. William Cross Collection, Newport/Tilly Losch.

47 *St Petersburg Times*, 15 December 1936.

48 Mosley, Leonard, *Castlerosse* (Arthur Baker, London 1956) p. 146.

49 Cholly Knickerbocker's column, *Syracuse NY Journal*, 20 December 1936.

50 '... Now, as regards to the Castlerosse and Hoffman Pictures. I cannot imagine what could have happened to them ... I have been to the Post Office where I posted them and filled in a claim and enquiry form.' Letter from Dorothy Joseph to Cecil Beaton, 10 December 1936. GBR/0275, Papers of Sir Cecil Beaton, St John's College Library.

51 *Daily Express*, 1936.

52 *The Southwestern Missourian*, 15 December 1936.

53 Letter from Doris to Winston Churchill circa September 1936. CHAR 1/285/178, The Churchill Papers, Churchill Archives Centre (Cambridge), Churchill Archive.

54 Telegram sent by Winston Churchill to Doris, 20 September 1936. CHAR 1/285/177, The Churchill Papers, Churchill Archives Centre (Cambridge), Churchill Archive.

55 Writ issued to Robert Heber Percy (Mad Boy), 10 August 1937. Browne versus Browne divorce petition. Divorce Court File: 4678. Appellant: Valentine Edward Charles Browne, Viscount Castlerosse. Respondent: Jessica Doris Browne, Viscountess Castlerosse. Co-respondent: Sir Alfred Lane Beit, baronet. Type: Husband's petition for divorce. J 77/3073/4678, The National Archives, Kew.

56 'Unless sufficient cause be shown to the Court why the said Decree should not be made absolute, within six months from the making thereof and no such cause having been shown, the Court on application of the said Petition by final decree pronounced and declared the said Marriage to be dissolved. Certificate of Decree *Nisi*. 17 December 1937. Divorce Court File: 4678. Appellant: Valentine Edward Charles Browne, Viscount Castlerosse. Respondent: Jessica Doris Browne, Viscountess Castlerosse. Co-respondent: Sir Alfred Lane Beit, baronet. Type: Husband's petition for divorce. J 77/3073/4678, The National Archives, Kew.

57 Miss Cowell (referred to as Miss Brown in Leonard Mosley's book) recalled: 'I remember he was wearing a dressing gown of chocolate and red stripes, and it made him look like an enormous Mephistopheles. After he had read the letter, he turned upon me and practically began to spit with rage. He said Lord Beaverbrook had discovered that he had been going to the boys, and who could have told him but me. I had betrayed his trust. I was a traitress. I would betray my own mother. It was terrible the way he went on.' Miss Brown went to her room and packed her bag. She slipped out of the house and prepared to walk to the nearest station, but was only halfway down the driveway when Castlerosse burst out the house and dragged her back. She was crying and he sat her on his knee and dried her tears with his handkerchief. 'My poor Miss B,' he said. 'How could I have thought you could possibly betray me? I'm a miserable scoundrel, treating you like this. That's the sort of chap I am, filthy to his friends.' Mosley, Leonard, *Castlerosse* (Arthur Baker, London 1956).

58 Mosley, Leonard, *Castlerosse* (Arthur Baker, London 1956) p. 148.

11. Playing to the Gallery

1 'I always knew he liked me best,' Diana was reported to have said. Daley, Jan, *Diana Mosley: A Life* (Faber and Faber, London 1999) p. 204.

2 *The Daily Worker* 13 April 1932.

3 Irene Curzon had written in her diary. Dalley, Jan, *Diana Mosley: A Life* (Faber and Faber, London 1999) p. 134.

4 Dalley, Jan, *Diana Mosley: A Life* (Faber and Faber, London 1999) p. 134.

5 Mosley, Leonard, *Castlerosse* (Arthur Baker, London 1956) p. 152.

6 Mosley, Leonard, *Castlerosse* (Arthur Baker, London 1956) p. 81.

7 Mosley, Leonard, *Castlerosse* (Arthur Baker, London 1956) p. 153.

8 This behaviour was typical of Castlerosse. Seven years after an acquaintance had spoken badly of Doris, Castlerosse challenged him to a duel. 'The honour of the family is at stake,' Gerald told Castlerosse. 'You must challenge the man to a duel.' The two men consulted library books on the subject and were discouraged to learn it was illegal. However, they were momentarily cheered when they discovered it was legal in Nazi Germany. Needless to say the recipient of such an invitation refused to take it seriously and the duel never commenced.

9 Mosley, Leonard, *Castlerosse* (Arthur Baker, London 1956) p. 155.

10 Gourlay, Logan (ed.), *The Beaverbrook I Knew* (Quarter, London 1984) p. 25.

11 'Please wire me if Castlerosse is going to Cannes with you if so shall not go to Maxine's.' Telegram from Doris to Lord Beaverbrook, Grand Hotel Venice, circa 1935. BBK_C_19, Parliamentary Archives.

12 The monkey would not eat his strawberries unless they were sprinkled with sugar.

13 A detective had barged in on a disgraced socialite and found her wearing nothing but her husband's self-winding watch. 'I had to wear it to keep it wound,' she said.

14 It was said that two versions of the painting were made, one was painted at the poolside, and later a larger version was made. 'It was a provocative pose that courted controversy,' observed Rory Guthrie of de Veres, where the painting was sold in 2014. The larger version was sold at Sotheby's in 1997. *The Irish Times*, 20 September 2014.

15   The location of the painting has also been listed as Palm Beach, Florida. The exhibition was called Winter in Florida. Mosley, Leonard, *Castlerosse* (Arthur Baker, London 1956) p. 160.

16   Letter from Doris to Winston Churchill, circa 1938. CHAR 1/299/77, The Churchill Papers, Churchill Archives Centre (Cambridge), Churchill Archive.

17   Purchased in 1948 by the American heiress and art collector, Peggy Guggenheim. Today it is the home of the Guggenheim collection.

18   A rumour, originated in the eighteenth century, maintained that construction was halted by the Corner family across the canal, who did not want their sunlight to be blocked by a palazzo bigger than theirs. Owing to its one storey it is often called the Palazzo Nonfinito.

19   The Marchesa brought a boa constrictor to Faringdon, and Gerald Berners's mother, Mrs Tyrwhitt, asked if it would like something to eat. 'No, it had a goat this morning,' said the Marchesa. 'It does seem rather inhospitable,' bemoaned Mrs Tyrwhitt. Dickinson, Peter, *Lord Berners: Composer, Writer, Painter* (Boydell Press, Suffolk 2008) p. 82.

20   'Doris's palazzo is evoked in one of Cole Porter's satirical café society ditties.' Richardson, John, *Sacred Monsters, Sacred Masters: Beaton, Capote, Dali, Picasso, Freud, Warhol, and More* (Random House, New York 2001) p. 163.

21   'Why did Britain want the old Emperor of Abyssinia represented at the coronation?' Letter from Doris to Winston Churchill, February 1938. CHAR 1/298/49/51, The Churchill Papers, Churchill Archives Centre (Cambridge), Churchill Archive.

22   Letter from Doris to Winston Churchill, February 1938. CHAR 1/298/49/51, The Churchill Papers, Churchill Archives Centre (Cambridge), Churchill Archive.

23   Letter from Doris to Winston Churchill, February 1938. CHAR 1/298/49/51, The Churchill Papers, Churchill Archives Centre (Cambridge), Churchill Archive.

24   Letter from Doris to Winston Churchill, February 1938. CHAR 1/298/49/51, The Churchill Papers, Churchill Archives Centre (Cambridge), Churchill Archive.

12. Doris Dreams of Stardom

1 *Auckland Star*, 28 August 1937.
2 George Cukor had directed Greta Garbo in *Camille*, released in 1936, and was not to direct her again until *Two-Faced Woman* in 1941. Therefore Doris's talk of appearing in a Garbo picture appeared to be nothing more than an idle fantasy. As for Cukor's offer for Doris to appear in his next picture, circa 1937–38, those pictures would have been *Holiday* (1938) and *Zsa Zsa* (1938). She did not appear in either, nor does any evidence exist to suggest she had been considered for a part.
3 *Auckland Star*, 28 August 1937.
4 As was the address given on her divorce petition from Castlerosse in 1937.
5 David O. Selznick and George Cukor could not agree on a principal cast, so various scenes such as the burning of Atlanta were shot with stand-ins.
6 In Margaret Mitchell's *Gone with the Wind* (Macmillan, New York 1936), Mammy asks Scarlett: 'Does you know a dyed-ha'rd woman?' p. 773.
7 Doris mentions her visit with Sir Shenton Thomas in a letter to Winston Churchill. She asked Churchill if he knew the former governor. Circa December 1937. CHAR 1/298/49_51. The Sir Winston Churchill Archive Trust.
8 Angela's father, Hamar Greenwood, served in Lloyd George's Cabinet as chief secretary for Ireland from 1920 to 1922 and was involved with the Republican fight for independence. Owing to this, Greenwood hired policemen to chaperone his family. The attempt to kidnap Angela from Harrods was thwarted when her detective knocked the assailant to the floor.
9 According to Peter Watson. Clark, Adrian and Dronfield, Jeremy, *Queer Saint: The Cultured Life of Peter Watson* (John Blake, London 2015) p. 126.
10 Clark, Adrian and Dronfield, Jeremy, *Queer Saint: The Cultured Life of Peter Watson* (John Blake, London 2015) p. 126.
11 Half a year's rent in London or Paris.
12 Clark, Adrian and Dronfield, Jeremy, *Queer Saint: The Cultured Life of Peter Watson* (John Blake, London 2015) p. 126.

13   In 1927 the 'quota quickie' was introduced by the Cinematography
      Films Act in a bid to stimulate the declining British film industry.
      It introduced a requirement for British cinemas to show a quota of
      British films, for a duration of ten years.

14   'The story of *Diamond Cut Diamond* was suggested by Viscountess
      Castlerosse ...' *The Advertiser*, 26 August 1933.

15   The memoir included amusing tales such as the time Castlerosse
      went to the Four Arts Ball in Paris, dressed in animal skins. When
      he returned to his hotel, he encountered a maiden lady who
      remarked, 'My God.' 'Yes, madam,' Castlerosse replied, 'but strictly
      incognito.' He also wrote of a visit to a country hotel in Eire, where
      he discovered that his boots, which he had left outside his door,
      had not been cleaned. 'Tell me,' he said to the servant, 'why do you
      think I put my boots outside my door?' 'I couldn't say, sir,' replied
      the servant. 'Unless, God forgive me, your honour was drunk.'
      Castlerosse, Lord, *Valentine's Days* (Methuen, London 1934).

16   '... It was a humiliating experience. I had no idea how bad a writer
      I was till I saw a conglomeration of my own writing in book form
      ... As I read on I came to the conclusion that it might have been
      called *Valentine's Mornings After.*' *The Sunday Times*, 3 June 1934.

17   *Daily Express*, circa 1932.

18   '... a party of diversified personalities barged in, headed by Lady
      Castlerosse and including Margot Flick Hoffman, Enzo Fiermonte
      and Cecil Beaton.' *St Petersburg Times*, 19 October 1937.

19   'I'll only run into tempting friends if I go to any of the usual
      places.' Mosley, Leonard, *Castlerosse* (Arthur Baker, London 1956)
      p. 161.

20   *Action*, 23 April 1936.

21   Mosley, Leonard, *Castlerosse* (Arthur Baker, London 1956) p. 162.

22   Lewis, Alfred Allan, *Ladies and Not So Gentlewomen* (Penguin, London
      1995) p. 464.

23   Doris later bequeathed the Palazzo Venier dei Leonie to Dudley's
      children, who sold it to Peggy Guggenheim in 1949.

24   Whistler, Laurence, *The Laughter and the Urn: The Life of Rex Whistler*
      (Weidenfeld & Nicolson, London 1985) p. 221.

13. A Last Resort

1   Thomson, George Malcolm, *Lord Castlerosse* (Weidenfeld and Nicolson, London 1973) p. 159.
2   'Love is one thing, marriage is another. He should have known.' Thomson, George Malcolm, *Lord Castlerosse* (Weidenfeld and Nicolson, London 1973) p. 100.
3   'A nurse complained that one whose liver, heart and breathing were gravely impaired and who had a high temperature ought not to stand naked in front of an open window practising his golf swings.' Thomson, George Malcolm, *Lord Castlerosse: His Life and Times* (Weidenfeld and Nicolson, London 1973) p. 146.
4   Thomson, George Malcolm, *Lord Castlerosse: His Life and Times* (Weidenfeld and Nicolson, London 1973) p. 148.
5   Thomson, George Malcolm, *Lord Castlerosse: His Life and Times* (Weidenfeld and Nicolson, London 1973) p. 148.
6   Mosley, Leonard, *Castlerosse* (Arthur Baker, London 1956) p. 163.
7   de Courcy, Anne, *The Last Season* (Weidenfeld and Nicolson, London 2003) p. 15.
8   Letter from Doris to Winston Churchill, 28 December 1939. CHAR 1/272/114–115. The Sir Winston Churchill Archive Trust.
9   Letter from Doris to Winston Churchill, 28 December 1939. CHAR 1/272/114–115. The Sir Winston Churchill Archive Trust.
10 Mosley, Leonard, *Castlerosse* (Arthur Baker, London 1956) p. 177.
11 'Thought you were another ship; please go on, go on!' the Germans said. Taken from an account by the SS *Washington*'s captain Harry Manning. http://www.usmm.org/washington.html.
12 The trial was one of the most sensational of the 1940s. Wayne Lonergan, a corrupt playboy from humble beginnings, apparently murdered his wife by strangling her and hitting her over the head with a candelabra for motives relating to her $7 million inheritance. Although Lonergan escaped the electric chair, he was sentenced to life in prison and would go on to serve thirty-seven years behind bars.
13 'He was well known to be rich in friends, some of whom bestowed their riches on him. When Billy McCarty-Cooper knew he was dying he settled an annuity of $50,000 a year on John for the rest of his life.' *New York Social Diary*.

14. Out of Luck

1 James Douglas, editor of the *Sunday Express* newspaper, began a campaign to suppress the book with poster and billboard advertising. Publisher Jonathan Cape panicked and sent a copy of *The Well of Loneliness* to the Home Secretary, William Joynson-Hicks (a Conservative), for his opinion; he took only two days to reply that *The Well of Loneliness* was 'gravely detrimental to the public interest' and if Cape did not withdraw it voluntarily, criminal proceedings would be brought against him. Cape suppressed the book after only two editions.

2 Richardson, John, *Sacred Monsters, Sacred Masters: Beaton, Capote, Dali, Picasso, Freud, Warhol, and More* (Random House, New York 2001) p. 163.

3 As mentioned in the *New York Times*, 27 June 1941.

4 Doris was keeping a low profile during this period and her social life was pitiful in comparison to the past. I have used the *New York Times* as a guide to her whereabouts in 1941.

5 Dunne, Dominick, *Fatal Charms and Other Tales of Today / The Mansions of Limbo* (Crown, New York 1987) p. 352.

6 Randolph Churchill saw her in New York around this period and commented that 'she seemed less confident than he had ever known her'. Mosley, Leonard, *Castlerosse* (Arthur Baker, London 1956) p. 181.

7 'Exactly what that cable said no one knows, but it certainly reached her at a dismal moment in her career as an international beauty.' Mosley, Leonard, *Castlerosse* (Arthur Baker, London 1956) p. 181.

8 As reported by Walter Winchell in his column for the *Syracuse Herald Journal*.

9 'Owing to my bad health I cannot sleep in New York.' A letter from Doris to Winston Churchill, 23 June 1942. The letter is in the Harry Hopkins archive at FDRL, box 136 'Churchill and family'.

10 'I am very very desperate.' Doris wrote in a letter to Lord Beaverbrook, March 1942. BBK_D_518, Parliamentary Archives.

11 A letter from Doris to Lord Beaverbrook, March 1942. BBK_D_518, Parliamentary Archives.

12 Thomson, George Malcolm, *Castlerosse: His Life and Times* (Weidenfeld and Nicolson, London 1973) p. 160.

13   The letter, dated 23 June 1942, is in the Harry Hopkins archive at FDRL, box 136 'Churchill and family'.

14   The letter, dated 23 June 1942, is in the Harry Hopkins archive at FDRL, box 136 'Churchill and family'.

15   Enid attended the wedding of Grace Kelly and Prince Rainier, and as she left the church she was cheered by crowds who mistook her for a visiting monarch. Dunne, Dominick, *Justice: Crime, Trials and Punishment* (Broadway Books, New York 2002) p. 316.

16   Dunne, Dominick, *Fatal Charms and Other Tales of Today/The Mansions of Limbo* (Crown, New York 1987) p. 305.

17   He told her when he was 40 and, although it came as a surprise, she took the news well and supported him.

18   Dunne, Dominick, *Fatal Charms and Other Tales of Today/The Mansions of Limbo* (Crown, New York 1987) p. 316.

15. The Jig is Up

1   He was known to exert his power to make exceptions towards those he knew. Although his cousin Diana Mosley was imprisoned under his own wartime enforcement, Regulation 18B, he ordered Holloway prison to ensure she got a bath every day.

2   Cavendish O'Neill, Pat, *A Lion in the Bedroom* (Jonathan Ball, Cape Town 2004) p. 122.

3   'She sat on my father's right, saying scarcely a word, but inspiring him to talk more freely than usual, with her almost bare bosom, held up by a red velvet dress, and her Carrara marble face poised motionless above the mirror, as if she was sitting for a portrait of herself at the Court of Versailles, or in Regency Brighton.' Murphy, Richard, *The Kick: A Life Among Writers* (Granta Books, London 2003) p. 110.

4   Cavendish O'Neill, Pat, *A Lion in the Bedroom* (Jonathan Ball, Cape Town 2004) p. 150.

5   Mosley, Leonard, *Castlerosse* (Arthur Baker, London 1956) p. 183.

6   Malcolm Thomson, George, *Lord Castlerosse: His Life and Times* (Weidenfeld and Nicolson, London 1973) p. 98.

Afterword

1   Thomson, George Malcolm, *Lord Castlerosse: His Life and Times* (Weidenfeld and Nicolson, London 1973) p. 167.
2   Letter from Enid Kenmare to Lord Beaverbrook, October 1943. BBK_C_19, Parliamentary Archives.
3   Davenport-Hines, Richard, *Ettie: The Intimate Life and Dauntless Spirit of Lady Desborough* (Weidenfeld and Nicolson, London 2008) p. 350.
4   O'Neill Cavendish, Pat, *A Lion in the Bedroom* (Jonathan Ball, Cape Town 2004) p. 159.
5   O'Neill Cavendish, Pat, *A Lion in the Bedroom* (Jonathan Ball, Cape Town 2004) p. 159.
6   Mosley, Leonard, *Castlerosse* (Arthur Baker, London 1956) p. 167.
7   Dunne, Dominick, *Fatal Charms and Other Tales of Today / The Mansions of Limbo* (Crown, New York 1987) p. 310.
8   Thomson, George Malcolm, *Lord Castlerosse: His Life and Times* (Weidenfeld and Nicolson, London 1973) p. 167.

SELECT BIBLIOGRAPHY

Aitken Kidd, Janet, *The Beaverbrook Girl*, Collins, 1987.

Arlen, Michael, *The Green Hat*, Collins, 1924.

Cavendish O'Neill, Pat, *A Lion in the Bedroom*, Jonathan Ball, 2004.

Chisholm, Anne, and Michael Davie, *Beaverbrook: A Life*, Hutchinson, 1992.

Clark, Adrian, and Jeremy Dronfield, *Queer Saint: The Cultured Life of Peter Watson*, John Blake, 2015.

Davenport-Hines, Richard, *Ettie: The Intimate Life and Dauntless Spirit of Lady Desborough*, Hachette, 2012.

de Courcy, Anne, *The Viceroy's Daughters*, Weidenfeld and Nicolson, 2001.

Dunne, Dominick, *Fatal Charms and Other Tales of Today / The Mansions of Limbo*, Crown, 1987.

Dunne, Dominick, *Justice: Crime, Trials and Punishment*, Broadway Books, 2002.

Fielding, Daphne, *The Duchess of Jermyn Street*, Penguin, 1978.

Morgan, Janet, *Edwina Mountbatten: A Life of Her Own*, HarperCollins, 1991.

Morley, Sheridan, *Gertrude Lawrence*, Weidenfeld and Nicolson, 1981.

Mosley, Charlotte, ed., *Love from Nancy: The Letters of Nancy Mitford*, Hodder and Stoughton, 1993.

Mosley, Leonard, *Castlerosse*, Arthur Baker, 1956.

Nichols, Beverley, *A Case of Human Bondage*, Secker and Warburg, 1966.

Osborne, Frances, *The Bolter*, Virago, 2008.

Pugh, Martin, *We Danced All Night: A Social History of Britain Between the Wars*, Vintage, 2009.

Soames, Mary, *Speaking for Themselves: The Personal Letters of Winston and Clementine Churchill*, Doubleday, 1998.

Thomson, George Malcolm, *Lord Castlerosse: His Life and Times*, Weidenfeld and Nicolson, 1973.

Vickers, Hugo, *Cecil Beaton: The Authorized Biography*, Weidenfeld and Nicolson New Ed., 2002.

Young, Kenneth, *The Diaries of Sir Robert Bruce Lockhart: Vol. I, 1915–38*, Macmillan, 1973.

Zinovieff, Sofka, *The Mad Boy, Lord Berners, My Grandmother and Me*, Jonathan Cape, 2014.

ᑫNDEX

Abyssinia 145
    Abyssinian Crisis 146, 149
adultery 38, 75, 79, 92, 103, 105,
    124–6, 130–1, 134–5, 144
Aitken, Max 156
alcohol 16, 35–7, 59, 168
America 18, 20–1, 24, 29, 31, 37–40,
    42–3, 45, 50–1, 58–9, 86, 92,
    98, 101, 104, 117–20, 128, 132,
    135, 140–2, 145–6, 149–50,
    152, 158–64, 166–7, 169–71,
    173–5, 177–8
Amsterdam 39, 87
aristocracy 10, 12, 19–20, 36–7,
    39, 42, 45, 50–2, 54–5, 58, 64,
    79–80, 86, 97–8, 108, 113,
    117–18, 142, 150, 153, 169,
    177
Arlen, Michael 10, 19, 74, 94, 97
Ascot 128–9, 144

Ashcombe 110, 119
Ashley, Sylvia 94, 129, 146–7, 162
Astley, MC, Captain Philip 17, 19,
    21, 40
Astor, Nancy 114, 161

Baden Baden 86–7, 121, 152
Balfour Place 69, 78
Bank of England, the 10, 25
Bankhead, Tallulah 9, 148
bankruptcy 45–6, 81, 83, 87, 135,
    177
barbiturates 178–80
Baring Brothers 47, 49
Baring, Maurice 26, 81, 104
Baring trust fund 66, 74, 80–1
Bavaria 87, 152
Beaton, Cecil 10, 36, 94, 106,
    108–13, 116–21, 124, 128, 133,
    149–50, 167

Beaverbrook, Lord/Sir Max Aitken
    9–10, 24, 31, 49, 51–5, 61–2,
    64–6, 68, 70–4, 76, 79–94,
    100, 103–5, 115, 121–2, 129,
    132–3, 135–6, 139–40, 143,
    152, 156–7, 159, 164, 170, 175,
    177, 180–1
Beckenham 11, 15–17, 35, 140
Beit, Sir Alfred 99, 103, 116–17, 132
Belgravia 41, 57–8
Bennett, Arnold 52–3
Berlin 53, 85, 87, 103
Berners, 14th Baron, Gerald
    Tyrwhitt-Wilson 10, 106, *111*,
    124, 144
Beverly Hills 147–9
Bright Young Things, the 36, 58, 71,
    93
Britain 12–13, 17, 20, 24, 27, 35, 37,
    42, 45, 50, 58, 61, 102, 125,
    129, 133, 145, 150, 153, 159,
    161–2, 164, 169–70, 175, 178
British Union of Fascists (BUF), the
    109, 138–9
Broadway 40, 132, 149
brothels 37, 80, 148

Café de Paris, the 45, 155
Cairo 25, 129–30
Cambridge University 26, 112
Cameron (née Lindeman), Enid/
    Viscountess Furness 31–3,
    129–31, 164, 166, 171–3,
    175–7, 181, *182*, 183
Canada 45, 51, 82, 103, 105
Cannes 65, 95, 115, 119
Capri 42, 133
Carrington, Dora 93, 118
Cartland, Dame Barbara 38, 75
Casati, Marchesa Luisa 144–5
Castlerosse, Viscount/Valentine

Edward Charles Browne 10,
    23–7, 29–33, 47, *48*, 49–56,
    59–89, 91, 93–5, 97–105, 107,
    113–15, *116*, 120–6, 128–36,
    138–43, 150–2, 155–62, 164,
    166–8, 171–3, 175–8, 180–1,
    182, 183
Cavendish, Brigadier General
    Frederick 'Caviar' 32, 129–30
Cavendish Hotel, the 37–8, 41
Chamberlain, Lord Neville 144, 152
Channon, Chips 101–2, 110
Chaplin, Charlie 126, *127*, 149
Château de l'Horizon 94, 114, 141
Cherkley Court, 71, 140
chorus girls 15, 34–5, 38, 40, 49
Churchill, Randolph 41, 93,
    99–103, 109, 117, 156
Churchill, Winston 9–10, 18, 23,
    91–3, 99, 102–3, 114–15,
    126, 129, 133–4, 141, 144,
    146, 153–6, 158–9, 161, 166,
    169–71, 174–5, 178–9
Clapham 16, 19
Claridge's 93, 98, 122–3, 135, 154,
    156–7, 159–60, 171, 176
clientele 15, 34–5, 45, 86, 126
clothes 14–16, 19, 22, 37–8, 40–1,
    43–4, 66–7, 102, 108, 114, 138,
    140, 175
Cochran, C.B. 97, 150
    Cochran's Revue 35, 44
Cocteau, Jean 126, *127*
Colefax, Sybil 107, 120, 126
Cooper, Alfred 'Duff' Gordon 53–4,
    85, 102, 109–10, 153
Cooper, Lady Diana 10, 52–4, 67,
    71, 85–6, 101, 109–10, 126
Copers Cope House 11, *18*
courtesans 25, 29, 35, 46, 92, 113,
    174, 180

Coward, Noel 10, 19, 40, 42–3,
    93–5, *96*, 97–8, 108, 129, 137
Cowell, Miss Marjorie 122–3, 135
crêpe de Chine sheets 69, 129, 138
Cukor, George 147–8
Culross Street 91, 98, 103, 122
Cunard, Lady Emerald 79, 93, 98,
    107, 109, 172
Curzon, Lady Irene 138–9
Czechoslovakia 152–3

Daily Express, the 54, 88, 101, 115
Daily Mail, the 74, 122
Deanery Street 40, 45, 69, 78–80,
    83–4, 88, 97
Deauville 44, 95, *143*, *165*
debutantes 21, 53, 58, 109
decree nisi 134–5, 140
de Janzé, Phyllis 118, 180
Delevingne, Edward Charles 11–12,
    90
Delevingne, (Edward) Dudley 13,
    42, 65, 104, 112, 149, 153, 170
Delevingne/Delavigne, (Jessie)
    Doris 9–17, *18*, 19–24, 33–46,
    57–95, *96*, 97–110, *111*, 112–
    15, *116*, 117–26, *127*, 128–42,
    143, 144–50, *151*, 152–64,
    165, 166–81, 183
demi-mondaine 10, 34, 40, 92, 110
Dengler, Dr F. 86–7, 121–2, 152
Derby, Lord 23, 32
divorce 45, 56, 63, 73, 78–80, 89, 95,
    98–9, 102–5, 113–14, 121–2,
    124–5, 130–4, 136, 140–1,
    143–4, 147–8, 156, 167
Dorchester Hotel, the 40, 103, 123,
    175, 178–9, 182
drugs 108, 172

East End, the 13–14, 41, 162
Eaton Square 118, 137
Edgar, Sir Edward MacKay 'Mike'
    45–6
Edward VII, King 21, 29, 37, 44
Edward VIII, King 133, 141
Elliott, Maxine 94, 114–15, 119,
    141, 158–9
Embassy Club, the 44–5, 67, 155
England 14, 29, 38–9, 41, 43, 55,
    120, 128, 152–4, 160–1, 164,
    170–1, 175, 178–80
Eton 17, 27, 92, 106
Europe 50, 80, 86, 92, 94, 117–18,
    145, 148, 152, 154, 159, 167
Evening Standard, the 65, 67

Fairbanks, Douglas 35, 79, 86, 123,
    129, 146–7, 162
Faringdon House 107–8, 110, *111*,
    144
fascism 94, 124, 138, 145, 153
Federated Malay States 125, 128, 149
First World War 14, 20, 36, 45, 53, 177
Fitzgerald, F. Scott 38–9
Florence 56, 118
Florida 141
Forzane, Jacqueline 30–1, 33, 49,
    61, 64
France 12, 27, 31, 42, 81, 114, 145,
    159, 164, 171
    south of *116*, 164
Furness, the 1st Viscount/
    Marmaduke Furness 130, 164,
    166, 172, 176–7, 181, 183

Gable, Clark 35, 149
Galliher, John 'Johnny' 162, 166–8
Galway 159–60
gambling 23, 32, 46–7, 49, 55, 60,
    66, 76, 80, 92, 171

Garbo, Greta 109, 142, 148
George V, King 27, 72
Germany 27, 29, 52, 67, 86, 93, 139, 145, 152–3, 159–60, 166, 178
Goddard, Paulette 126, *127*, 148–50, *151*
Golfe-Juan 114–15, 141
Gone with the Wind 147–9
Gordon, John 55, 65, 139
Grafton Galleries 34–6, 79
Grand National, the 38, 43
Great Gatsby, The 38–9
Green Hat, The 10, 19, 97
Grosvenor, Lord Edward 72, 89
Guinness, Bryan 84, 93, 97, 109, 117–18, 139

haberdashery 12, 15, 90
Hall, Radclyffe 108, 163
Halsey, Captain Gordon 35–7
Hammersmith Register Office 65, 68–9, 72–3
Hamsell Street 13–15
Harjes, John 168
Hawaii 149, *151*
Hawkes, Sylvia 35, 37, 79
Haxton, Gerald 42–3
Hearst, Millicent 50–1, 77
Hearst, William Randolph 50–1, 92
heart attack 152, 156, 170, 176, 183
high society 11, 13, 36, 40, 80, 109
Hitchcock, Tommy 38–9
Hitler, Adolf 144–5, 152–3, 164
Hoey, Fred 29–30
Hoffman, Margot Flick 126–9, 131–6, 140–2, 144–6, 149, 152–4, 156, 158–9, 161–4, *165*, 166
Hoffman, Richard 131, 156
Hollywood 35, 41, 50, 79, 94, 126, 132, 141–2, 147–51

homosexuality 80, 92, 107, 109, 111, 117, 124, 163, 167–8
Hong Kong 126, 149
Honolulu 149, *151*
Hopkins, Harry 170
Hurricanes, the 39, 58
Hyde Park 17, 25, 102, 137, 172, 178

India 39, 86, 126
    West 85
inheritance 24, 31, 44, 51, 82–3, 91, 99, 164, 166–7, 178, 181–3
insomnia 180
Ireland 25, *28*, 51, 70, 113, 157, 159
Irish Guards, the 27, 29
Italy 124, 145, 152–3, 159, 166

James, Edward 93, 109
jewellery 22, 29, 44, 61, 70, 76, 80, 82–3, 97, 107, 117, 151, 161, 166, 174, 179
    Cartier 40, 45, 108, 118

Karlsbad 152
Kenmare, Dermot 25, 29, 31–2, 49, 55, 72, 177
Kenmare, Gerald 25, 29
Kenmare, Lady 23, 25–6, 29–32, 49–50, 61, 64–6, 69, 71–4, 78, 81–3, 91, 97, 103–4, 113–14, 152, 157, 159, 177, 182–3
Kenmare, Lord 23–7, *28*, 29, 31, 61, 64–6, 72, 78, 81–3, 103, 114, 159, 167
Killarney House 24–5, *28*, 29, 49–51, 64, 70, 73, 80, 82, 104, 123, 157, 159, 167, 179, 182–3
    Lower Lake 29, 50
Kit-Kat Club, the 75, 100

Lavery, Lady 79, 114
Lavery R.A., Sir John 10, 79, 114–15, 131, 134, 142
Lawrence, Gertrude 'Gertie'/ Gertrude Alice Dagmar Klasen 15–17, 19–21, 33–6, 38, 40, 62, 97, 162, 166
Le Touquet 42, 92, 172
Lewis, Rosa 37, 41
Licensing Act 35–6
Lido 89, 102, 109
Lockhart, Sir Robert Bruce 79, 93
London 11–13, 16, 19–21, 24–5, 27, 29–32, 35–6, 38, 40–7, 50–1, 53, 58–9, 61–2, 64–7, 71, 74–5, 79, 81–2, 87, 90–1, 93, 95, 97, 99–100, 102, 104, 109–10, 113, 117–19, 122, 125, 130, 132–4, 136–8, 140–2, 145–7, 149, 154–60, 162, 166, 168–71, 178–80
Londoner's Log 52, 54–6, 59–60, 62, 66–7, 69, 71, 74–5, 77, 84, 89, 93, 104, 115, 122, 133, 139, 143, 157, 167
Lonergan, Patsy 167–8
Lonergan, Wayne 162, 166–8
Long Island 38–9, 44, 59, 166
Los Angeles 149, 162
Losch, Tilly 93, 109, 132, 161
Lusitania, RMS 45, 160

MacDonald, Ramsay 38, 114
Marian (née Homan), Jessie 11–13, 21, 90–1
marriage 12–14, 16, 21–2, 38, 43, 50, 56, 58, 62–74, 77–9, 84–5, 88–9, 93–4, 103–4, 109, 113, 116–17, 126, 130–1, 135, 143, 148, 164, 167, 172, 176, 182–3
Maugham, Syrie 42–3

Maugham, W. Somerset 42–3, 78
Mayfair 17, 23, 32–4, 37, 41–2, 47, 57–8, 61, 72, 74–6, 79, 81, 107, 129, 141
Mendl, Elsie 95, 117, 166
Messel, Oliver 95, 108–9
MGM 149–50
Mitford/Guinness/Mosley, Diana 10, 84, 92–3, 97, 106, 108–9, 116–19, 137–9, 144, 150, 159, 179
Mitford, Nancy 90, 92–3, 98, 110, 116, 137, 162
Mitford, David 92–3
Mitford, Tom 92, 94, 109, 117, 156
Mitford, Unity 137
Montagu, Venetia 52, 158
Monte Carlo 52, 94, 130, 146, 171
Mosley, Cimmie 109, 118–19, 138
Mosley, Sir Oswald 94, 109, 117–19, 126, 137–9, 159
Mountbatten, Edwina 43–4, 58, 162, 164, 171
Mountbatten, Lord 'Dickie' 43–4, 58
Munich 87, 93, 152

Nevada 131–2
Newmarket Races 59–60, 128
New York 31, 39, 59, 67, 88, 109, 113, 116, 119, 126, 128, 131–2, 147, 154, 156, 159–62, 167–8, 170–1, 174–5, 179
New York Herald, the 24
New York Times, the 161
Nichols, Beverley 42–3
Norton, Jean 53, 58

O'Connor, Anthony 99–100
Odom, William 117–18
Official Secrets Act, the 180–1

Olivier, Edith 10, 110
Orient, the 39, 125, *127*, 128
Oxford 42, 92, 107, 135

Palazzo Venier dei Leoni, the 144–7, 149, 152–4, 159, 166
   renovation 135, 146, 149, 153
Palm Beach 141, 166
Palm Court 45, 77, 160
Palm Springs 141–3
Paris 19, 23–4, 30–1, 40, 42, 47, 53, 58, 69, 81, 85–7, 92, 95, 103, 115, 119, 124, 129–30, 135, 146, 155, 157, 159, 164, 166
Park Lane 17, 22, 40, 46, 69
Parker, Hubert 125–6, *127*
Parliament 37, 92, 99
parties 21, 34, 36, 38, 41–2, 44, 54, 59–60, 71, 75, 79–81, 83, 85–6, 94, 100–2, 106, 109–10, 114, 125–6, 129–30, 134–5, 144–5, 149, *151*, 153–4, 168, 172, 176, 182, 189
   dinner 41, 59, 79, 84–5, 120, 161, 168–9
pawnbroker 82–3, 179
Piccadilly 16, 37
   Circus 120
Pickford, Mary 86, 147
playboys 21, 39
polo 38–40, 43, 58, 127, 130, 164
prison 109, 159, 179
Private Lives 95, 97–8

rag trade 14, 16, 40, 150
Rainbozend 135, 139–40, 143, 152
Regent Street 37, 39
Reno 131–3, 141, 156
Revelstoke, Lord 25–7, 30, 47, 49, 64, 74, 81

Ritz Hotel, the 30, 77, 86, 92, 103, 115, 117, 119, 124, 146
Roaring Twenties, the 57, 180
Rolls-Royce 19, 40–1, 75, 77, 79, 108, 129, 154, 159, 161
Rome 40, 118–19, 124
Roosevelt, Franklin D. 169–70
Rootes, Geoffrey 125–6, *127*
Rootes, William 'Billy' 75, 124–6, *127*, 128, 132
Rothermere, Lord 122
Rules restaurant 21

sanatorium 86–7, 121–2, 152
Sanford, Stephen 'Laddie' 38–40, 42–6, 58–9, 62, 64, 97, 140–1, 147, 164
scandal 9, 16, 30, 34, 41, 66, 74, 79, 86, 105, 109, 133, 145
Scotland Yard 179, 181
Second World War, the 57, 155, 166–7, 180
Selznick, David O. 148–9
sex 21, 33–4, 36, 38, 46, 56, 65, 70, 80, 90, 92, 108, 110–11, 119–20, 124, 128, 150, 162–3, 166, 180, 183
Singapore 125–6, 128
Sketch, The 60, 114
Smith, Lady Eleanor 54, 85
South Africa 39, 99, 117
St James nightclub 33, 47, 60
St James's Palace 21, 95
Stanley of Alderley, 5th Baron Lord 79, 150
stockbroking 26, 47, 49
Streatham 11
   High Street 11, 13
suicide 31, 46, 107, 120, 156, 172, 180–1

Sunday Express, the 24, 52, 54–5, 63, 65, 86, 139, 167
Surrey 71, 135, 156
Sutton Place 166, 169

Tatler magazine 110, 112, 114
Thames, the 16–17, 20, 79
Time magazine 38–9
Times, The 112, 134–5
Tyrwhitt-Wilson, Gerald 106–8, 110

U-boats 159–60
unemployment 14, 20, 57

Valentine's Days 124, 151
Vanderbilts 29, 161, 166
Venice 89, 95, *96*, 101, 103, 109–10, 129, 135–6, 140, 143, 145–6, 148–9, 153–4, 159
  Grand Canal, the 135–6, 140, 143–5

Vile Bodies 54, 93, 97–8, 106
Vogue 10, 109, 113, 117, 140
Vreeland, Diana 117, 153

Wales, Prince of 16, 21, 42, 45, 51, 53, 67, 104, 130, 133
Washington 160, 162, 169–71
Washington, SS 159–61
Watson, Peter 10, 108–9, 112, 117, 119–20, 149–50
Waugh, Evelyn 54, 93, 97–8, 100, 106, 112, 158
Well of Loneliness, The 108, 163
West End, the 15–16, 74, 93, 104
Weymouth, Daphne 77, 79, 81, 88–9, 110, *111*
Weymouth, Lord Henry 81, 88–9
Whistler, Rex 43, 58
Whitney, Jock 38, 85
Wilson, Jack 42–3, 108
Wimborne House 134, 143

If you enjoyed this book, you may also be interested in…

Mrs Guinness: The Rise and Fall of Diana Mitford the Thirties Socialite
LYNDSY SPENCE

Before Diana Mitford's disgrace as a social pariah, she was a celebrated member of the Bright Young Things, moving at the centre of 1920s and '30s London high society. As the young wife of Bryan Guinness, heir to the Guinness brewing empire, she lived a gilded life until fascist leader Sir Oswald Mosley turned her head. Unpublished letters, diaries and archives bring an unknown Diana to life, creating a portrait of a beautiful woman whose charm and personality enthralled all who met her, but the discourse of her life would ultimately act as a cautionary tale. This groundbreaking biography reveals the woman behind the myth.

978 0 7509 5973 5

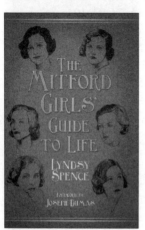

The Mitford Girls' Guide to Life
LYNDSY SPENCE

The six Mitford girls were blessed with beauty, wit and talent, yet they led very distinct, cultural lives and not one sister, except for Diana and Unity, shared the same opinion or ideology. As individuals they exploited their attributes to the best of their abilities, and through difficult times they used laughter as their remedy. Their life experiences, although sometimes maddening, are a lesson to us all. How would the Mitford girls cope with the pressures and turmoil of modern life? Whether it is Pamela's guide to throwing a jubilee party, Nancy's guide to fashion or Diana's tips on how to stay young, this quirky and fact-filled book draws on rare and unpublished interviews and information to answer that question.

978 0 7524 9694 8

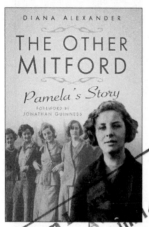

The Other Mitford: Pamela's Story
DIANA ALEXANDER

Pamela Jackson, née Mitford, is perhaps the least well known of the illustrious Mitford sisters, yet her story is just as captivating, and more revealing. Despite shunning the bright city lights that her sisters so desperately craved, she was very much involved in the activities of her extraordinary family, picking up the many pieces when things went disastrously wrong – which they so often did. Joining her sisters on many adventures, including their meeting with Adolf Hitler in Nazi Germany, Pamela quietly observed the bizarre, funny and often tragic events that took place around her. Through her eyes, we are given a view of the Mitfords never seen before.

978 0 7509 6699 3

The
History
Press

The destination for history
www.thehistorypress.co.uk